PRAISE FOR *FEASTING WILD*

"*Feasting Wild* is indeed a feast—a memorable, genre-defying work that blends anthropology and adventure, love and loss. Gina Rae La Cerva is a keen observer and a wonderful writer."

ELIZABETH KOLBERT, *New York Times* bestselling author of *The Sixth Extinction*

"A curious, passionate, and beautifully poetic book. La Cerva uncovers something essential about our enduring desire for wildness in a world where it is rapidly vanishing."

JAMES PROSEK, artist and author of *Trout: An Illustrated History*

"Intrepid anthropologist Gina Rae La Cerva has set herself what some might consider a Sisyphean task: to seek out, and where possible, savor, what remains of the wilds on a planet comprehensively domesticated by *Homo sapiens*. What she discovers—whether it's wild boar in a Polish forest, birds' nests in Borneo, or love as she investigates the culture of bushmeat in the Congo—is the human passion for an untamed world that survives, against all odds, amidst our monocultures and megacities. By turns lyrical, melancholy, and invigorating, *Feasting Wild* is an enthralling and necessary meditation on what it means to love the feral in a world increasingly of our making."

TARAS GRESCOE, author of *Possess the Air, Straphanger,* and *Bottomfeeder*

T0053717

"This book pulled at my heartstrings and awakened a deep hunger for connection: to the foraged foods that once sustained us but have become lost or commodified, to my landscape and community, and to the wild nature that surrounds us all."

ANDREA BEMIS, author of *Dishing Up the Dirt*

"This is the food book I've always wanted to read—a witty, illuminating, and beautifully written travelogue that rightly centers the historical role of women and the importance of Indigenous knowledge. Throw away the trite faux-wisdom of dietitians and gorge yourself instead on the charming platter that Gina Rae La Cerva has served up."

ED YONG, author of *I Contain Multitudes*

"It is rare these days to find a food book with a truly original take on food. *Feasting Wild* gives you a great deal to think about and at the same time is a pleasure to read."

MARK KURLANSKY, *New York Times* bestselling author of *Salmon* and *Salt*

"*Feasting Wild is* a rich literary banquet, its pages a smorgasbord of intrepid travelogue, unflinching memoir, and keen ecological history. Where the worldviews of Cheryl Strayed and Michael Pollan converge, you'll find this perceptive, big-hearted, beautifully crafted book."

BEN GOLDFARB, author of *Eager*

"La Cerva's engrossing book celebrates wild-harvested food but also mourns it, showing how plentiful staples have dwindled time and again to overexploited luxuries. Mixing memoir, travelogue, and environmental history, *Feasting Wild* is a lyrical and lucid exploration of hunger and fulfillment, richly detailed and beautifully told."

THOR HANSON, author of *Buzz* and *The Triumph of Seeds*

"La Cerva is a modern-day hunter-gatherer, scouring the planet to bring us delicious stories and lessons about our world. Her writing is original and thought-provoking, and even though it's not always palatable how we've transformed our native flora and fauna, her adventurous storytelling is endlessly satisfying."

DANIEL STONE, author of *The Food Explorer*

"An extraordinary book, full of powerful, troubling, and important stories, beautifully evoked. My mouth watered, my mind expanded, and my heart broke and was remade through this superb writing. A must-read demonstration of how our senses and desires are entangled with the justice and well-being of life's community."

DAVID GEORGE HASKELL, author of *The Forest Unseen*

FEASTING WILD

GINA RAE LA CERVA

FEASTING WILD

In Search of the Last Untamed Food

GREYSTONE BOOKS

Vancouver/Berkeley

Greystone Books Ltd.
greystonebooks.com

Cataloguing data available from Library and Archives Canada
ISBN 978-1-77164-915-5 (pbk)
ISBN 978-1-77164-533-1 (cloth)
ISBN 978-1-77164-534-8 (epub)

Editing by Paula Ayer
Copy editing by Linda Pruessen
Proofreading by Stefania Alexandru
Cover design by Michelle Clement and Nayeli Jimenez
Illustrations by Michelle Clement
Text design by Nayeli Jimenez

Printed and bound in Canada on FSC® certified paper at Friesens.
The FSC® label means that materials used for the product have
been responsibly sourced.

Greystone Books gratefully acknowledges the Musqueam, Squamish,
and Tsleil-Waututh peoples on whose land our office is located.

Greystone Books thanks the Canada Council for the Arts, the British
Columbia Arts Council, the Province of British Columbia through
the Book Publishing Tax Credit, and the Government of Canada for
supporting our publishing activities.

Canada

For my parents, Laura and Victor,
and for my sister—whom I know by many names.

CONTENTS

Prologue

HEARTBREAK MOOSE

IN THE MIDDLE of July, I invite some friends over to eat Heartbreak Moose.

I light the BBQ and a few candles. A kousa dogwood tree casts shadows over our dinner party. The occasional errant seed-pod bounces among the plates and silverware.

I have smuggled the Heartbreak Moose meat back from Sweden—frozen, vacuum-sealed, and hidden between sweaters in my suitcase. When I went through customs at JFK, I was as nervous as a novice drug runner.

I prepare the Heartbreak Moose as small burgers, mixing the wild meat with pork lard, caramelized onions, pressed garlic, and herbs my sister grew. As I cook, I remember watching the animal die in a lush forest next to a misty lake. I serve the burgers on toasted buns with shiitake mushrooms and heirloom tomatoes from a farm on a marsh river down the road. We taste the untamed. I think of the man who killed the beast. We digest my grief into a million little morsels.

For 99 percent of our history, humans ate hunted and gathered foods. Hunters patterned their lives after the lives of the animals they pursued. Gathering tied us to places and seasons. As recently as two hundred years ago, nearly half the North American diet still came from the wild—venison, game fowl, abundant and cheap seafood, even turtle in some places. Today, most people will never eat anything undomesticated or uncultivated. Eating something truly untamed has become incredibly rare.

What was once sustenance—and often associated with poverty and subsistence—is now becoming a luxury. The top restaurants in the world serve gathered weeds to their elite clientele. "Foraged" flavors and "gamey" flesh have become marks of wealth, refinement, and purity. The price of "wild caught" fish is much higher than farmed fish, and steadily on the rise. And the most desirable wild foods—like game meat from tropical rainforests and edible bird's nests from Southeast Asia—are becoming globally traded commodities associated with black markets, counterfeit products, and violence. At the same time, those who still depend on wild foods for survival are finding their lifestyles rapidly changing, even in the most remote of places.

It seems some shift is occurring in our desire for foods we can't grow or produce ourselves. Eating remains the closest, most consistent relationship we have to nature. Yet it's often the most unconscious. When I go to the grocery store, I am overwhelmed by the variety. But the options pale in comparison to the biodiversity of flavors we once consumed. As we have domesticated our diets, we have unintentionally domesticated ourselves. What pleasures are we missing? We mourn the loss of something we don't fully understand.

The disappearance of wild places has diminished our food options. It is estimated that we will lose 30 to 50 percent of other life forms with whom we share the planet by mid-century. Dozens go extinct every day. So many edible species and varietals have vanished to standardization, uniformity, and predictable tastes. It is easy to feel as though we are lacking some vital nourishment.

The preference for wild foods has a long history, and protecting the natural places where wild edibles were sourced was the primary motivation behind some of the earliest environmental conservation laws. The story of our relationship to wild food is therefore inseparable from our concept of wildness itself. Wildness was once a stand-in for the unknowable, for a kind of nature that could never be entirely understood or controlled. But as settler-colonialism spread across the globe, "wildness" took on negative connotations and was used to justify violent appetites and the domination of unfamiliar cultures and places. The idea that Wild Nature was separate from Tame Culture took hold, and our ecosystems became increasingly cultivated. In just a few centuries, the world traded wild edibles at home for exotic domesticates from abroad.

Despite women being the primary food producers around the world, and intimately familiar with its fields and forests, their knowledge of the wild was largely silenced throughout history. Women were characters in natural histories only by their absence, invisible objects set in the margins, relegated to footnotes, sharing space with the Indigenous people, the enslaved, and the exploited lands.

Saving wild foods is, therefore, fundamentally about recovering our common heritage. The urgency of the environmental crisis is precisely why we must slow down, take time, become complicated in our actions. Hunting and gathering divert us from the clock and demand we look at everything and nothing all at once.

What does it feel like to consume the least processed foods, the most unadulterated, which haven't been overbred, monocultured, and passed through innumerable unseen hands? What does it mean to eat *wild* food—or the closest thing to it in a world so thoroughly dominated by humans?

My appetite drove me forward.

This book is a collection of impressions, all caught in the same fine mesh, important because of their coincidence more than anything else. It can be read in two ways: as a tragedy or a story of hope. If you believe the tale is one of decline, you might discover a manufactured wasteland. If instead you wish to see promise, our closing landscape will be an untamable garden. Perhaps it will contain vestiges of both. The text of this book, like the book of nature, cannot offer a singular meaning.

Before we eat the moose burgers, I stand to make a toast. I think of the Congolese women I met during my research, with their own suitcases of illegal bushmeat.

"The thing about wild food—unlike domesticated food—is that it has its own story. I want to tell you the story of my Heartbreak Moose."

"Isn't that a long story?" a friend who's heard it before interrupts.

"Then I will begin in the middle," I reply.

And so it is, with a generous heart and an empty stomach, I give you my account of this quest to understand the wild foods we still eat and the ones we have forgotten. To regain contact with the essential. To journey outside of history and into time.

We will taste the untamed, and the flavors will bring to mind a vast unstructured record of the past. Each dish an artifact of a vanishing way of life and a promise of a new tradition.

Let the Wild Feast commence!

PART I

ON MEMORY AND FORGETTING

❖ I ❖

HERBS AND INSECTS

The Test Kitchen—A Wallet Lost—Foraging with
Kierkegaard's Ghost—The Savage Arts—A Map of Flavor—
The Punk Rock Chef—The Opulence of Time

I AM IN THE test kitchen of the "best restaurant in the world" and I'm on the verge of throwing up. Around the room, chefs are bent over their culinary investigations. A soundtrack of downbeat reggae plays overhead.

A tall, handsome Australian chef named Brad has just taken me on a tour of Noma's four kitchens and the private dining room where Metallica ate the week before. At the back of the restaurant, we paused to watch a man in a small shed sweating over a nine-hundred-degree fire cooking charred fish, a bandana obscuring half his face, and I thought about him standing there all day, sixteen hours, full of pride and secret doubts that intensified with each tiring moment.

Noma only uses ingredients sourced within the Nordic region (Scandinavia, Finland, Iceland, Greenland, and the Faroe

3

Islands). No lemons. No olive oil. It is a challenge to prepare a meal without such basic staples. The chefs must find similar flavors in wild ingredients. The menu changes about five times each month to keep up with the seasonal changes in ingredients, and the restaurant employs a full-time forager.

Now in the test kitchen, Brad and I stand next to shelves lined with jars of experimental foods. "These are the scallops. This is how we dry them," Brad says as he opens a jar, "and then we emulsify them—with the wax of bees. And that's how you get that fudge." The things in the jar look of indeterminate origin and stink something like rancid, dirty laundry. The smell travels through my nose and into my brain, and there in the neocortex it meets signals from my stomach that say I am quite too full from the twenty-one-course lunch I've just eaten, and quite too nervous in the presence of this tall man, for such a smell. I start to retch. René Redzepi, the master artist himself, turns around from the photo shoot he is conducting and stares in horror. How dare I gag in his test kitchen. How dare I, indeed.

Let me begin again. As soon as I arrived in Copenhagen, I lost my wallet. Somewhere between the train station and my accommodations, it decided to jump out of my bag. I retrace my steps. As with foraging, it is only when you are looking for something very specific that you notice everything else that has been lost to the world. I find: a pink button, plastic wrappers, used train tickets, cigarette butts, and an old cemetery headstone set into the sidewalk, engraved with the words "The Earth Bears Your Mark." At the ATM near the train station, I find a woman sitting in rags, her wide eyes tired and scared.

I imagine the person who has found my wallet. What would they know of me? My Yale ID—the one where I look like a

Russian spy. Currencies from three different countries. A heart-shaped nugget of amber and a lightweight shard of volcanic rock. A blackened fossilized bone I found on a beach. A small feather. So many credit cards from so many banks. Expired health insurance. Slips of paper obscured by written observations, to-do lists, and passing thoughts, the overheard words of strangers, fragments that I hold onto with a stubbornness bordering on obsession. My driver's license—the one where I look like a con woman who's just hit up a bank and is mad about it. I was terribly hungover in that picture, because the night before I had met Bill Murray in a bar, asked him for a job, confessed to him that I was in love with my best friend, and then threatened him into never revealing my secret. Who is this woman? Does she have a coherent life, beyond these broken pieces? Is there someplace she belongs?

———

I have come to Copenhagen to try to understand why the seemingly archaic practice of gathering wild plants is having a resurgence, to follow the trend of *time* and *place*. Before I eat lunch at Noma, I join a group of food researchers from the Nordic Food Lab to forage in Assistens Cemetery. No one can remember if foraging here is legal, but all the city's finest chefs do it.

The graveyard is renowned for having the tastiest wild onions within city limits. Ramson (*Allium ursinum*), also called broad-leaved garlic, wood garlic, or bear's garlic, is part of the lily family and related to chives. Ramson grows in damp, shady places and produces clusters of tiny white flowers, which become hard little green seed pods by midsummer. The chefs are hoping to pickle the ramson seed pods as part of their research into the process of flavor creation during preservation.

They are working on a project to map the functions of various compounds within fermented foods. For instance, both chili and garlic contain antimicrobial compounds that affect the rate of lactic fermentation. By adjusting the ratio of these elements, they hope to create more flavor with less acidity.

We do not, technically, have a sense of flavor. Flavor emerges in our brains from the synthesis of all other sensory inputs—touch, taste, sight, smell, sound—combined with the much more elusive quality of memory. While some taste preferences and concerns of generations past are difficult to understand, others are so firmly entrenched in our collective minds that they have survived the rise and decay of empires. Generally, we crave flavors that are sweet or fatty because these were limiting factors in our diets for the majority of human history. We like complex flavors because they signify micronutrients that are necessary to our cells, and while we might naturally be averse to bitterness, we learn to enjoy it. Many of our most beloved medicines and stimulants are bitter, which signifies potency—a result of molecules called allelochemicals that plants make to fight off pests.

Acquiring a taste for something is similar to learning a new language. At a young age, our brains—and taste buds—are primed and ready for novel flavor experiences. As we age, our tastes become rigid and ingrained. But because our brains are malleable, tastes can change or be augmented over time, both in individuals and in societies at large. Flavor is a way to pass down the wisdom of one generation to the next. In sitting down for a meal, we can update and modify that which we know to be true about our environment. The act is the data itself.

Perceiving flavor evolved to be so complex because it is fundamental to keeping us alive. Early humans had to balance the potential reward of discovering a novel flavor or nutrient source with the risk of ingesting poison. This contradiction between being attracted to and wary of new foods—between freedom and control—is deeply rooted in our psychology.

Of course, what is deemed delicious is very much context specific, and the madness of hunger has driven humans to eat all manner of foods. Tastes change with desperation. In many ways, we are desperate today, too. Although thirty thousand plant species have been used at some point for food or medicine, we now rely primarily on just thirty. Sixty percent of our diet is made up of just three annual crops—rice, wheat, and corn—two of which are only edible when cooked. Eighty percent of our agricultural crops are annuals that must be ripped up and replanted each year.[1] Almost all of them are heavily inbred and generally less flavorful or nutritious than their wild counterparts, which tend to contain higher concentrations of essential nutrients such as vitamins A and C, thiamine, riboflavin, iron, and trace minerals. Eating a diversity of wild foods is associated with higher rates of gut flora diversity, which correlates to better measures of health. The increasing homogenization and standardization of agriculture is making us sick. Our psyches, palates, and physiques were not made for such uniform food.

"Perhaps we will find the ramson growing near a chef's grave," John, a young food researcher from Canada, jokes as we head toward a back corner of the cemetery. As we ramble onward, I notice the numerous other edible plants growing in the cemetery. Most have been planted as decorative ornamentals, but that doesn't stop people gathering them. Foraging in urban areas like this is far from new—immigrants have long used city parks and green spaces to harvest familiar plants in their new homes, and it continues to be a subsistence practice for many groups.

But urban foraging is also an increasingly popular activity among "foodies," despite the potential health risks (plants growing in cities may be polluted with lead and other heavy metals) and the fact that it is illegal in many places. Perhaps the first high-profile case of criminal urban foraging was in 1986, when Steve "Wildman" Brill—dubbed "The Man Who Ate Manhattan"—was arrested in Central Park for illegally gathering plants. He continues to lead foraging tours around the city. And he is not alone; social media and cell phone apps that identify edible plants have both fueled the rise in urban gathering.

"What do you think about the recent trendiness associated with foraging?" I ask John as the sound of a grass cutter motors nearby.

"It's a double-edged sword," he says. "While it's great more people are interested, it's dangerous that the interest is growing without the corresponding knowledge—how to not pick things that will kill you or make you sick. Knowing not to pick everything and how to not destroy the habitat, which is even more important."

As one of the first wild plants to emerge in spring, ramson was traditionally a welcomed bit of edible green and vitamins after many cold months of preserved foods and dried meats. In the United States, the related species called ramps were a highly valued and spiritually important plant for numerous Indigenous American tribes, including the Cherokee, Ojibwa, Menominee, Iroquois, and Chippewa. They were eaten boiled, fried, or dried for winter use, and made into tonics to fight various ailments.

Ramps were so widely consumed by the first colonists during periods of hunger that their smell came to be associated with poverty. Today, they are a coveted ingredient. One of the more typical uses of the leaves is to make pesto, capturing the flavor of both herb and garlic in the same ingredient. Unfortunately, the increasing demand is threatening the plant's existence. Ramps are in danger of being overharvested, in part, because they are incredibly slow-growing: it takes anywhere between three and seven years for a seed to become a plant large enough to be eaten. If harvested correctly—by cutting above the roots, leaving some of the bulb in the ground—ramps will eventually regenerate. A general rule of thumb for foragers is to only take 10 percent of what you find and leave 90 percent behind for nature, but this highly depends on the specific plant and the number of other people also gathering it in the same area. According to one experiment, harvesting ramps sustainably would require collecting just 10 percent every ten years.

Ramps continue to be of high value to many Indigenous Americans, though modern environmental regulations have disrupted the link to their heritage. Harvesting wild species is banned across all U.S. national parks, but individual park super-intendents can regulate the picking of certain plants and fungi as they see fit. In 2009, a member of the Eastern Band of Cherokee Indians was charged with illegally harvesting ramps in Great Smoky Mountains National Park, the site of traditional family gathering plots for thousands of years. The Cherokee continue to fight for their sovereign right to harvest on ancestral lands and have set up projects to cultivate the plants in order to reduce reliance on wild populations.

Wild plants have been loved to death before. Silphium was a fennel-like vegetable used extensively in classical antiquity as a prized seasoning, and as grazing fodder for meat animals because it was said to improve the taste of their flesh. It was also a popular contraceptive and a treatment for numerous other maladies—indigestion, cough, sore throat, fever, warts, and pains. The plant became so revered and economically important that the North African city of Cyrene stamped an image of its heart-shaped seedpods onto their coins. By the second century BCE, silphium was so overharvested that it was headed toward extinction. The last remaining stalk, so the ancient chronicle goes, was given to Emperor Nero as a curiosity.

The act of gathering means there is no guarantee of a harvest, and I am starting to think the ramson will remain elusive. But near Kierkegaard's grave, we find some growing beneath a towering pine.

"Foraging in Scandinavia died out like two centuries ago," John says as he hands me a ramson leaf. "It was perceived as a poor thing to do."

"So I just eat this?" I say, holding up the leaf for inspection.

"Yeah."

"It's pretty mild." It has a sweet pleasing flavor, like a young leek but also a bit like peas.

"Early in the season, the leaves are really strong, but once they start to go to flower, they lose a lot of their flavor because the plant is focusing on going to seed."

"Do you tend to take everything you can find?" I ask John as he puts some of the little green seed pods into a Tupperware container.

"It depends on the plant. Ramson, like all allium species, has bulbs that will split. So they don't just propagate through seed. And now it's also late. You can see that some of the clusters have dropped already"—he points to a smattering of the seed heads lying on the ground—"so there are probably already viable seeds out there."

I pop one in my mouth and chew, releasing the explosive pungency of an entire clove of garlic.

It is difficult to pinpoint exactly when the resurgent interest in gathering wild plants began. Fascination with eating foraged foods, and culinary movements that romanticize simplicity, are not especially modern sentiments. They seem to be a whimsy particularly suited to times of excess. The late Roman Empire poet Horace wrote nostalgically for the days of the Republic when no one had a personal chef. He was tired of the elaborate dinners he attended and longed for the kinds of meals eaten by the hunter returned from the hunt, and the farmer from his field, exhausted by the toil, who sat before a basic meal of grain porridge, ground by the hands of his wife.

In the high Middle Ages, perhaps in reaction to the gluttony of medieval feasts, Wild Nature was cast as a place to regain a sense of temperance, self-discipline, and purity. Jean de Hauville's twelfth-century satirical poem, *Architrenius,* chronicles the journey of the titular young hero, who visits the Land of Gorging, where the "Stomach Worshippers" live in extreme sensuality—an allegory for the era's gourmands. After experiencing the wickedness and vices of civilization, Architrenius eventually meets Nature, who resides in a field speckled with flowers. As a remedy for what ails Architrenius, Nature suggests that he marry a beautiful, youthful woman named Moderation.

During the height of the Renaissance, when lavish banquets were once again in style, a countermovement arose inspired by a renewed interest in ancient Greek and Roman moral philosophy, which cast human artifice as contaminating the most basic aspects of life. Numerous dietetic manuals were published discussing ancient recipes and health advice, often emphasizing that the key to a happier, more productive existence was eating closer to the source, as well as exercising self-control in the face of hunger pangs. Foraged plants show up in the form of condiments, along with sugar and spices, but it was important not to use these in "luxury, lust, and intemperance," as one manual admonished.[2]

12

Several hundred years later, during the period of American Romanticism in the nineteenth century, people rebelled against the new methods of domestic scientific cookery and the influx of foreign ingredients, and went out into the woods, as one author put it, in search of "a perfect digestion."[3] After a day of foraging, Henry David Thoreau wrote admiringly of the quality of "gatheredness" and mused that "the bitter-sweet of a white-oak acorn which you nibble in a bleak November walk over the tawny earth is more to me than a slice of imported pine-apple."[4]

More recently, in the 1960s, as part of the growing back-to-nature movement, Euell Gibbons—who grew up poor and learned to forage to supplement his family's meager diet—wrote *Stalking the Wild Asparagus*, a surprise bestseller that advo-cated eating cattails, parts of pine trees, and the edible tubers of wildflowers, among many other foraged foods. He became a mild celebrity, appearing on numerous TV shows, including the highly popular *Tonight Show Starring Johnny Carson*, and even starred in a commercial for Grape-Nuts cereal. Gibbons published numerous books, advocating "wild" dinner parties, and many of the plants he espoused—such as lamb's-quarters, dandelions, and purslane—are now commonly found in local farmers' market salad mixes.

It takes little stretch of the imagination to see this trend per-sisting into the present day. In a world of unpleasantness and excess, of decay and extinction, of pollution and crisis, wild food is an intoxicating symbol.

As we skirt Hans Christian Andersen's grave, the chefs decide the cemetery is too manicured and picked over to find enough ramson seed pods. On our way out of the graveyard, we pause at the headstone of nuclear physicist Niels Bohr. "Is it weird to take stuff from an actual grave?" John asks. "Cause that St. John's wort is looking really good... very, very fresh!"

We say our goodbyes. The experimental chefs go in search of undisturbed shadows, and I am off to a very expensive lunch.

When I enter the front doors of Noma, a crowd of waiters and chefs stand at attention and welcome me by name. The walls are whitewashed stone. The wooden chairs have been made to look like weathered bone, and sheepskin furs drape off the backs as cozy cloaks. Black earthenware is scattered across the tabletops like boulders thrown from a rockfall, with plain white candles in the center evoking frozen-over cascades of water.

Perhaps Chef Redzepi is attempting to emulate the trappings of the most famous hunter-gatherers in Denmark, the Ertebølle, a culture that dates to the very late Mesolithic period (4500 BCE). They lived a semi-settled existence along the coast and traded with inland farmers for polished stone axes. The wooden hurdles they built to trap fish in the estuaries were so well-made that some have survived for six thousand years.

There is no written menu to follow at Noma, so each course comes as a sensory surprise, a nature walk with a cryptic message.

A tiny speckled quail egg—cooked, pickled, seasoned with smoked hay, and nestled in burlap. Is it meant to mimic the smell of a burning field? A memory device to invoke the feeling of harvest time?

Fried reindeer moss foraged from northern Sweden—a tiny portion served in a terra-cotta dish, with a rock and a stick to imitate the landscape where it was gathered. It tastes like french fries but feels like chartreuse velvet on the tongue.

Ice cream of wild mushrooms and gathered seaweeds. "Superhealthy. Full of vitamins and antioxidants. You almost levitate after," the waiter beams.

Turbot with a sauce of nasturtium, wild wood sorrel, and horse-radish-infused cream.

The group next to me is talking about losing weight, diet regimens, how to be healthier.

14

Sloe berries and aromatic herbs.

At another table, the conversation is about a restaurant with a mineral-water sommelier, forty kinds of bottled water.

Caramel made from sourdough bread yeast served with Icelandic yogurt and sea buckthorn flower marmalade.

"Try foraging in Philadelphia. Dirty. Needles," someone nearby says between bites.

Red currant and lavender.

"We used to be more experimental," my waiter says as he sets down a wooden spoon and a stoneware bowl of peas with chamomile potpourri. "To be number one is limiting."

White cabbage and samphire.

Some dishes, like the congealed block of caramelized milk and cod liver, elicit no emotion in me, no memory, no environment. It just tastes overpowering, the flavor too distracting to place the dish within a familiar context.

Burned beets, scraped to the heart.

Others bring me to my childhood, in the New Mexico high-mountain desert where I grew up. The deliberately burnt petals of the flower tart remind me of the riotous blooms of my mother's garden. Perched on the edge of a dry arroyo, I constructed dirt and dust pies, topped with fuchsia pansies and deep-purple bottlebrush, a miniature chef dwarfed by the dry heat of the noonday. The sweet, earthy taste of edible Indian paintbrush, juniper berries, and red-ripe prickly pear fruits mingled in my mouth for years.

White asparagus, black currant leaves, and barley.

The waiter has something on his nose as he places the next

dish before me, a grilled pike head, skewered and cooked over low flames. The charred taste reminds me of a day on an idyllic beach, when I was still too young to appreciate the preciousness of the experience. I ate fresh-caught dorado, cooked over an open fire, while the setting sun melted into impossible Caribbean waters, and I smiled shyly at a teenage boy across the way, raw lime juice running down my chin, and my newfound teenage sexuality blooming somewhere unseen.

Lovage and parsley.

A wooden saucer of glistening pink beef tartare dotted with flash-frozen wood ants is set before me. I take a bite. The little black creatures burst in my mouth like sour-green sprinkles of lemongrass and pine.

To eat ants outside of periods of extreme scarcity, without the motivation of an empty belly, holds within it the paradox at the center of Noma's dishes—the fetishization of need. It is no surprise that Redzepi consulted a 1960s Swedish army survival guide as one of his earliest sources for identifying edible wild ingredients. Even if you have never experienced famine, Noma is happy to invent this memory for you, so that you might experience the delight that can only come from killing extreme hunger.

Of course, eating insects is only a rarity in the Western world. There are some nineteen hundred insect species that are part of human diets for people all over Asia, Africa, and South America. The recent Western interest in making cricket-meal protein bars is merely us catching up with the rest of the world. Still, the fear of eating the unknown is deep, and for the Western palate, insects seem to be particularly taboo, despite attempts to introduce the practice. In 1885, Vincent M. Holt published his manifesto *Why Not Eat Insects?* He meticulously went through the benefits, which ranged widely, from the

15

nutritional advantages to pest control on crops. He was baffled that people would eat lobster—"such a foul feeder"—but were averse to insects, which lived off healthy plants and flowers.[5]

I take another taste of wood ants. I remember the first time I ate bugs. It was a glorious preteen summer of rollerblading around downtown, getting into mild trouble—giving tourists the wrong directions, stealing traffic cones, making pay phones ring and watching the confused looks of people passing by the ghostly calls—and I reveled in being a nineties grunge-kid plaza-rat in cutoff jeans and a scrunchy ponytail reeling against something I couldn't fully articulate.

One hot, lazy afternoon, after returning from mischief in the town square, a friend and I decided to forage for grasshoppers in her overgrown yard. We were not hungry, merely at the cusp of adolescence and inherently bored. We found it easy work. The pellucid New Mexico sun made each insect vivid against the blades of dry grass. We fried them up in olive oil until they sizzled and crisped, then dared each other to eat the shriveled bugs. When I finally got up my courage and bit the head off the charred corpse, it tasted like some kind of discordant freedom.

———

Flavor is a map of our desires. But it is not the territory. As the world changes, the map must change too. How have wild plants become a rarefied luxury? In order to understand the resurgence in foraging, we must follow the lines of loss of this common knowledge.

Gathering has long been seen as women's work, perhaps because we seem to hold a special capacity to observe the seasons and reckon with change. Perhaps the first conceptual thought emerged to organize the array of plants we ate. Women gained intimate knowledge of the plants they collected. Some herbs—and the women who knew how to use them—held magic, held the power to cure or curse.

By some estimates, it was women who were responsible for providing the majority of calories eaten in early human societies. Nevertheless, petroglyphs rarely show food-gathering along-side their depictions of epic hunts, although in the Cuevas de la Araña in Spain, a Mesolithic drawing depicts the collection of honey. The first tools humans made were likely satchels woven from bark to carry gathered food home. We do not know for sure. These archives are lost to history—the satchels degraded while the stone tools survived the crush of time.

Similarly, no one knows exactly when or why plant and animal domestication first arose. Some argue that farming gradually displaced hunting and gathering because of a series of pulls: a desire for plants with more sweetness and animals with more fat. Other evidence points to a series of pushes: climatic shifts about twelve thousand years ago that ended the Ice Age and ushered in the Holocene epoch, which dramatically altered the ecosystems in which we had evolved; increasing population sizes that could no longer rely on sparse wild supplies; or more sedentary groups amassing larger stores of food and dominating nomadic gatherer-hunter populations.

Likely, the first agriculture was an accident. Bits of gathered root fell out on the way home and re-rooted. Seeds thrown away during dinner sprouted near the extinguished fires. Given women's role in gathering, it is likely they took notice of these events and began to coax plants into domestication. We do know that the first major agriculture crops evolved from wild versions that were already a major part of the diet: cereals in the Near East, maize and beans in Central America, and rice in China.

In the process of domestication, organisms become increas-ingly more dependent upon us to feed and shelter them, and we in turn become more dependent upon them. Surprisingly, the risk of going hungry was not dampened by agriculture, especially in the beginning, when crop breeding was in its nascent stages. Whereas for most of human history we ate what was seasonally available, with the rise of cultivation it became necessary to wait for crops to come in. Food storage was also risky—stockpiles could degrade or be raided.

By many physical health measures, agriculturalists were not as robust as hunter-gatherers: shortened life span, stunted stature, diabetes, cardiovascular disease, and tooth decay all became more common with the conversion to an agrarian lifestyle. Exposure to parasites and infections also increased as we settled into larger hamlets. The reversal in quality of life was particularly bad for women, who had less access to protein under agricultural regimes than in more egalitarian hunter-gatherer societies. It took much more labor to produce an agricultural crop than it did to gather. This need for extra help, combined with higher rates of child mortality due to new diseases and periods of starvation, meant women had more children—a primary burden of physical stress.

As agriculture became the dominant method for sourcing food, wild plants took on new spiritual value. During spring fertility rites in the Iron Age, human sacrifices were made to the goddess Nerthus to ensure good harvests. The victims first ate a ceremonial meal, which consisted, at least in one case, of more than sixty-three different varieties of seeds, mostly from species we would today consider weeds.

Wild plants were also increasingly sought out as remedies for the diseases caused by moving toward agriculture in the first place. Ancient Greek and Roman doctors believed that the power of herbs to cure was not inherent in their buds and leaves, but lay in their complementary resemblance to human needs and desires—a system called the doctrine of signatures. If a flower resembled an eye, it could treat eye infections. If the petals were triangular or flesh-colored, like the human heart, the plant would remedy chest pains and heartbreaks. This belief became popular again in Europe during the medieval period, and wild plant–based treatments were sought after for both spiritual and corporal ailments.

19

Wild plants were also eaten in times of distress. In the mid-1300s, the Black Plague lifted souls out of bodies by the millions, killing nearly 60 percent of Europe's population. With the population decline, there were fewer farm laborers, and many agricultural fields were abandoned to the weeds. Food became scarce. While the rich ate grand displays of game meat, wild birds, and exotic fruit, the poor survivors surveyed their deteriorated society and cooked pottages of whatever could be found free-growing in nearby fields, hedgerows, and woods: plantain and mallow, dock and nettles; woody roots of wild carrot, parsnips, leeks, skirret, and turnips; the leaves of wild strawberries, the leaves of violets and roses; moss, samphire, succory, colewort, nosesmart, peppergrass, bellflowers, scurvy grass, primrose, cowslip, beach mustard, and arrow grass; buttercup, yarrow, ryegrass, and smooth hawksbeard! One hundred herbs to add to the pudding. The strong, bitter flavors of these wild plants seemed to define the lives of those who ate them.

Initially, the church did not discourage foraging and the use of herbs. Many monasteries had extensive medicinal gardens, and the monks produced numerous herbal manuscripts. Most of these were based on texts first created in classical antiquity, such as the *De Materia Medica,* a five-volume encyclopedia about herbal medicine written in the first century by the Greek physician Dioscorides. Over the course of centuries, these books were copied and recopied by hand, modified bit by bit—ever-evolving manuscripts with new stories and quips inserted, slowly accumulating into the considerable tomes that existed by the Middle Ages. One of the most comprehensive was the *Leechbook of Bald*, a medical text written in the ninth century that laid out herbal cures for numerous afflictions, ranging from headaches to aching feet.

But until the printing press was developed in the fifteenth century, these handmade books remained rare and inaccessible to the ordinary person. Most herbal knowledge was therefore kept alive as folk medicine, handed down from mother to daughter, a kind of inheritance that might do her more good in staying healthy than any other sort of wealth a poor old country woman could offer.

Perhaps the most widespread use of wild plants was for contraception. Many species of the parsley family, such as wild carrot, contain estrogen-like molecules, and consuming them can prevent or terminate unwanted pregnancies. But a woman in control of her own body was a dangerous thing, and the church, along with male medical professionals, began to limit the unsupervised use and trade of gathered plants. The wise women who continued to practice their art were considered witches. Between 1450 and 1750 in Europe and North America, an estimated thirty-five thousand to one hundred thousand people, most of them women, were accused of wildcrafting and put to death.

The loss of common knowledge about wild edibles accelerated during the colonial period. Prior to European contact, the Americas were home to nearly 100 million Indigenous people, who between them spoke some one thousand to two thousand languages. The number of different plants they relied upon was enormous. Across North America, it is estimated that precontact people used over twenty-six hundred different species, nearly half exclusively for medicine. Less than one hundred of these plants were cultivated. The rest grew wild.

There was curly dock, rose hips, currant leaves, common arrowhead, and poke sprouts. There were chokecherries, western snowberries, and buffalo berries, the tart freshness of sassafras buds and wild ginseng. In spring, the young shoots of bigroot ladysthumb, and in the fall, the tubers of Maximilian sunflowers, which were sweetest after the first frost. The roots of butterfly weed were boiled, the seeds cooked with buffalo meat, and the buds dried for winter use. The wild turnip—timpsila—was so important to the Sioux that the location of hunting camps was often determined by where a supply could be found. Hidatsa hunters ate sunflower-seed balls stored in a piece of buffalo-heart skin as an energy snack. The Assiniboine picked rosebuds in summer, mixed them with tallow and dried berries. The Wasco tribe of the Pacific Northwest ate lichen with wind-dried salmon.

The origins of nearly 60 percent of what we eat globally today, including many of our most beloved foods, can be traced back to Indigenous Americans. It's no accident that we've forgotten this. Between 1492 and the late eighteenth century, land-use changes, imprisonment, wars, outright extermination, and the ravages of disease reduced the Indigenous American population to just 5 percent of its former size. With this genocide, thousands of years of environmental knowledge were lost.

The immense movement of people and goods associated with colonialism—often referred to as the Columbian exchange—transported so many species around the globe in just a few centuries that it fundamentally and irrevocably changed the composition of the world's ecosystems. Colonists brought medicinal and seasoning herbs from the old country to plant in their homestead gardens—many of which escaped into the surrounding countryside. Enslaved Africans smuggled seeds with them—watermelon, oil bush, gourd vine, gully root, okra, guinea corn, black-eyed peas, and prickly yam—so that they might grow a taste of home and feel somewhat less dispossessed. Like relics of freedom, these redemptive seeds sprouted into staple crops and outlasted the brief lives and violent deaths of those who planted them.

Naturalists were tasked with finding economically useful wild plants abroad that could be sold and domesticated back home. They bartered free passage on merchant ships and spread out to the far corners of the earth like some invasive weed. They went to China, North and South America, the Near East, the South Pacific and the Cape of Good Hope, Japan, and Borneo. With each round of colonial expansion, new plants were sent to colonies to be grown in plantations—sugar, sisal, tea, breadfruit, wild rubber, opium—while others were sent home as exotic specimens to be cultivated in greenhouses and studied. Many other plants unintentionally hitched a ride on these ships and took up root in new places.

Plants were dug up, placed in jars, thrust between sods or cuttings of moss, put in wooden boxes hammered shut with secure nails to prevent shipboard cats from getting in, or laid in small containers and kept moist until they could be transplanted. The hardiest specimens were planted in tubs and casks of dirt. Delicate seeds were coated in beeswax to protect them from moisture and mold, so that they might retain their vegetative powers until they could be relocated.

A few committed naturalists traveled with their collections to fend off jealous shipmates who wished to steal or damage the specimens. When fresh water onboard became scarce, they'd share their own small rations with the struggling plants. If the logistics of their lives made chaperoning specimens impossible, they'd beg the favor of ship surgeons, genteel passengers, and trusted friends to watch over their precious cargo.

The returning ships were thronged with more profitable goods from the colonies, and the captains often ignored the strict orders to store plant specimens in the "privilege of the cabin."[6] Instead, they were shoved into out-of-reach crevices and corners, placed in the cold, wet forecastle at the mercy of mildew and rats, or stowed in the storeroom, where they faced the perils of a lack of sunlight and putrid heat. Above deck, they were at the mercy of saltwater spray and negligent sailors. In many cases, these exotics arrived dead, stinking and rotten, reduced to bulbous roots and desiccated stems. It is estimated that fewer than one in fifty plants survived the trip. To have such lengthy work so thoroughly destroyed could only bring about spiritual enlightenment or mad decay.

Trial and error and experimentation greatly increased the success of keeping exotics alive. The key to transplant survival appeared to be sending plants during the appropriate seasons and the re-creation of the original ecology. Preserve the soil about the roots. Bury the Canadian trees in snow during the winter. Lay translucent cloches about the hot-loving and broad leaves of tropical ferns, and only send them on spring ships.

The study of wild plants was so esteemed that it became the root of much of the intellectual framework of the Enlightenment era. Ideas spun outward from the remote reaches of aristocratic estates to botanical gardens in London and Paris, crossed the Atlantic, whirled through the hands of a thousand plant collectors, revolved back again to Europe. Letters were collected into dictionaries of correspondence. Botanists painstakingly described, cataloged, and renamed wild plants that had previously been so commonplace and ordinary that they weren't mentioned in cookbooks or herbals. Exotic specimens were drawn on blank backgrounds, without the context of the landscapes where they grew. Encyclopedias were compiled over the course of a lifetime, updated with each new horticultural breakthrough. A great quantity of botanicals circled the earth.

Still, behind all this activity, naturalists relied heavily on Indigenous and enslaved peoples to gather specimens and knowledge for them. One of the first manuscripts describing plants in the Americas was the *Little Book of the Medicinal Herbs of the Indians*, an Aztec herbal translated from the Nahuatl original into Latin in 1552. Enslaved Africans had some of the most detailed knowledge of the natural environments of the Americas, as they often looked to wild foods to supplement their insufficient rations or foraged for medicinal and shamanistic herbs. Poisoning was one of the only ways enslaved people might overpower their masters, and knowing the properties of wild plants could mean the difference between freedom and bondage. Colonial naturalists utilized this knowledge in their own work. The physician and botanist Hans Sloane visited the West Indies from 1687 to 1689, and interacted extensively with enslaved peoples, eventually bringing home nearly eight hundred botanical specimens.

Some of the most intimate knowledge of plants came from Indigenous women, who, like women in Europe, had learned about the uses of plants from their mothers and grandmothers as tools for healing and contraception. Female colonists were also a source of information, as they tended to acquaint themselves with their new homes by foraging for familiar-looking potherbs.

The debt owed to these women who kept such wisdom alive through the centuries had been quietly acknowledged for hundreds of years. In the thirteenth century, Simon Corda of Genoa was taught the Greek names and uses of plants by an "old wife of Crete."[7] The fifteenth-century doctor Otto Brunfels called his botanical informers "highly expert old women."[8] The Swiss botanist Anton Schneeberger, who primarily worked in Poland, declared in 1557 that he "was not ashamed to be the pupil of an old peasant woman."[9] In the eighteenth century, Sir Joseph Banks paid herb-gathering women sixpence for every specimen they brought back to him.

25

But such folk knowledge was not considered scientific by Enlightenment standards. First, this botanical knowledge had to be purified for an elite European audience, silencing the contributions of those who had provided it in the first place. Colonial women's letters describing the plants they had found were rewritten and enclosed within the letters and pamphlets of male botanists. Botany was widely taught in medical schools, which women were not allowed to attend, just as they were not allowed to become members of the royal academies and botanical gardens. No matter how great their explorations or scientific publications, women were always considered amateurs or tourists.

Even as naturalists relied on women's knowledge, it was becoming increasingly difficult for poor women in Europe to practice their herb-craft at all. Land enclosures in England and other parts of Europe were turning common gathering lands into private property, making some types of agriculture more efficient—and freeing up labor for the Industrial Revolution— but destroying the diverse preexisting ecosystems where many wild plants had thrived. The swamps and fens were drained. The meadows were plowed up. The forests were cut down. The heaths were bounded by hedges and fences.

At the same time, the increasing rarity of once-common local plants enticed the upper class. Wild salads doused in sauces of butter and vinegar, or seasoned with sugar and spices, quickly

became an element of any aristocratic feast. The natural phi-
losopher Sir Kenelm Digby ate borage and bugloss, purslane
and sorrel, chervil and beet leaves. John Evelyn wrote an entire
treatise on edible plants to be used in salads called *Acetaria: A
Discourse of Sallets*. The lady's thistle, a wild spring plant that
was commonly boiled and eaten, was so popular that in the
year 1694, William Westmacott bemoaned its overharvest and
disappearance, writing, "As the world decays, so doth the use
of good old things and others more delicate and less virtuous
brought in."[10] Weeds even adorned the fanciest porcelain. In
1790, *Flora Danica,* a botanical atlas containing illustrations of
Denmark's wild plants, inspired an eighteen-hundred-piece
table setting made by the Royal Porcelain Factory in Copenhagen. Every dish was hand-painted.

By the beginning of the eighteenth century, plants had
become the most dominant symbol and tool of imperial expansion. The diversity of edible wild plants at home was traded for
a selection of domesticated plants from abroad. Foraged plants
had lost their link with feminine subsistence and survival. Land-
based practices, once taught by the doing of the action, were
translated into ethnographic documents, dead knowledge
stored in dusty libraries with the rest of the forgotten texts.

The day before my lunch at Noma, I have breakfast with the
Punk Rock Chef. He is a small Argentinian man with a dark
shock of hair and a rapid way of speaking. His words and ideas
blend into a torrent of competing streams. "Mostly foodies,
people just travel here to see Noma. It becomes this superfi-
cial thing," he says. "They are mechanical about wild food. They
just want one size. Everything else is wasted. You could start
a whole new restaurant just with the wasted produce! All this
food, it's fiction."

He pauses to take a sip of coffee.

"Yes, it's part of Danish culture to use herbs," the Punk Rock Chef continues. "It was a cheap thing to do, always. As a chef you go to the forest and pick stuff—it's a lot of work."

He smears jam on toast.

"But the business is pretend. The east coast of Denmark is very polluted. It's insane. There is so much boat traffic in the Baltic. You know this tourist island, Bornholm, famous for their fish? Well, the smoked herring they sell there is from Morocco. The west coast is much better—fish quality is one million times better—but the fish is very expensive, need to pay for the right to catch, have a boat. Very expensive to fish."

I dip my spoon into a fruit and yogurt parfait.

"We are surrounded by the sea, but people eat pork. It is a country made of pork. Forty million heads of pigs, you cannot see it but you can smell it. So many fields just with corn to feed the pigs. It's crazy how nations build their own image. Minimalism is big here, sure, but there are rules everywhere. Hiding. You cannot see it, but there are rules everywhere. This is a very flat place. Flat place leads to flat minds. Norway, they have wild minds. Because of the fjords, maybe."

The Punk Rock Chef grew up in a large city in Argentina and began cooking out of necessity—both his parents worked long hours. By age twelve, he was making dinners for himself and his sister. "Feeding is a very deep thing for me," he says, looking uncharacteristically serious for a moment before his face softens again. "Cooking, I compare to punk music. Like the Ramones, you can make it good with just three notes. You don't need to show how fast and how many you can play in thirty seconds."

The Punk Rock Chef moved to Copenhagen to work at Noma. After four years, he packed his knives and decided to open his own restaurant. But something went wrong. I don't completely understand how he "lost" his restaurant, but it had to do with a psychopath. And this psychopath changing all the locks. As psychopaths are wont to do.

Something in our conversation suddenly snaps the Punk Rock Chef into a new stream. His thoughts become turbulent and charged.

"It is like a sect. Nordic cuisine, with all its contradictions. For me, if you want to be dogmatic, be dogmatic, but nobody is dogmatic 100 percent, you cannot be halfway. You cannot be *almost* organic, you are or you are not. 'We don't use tomatoes because they don't come from the Nordic region.' Yes, but we do use potatoes and potatoes are originally from America. So where is the limit, when does it become Nordic? When does it become local? They all talk the same. It's a fucking brainwashing."

He shifts slightly in his chair. Leans forward. Sits back. Pushes on. "It helped me a lot as a human, being there, doing such extreme work, you know, because it made me free afterwards. Now I cook, and I don't think about it. I just do it. Before, I was scared—*What will I do, this is wrong*—and you are thinking too much. Drive me crazy! You heat up a sauce five degrees too much, which, yes, it's a mistake—it's all about details—but it wasn't the best environment for me to express myself. Two services a day with huge level of stress, so you are never, never relaxed. Sixteen, seventeen hours a day. Seventeen days in a row. That killed me! *Why am I doing this? For who?* Not for myself, this is someone else's dream."

The waters calm. The cataract of memory has passed.

"The world is fucked up in many ways. Now we have access to know that it's fucked up. Before we just didn't know. But to live these years is exciting. Coca-Cola, how powerful it was twenty years ago? I couldn't imagine opening a restaurant and not selling Coca-Cola. But now I don't serve it—'cause I don't want to, but also the people don't demand it. Yes, maybe it's trendy or hipster, but still, it's something, people drinking organic juice or tap water instead. But that's a small part of society. Big companies, they can push changes. Noma is avant-garde. Doesn't help change Denmark culture-wise."

The waitress sets down our check.

"Truly, truly, I am a cynical sarcastic ironic asshole, big-time asshole. But for me, being cynical is not about being dissatisfied. It's to be aware, awake, conscious. I don't believe in causalities. Coincidences. Home is where I am. I feel home many places."

Last I heard, he had joined the crew of a sailboat to explore unknown fjords in Greenland, cooking his philosophical food in tight quarters as the boat tossed back and forth with mid-winter storms.

We evolved to gather our sustenance on a daily basis, and eventually, this curiosity drove us across the blank spaces of the map, led us to wander in the wind-thrown seas and give new names to old places. We felt at home in the dark.

We found our way by touching and groping. A small taste of this, a bite of that. What we loved, we went back to again and again. It was an approach beyond the intellect, and so the first cuisines had an aesthetic of chance.

The oldest parts of our brains are those that tie together the senses with the emotions. The human gut has 500 million neurons, distributed across twenty different types, and the body responds to food much as it does to sexual stimulation. Both cause the mouth to water, stimulating sensitive nerve structures called Krause's end bulbs. These are found in the surfaces of the tongue and the folds of the lips, just as they are found in the sexual organs. We do not know which evolved first: our capacity for love or our desire to cook.

By the end of the meal at Noma, I feel like a culinary addict experiencing the diminishing return of excess. I have savored so many flavors, I feel desperate for the next fix and yet worn through from so much stimulation. I have reached saturation.

The neurologic phenomenon of desensitization is well known. We do not register every sensory perception equally. The logic of our nervous system is to find a signal in the noise—a sudden change from a former state. If a stimulus is repeated, each nerve cell dampens the messages it sends along a neural pathway until some new stimulus is observed.

In this way, eating is very much like falling in love. At first, the newness is startling. Each bite is remarkable. Then, as time passes, the dish becomes familiar, until one day, even our most rowdy decadence feels tame.

It is not so much that Noma presents us with novel flavors, merely that these common tastes are no longer mundane. We've lost them to over-domestication and standardization in an industrialized, monocultured food system. We've lost them as we've lost our wild places. Noma forces us to recognize the indulgence in eating something wild because it is the one thing we cannot make.

Weeds have become a delicacy only in the context of wealth, a luxury because access is limited. This is a meal for those most benefiting from the economic and social structures of modern-day capitalism, itself responsible for the vast destruction of species and ecosystems. Having consumed everything else civilization has to offer, we fetishize the wild because, in many ways, it no longer exists.

What does it mean for a plant to be from a specific place? With its own embedded history? Is it even possible to know anymore? Does it matter?

Noma isn't a local restaurant by any stretch of the imagination. The Nordic region is immense: if you were to flip Sweden upside down, it would extend past Sicily. In terms of distance, it would be more local to get sea urchins from the Mediterranean than the Norwegian Sea. But they taste different. Those from the Nordic arctic are sweet and voluptuous. In the Mediterranean, the poor urchins are merely briny.

The food travels long distances, within an arbitrarily constricted boundary, but the diners travel farther to eat it. There are none of the uncertainties associated with actual foraging, nor the boredom or long hours, or the need to really know a place. With money comes the ability to outsource all of that. The diner is paying for the opulence of time.

As if these acts of remembering might absolve us of all our sins. As if I wasn't complicit with my appetite, too.

I choke down the dessert served in an old cookie tin: a piece of fried pork chicharrón dipped in chocolate and a mushroom-shaped blob that tastes of cocoa and fungus. Chef Brad comes to collect me for the kitchen tour.

You already know how that goes.

And so it is, my brain alight in embarrassment and worry, my belly full of strange tastes, that I decide to wander a short distance away from Noma to Freetown Christiania, to see if I can make sense of my sudden nausea, or at the very least dull it.

Freetown is an anarchist village bordering two interconnected lakes that is generally considered exempt from the city's laws. A collection of handmade homes dot the feral, overgrown green space surrounding the water. I enter down a street lined with vendors, selling all manner of pot food and marijuana paraphernalia, a medieval affair that reminds me of peasants hawking their vegetables, and come to a central beer garden full of people lounging in the sun.

As I stroll along the dirt paths that circle the lakes, all in a pleasant cloud of smoke, *time* becomes unhinged and relative, *place* an intermittent dimension in which my senses become refined.

I digest my meal.

Is Noma presenting a myth of the past? A last-ditch effort to hold onto a vanishing set of relationships between people and the earth? Or is it a myth for the future? A re-articulation of the world we would like to create, where wild nature is highly valued, and there is a genuine desire to live closer to the land we have paved over and forgotten?

On some concrete steps overlooking the smaller lake, I meet a group of three men, all immigrants, each from a different African country. They live in a neighboring Swedish town, just over the border, and like to come to Freetown because it holds a different quality of interaction.

"Here, it is all about reciprocal acts of hospitality," one of the men tells me as he hands me a joint. One of the other men writes down his traditional name in my little black notebook, a name he no longer goes by in this new country, and says, "My village calls. I have been away too long." His features shift with this reflection, and beneath the joy of remembrance there is a sadness for something he is missing, and the uncertainty as to whether he will ever regain it.

The three men and I take a walk down the tree-lined trail that runs beside the larger of the two lakes. We pass a woman in the yard of a multicolored plywood house. She is planting flowers in old yogurt containers and plastic water bottles with the tops cut off. The light reflects off the lake, like a mirror casting prisms on her skin. The man from North Africa gestures toward this still-life and says to me, "This is love."

The men go their way and I go mine.

I walk down to the lake's edge. A hippie couple languishes in the sun on a flat rock overlooking the water. The man is from Copenhagen. The woman is a traveler from Poland. "My great-grandmother was from Poland," I say. There is something witchy about this woman, and she tells me a prophecy about my future, but I don't write it down and it will be forgotten.

"Why are people so cold here?" I ask.

"Sure, you could say it is the climate—the people match the 33 dark winters—but really I think it's because of our history," the man says. "So many generations of being colonized, waves and waves of intruders and wars. We became an insular people. Copenhagen is the most open city and the most racist—it is a city of contradictions." I leave them to their love.

While Noma's pastoral feast is about the unenclosed spaces, it cannot exist without the destructive act of enclosure. How easily we forget that this cuisine depends on the cemeteries where the foraged herbs grow, on the Christian ideologues who banished the trade of medicinal weeds by ordinary people so that they might consolidate their own power, on the wealthy tourists who support this experiment in living differently.

Next to a geodesic dome covered in tarps and fabric, I sit with a pretty Muslim woman in a pale-purple hijab who is waiting for her friend to return to his home. A couple of dogs sniff around the margins of the yard. "I want to write," she says, "to show that my culture is beautiful too. To explain why I don't drink and am not promiscuous. It is a fight to explain my world here. It is a foreign land, even though I was born and raised here. Even though Copenhagen is *my* city, too. Just because I am Muslim, it doesn't make me any less of a true Dane."

The afternoon is fading. I wander past a table laid out with a feast. Wine in crystal, tins of smoked fish, apples and cheese, bowls of salad. A group sits around the table looking jovial in the flaxen light. A robust man with blond hair and strong, genial features rises and approaches me. "I would ask you to join, but it is our monthly association meeting between the neighbors," he says with an apologetic smile. He then explains the history of the Freetown, gesturing energetically to a group of small neat houses with red-painted porches and a variety of bikes out front. "My parents, they came here, in protest. To squat the land. It was an abandoned military site. After many years, the government created an autonomous region and gave us ownership of this land. Now I raise my family here. We organize together for things like trash and schooling."

He radiates another kind smile. "Come again, another time, and you can eat with us."

His young wife walks up, two small children tugging at her legs. For the youth in his eyes, hers are rimmed in fatigue. I wander on.

Perhaps we can never truly abolish the past. The present merely holds on to the elements that have survived, now relics in our restaurants, like accumulated antiquities in our museums. But we remain addicted to the future, to becoming seers of that which does not yet exist, following our faulty sense of taste forward through the black night of history, ever in search of common memories.

And then I am in a completely different part of Copenhagen, at the French embassy. People are streaming in and out of the low stone entrance. I walk through a dark tunnel and emerge in a courtyard. There is a stage set up along the far wall, and a diplomat's teenage son is onstage, dressed in a tight leather jacket, crooning dramatically to bad-pop synths about the kind of deep romantic love he has yet to experience.

As the boy sings, the crowd of glamorous people sip champagne, pull at their cigarettes, and try to twist their drunken smirks into something resembling admiration. Green and orange lights bounce off the stone walls, jumping with the beat of the band, and the faces of the crowd turn into gargoyles in the intermittent shadows. The singer gives it everything his small body can give, and when he lets out his final note, he bows and beams, and feels himself to be important. His profuse thanks are genuine, even if the crowd's punctuated applause is not.

Perhaps this reverence for wild things is all an accident of history, 35 *an evolutionary artifact, ricocheting through the ages, even when we thought we were making decisions, even as we began to believe in the perception of free will. The pursuit of deliciousness became a bridge to new territories. As we pursued flavors more difficult to obtain, we exposed ourselves to a much more diverse set of foods. Chasing curious appetites created new kinds of men and women. It altered life histories. What began with the mouth, that external gatekeeper, became within the mysterious structures of the mind the undirected variants we call culture. And so, slowly, we forgot that the earth's history is our own. And soon, we no longer felt at home in the dark.*

On my way home, I stop in a small, loud bar to drink whiskey and watch the World Cup on a TV in the corner. The only remnant I have from this moment is a message in my little black notebook, written by the drunk guy who is sitting next to me. After the bar, I buy a falafel sandwich and get in bed and eat it quickly and fall asleep full.

HEAVY BEASTS
WITH MUSHROOMS
AND WILD HONEY

*Memories of Home—Shifting Borders—An Ancient Oak—The Value
of Tame and Wild—Prehistoric Beasts—A Small Revolt*

HAD A HOME once. It was in the desert, at the base of tall
snowy mountains with a wide valley of arroyos expanding to
the horizon. I was raised in a passive solar house my parents
built by hand, on twenty acres in New Mexico. The maze-like
structure was made of wood, tile, flagstone, and adobe. Their
bedroom was circular and had a mud wall, with flecks of hay that
bound it together. The *vigas,* or ceiling beams, were old electric
poles they'd salvaged, each with a hammered metal number in
the side. I spent hours imagining creatures in the wood grain
of the ceiling boards and frightened my little sister by telling
her snakes came out of the holes where the knots had fallen out.
Carved doors, secret compartments in the bookshelf, a hidden

drawer in the kitchen, wood stoves and fireplaces full of flames, *nichos* in the walls, sheepskins on the floors, and a row of purple lilacs out front. I was surrounded by earth and fire.

I was a feral child in this place. I used to sit in a little *piñon* tree just outside the garden. Three branches grew out of the base in such a way that they formed a nook just my size. I sat in this tree for hours, listening to the ravens laugh at the sunrise and the turtledoves moan their sunset laments. I'd snack on buttery *piñon* nuts picked straight from the cones, and watch ants carrying grains of crystal while the wind kicked dust into the perfect blue sky.

I usually came home dirty, picking cactus needles out of my legs and the fuzzy hairs of prickly pears out of my fingers, the tips stained magenta from peeling the fleshy fruit—a brief break of wild sustenance as I hunted rocks and searched for the elusive horned toad. On some evenings, my father would take me and my sister to gather tart wild raspberries, bitter miner's lettuce, and sweet red columbine in the blue-shadowed mountains just beyond.

Our pets were eaten by coyotes and hawks. Sometimes, wild dogs would show up on our doorstep, and we'd adopt them for as long as they felt like being domesticated. I never got too attached.

My mother's garden was a magical oasis. Each summer of my childhood, she coaxed lush plants from the dry desert soil, a kind of botanical alchemy I have yet to fully understand. One summer, a whole family of pastel-pink walking stick bugs took up residence on the plants. They sparkled in the pollen dust like savage jewels, until, one day, they all disappeared. I will always remember the bright verdure against the tawny sand and scrub, and the rattlesnakes among the tomatoes.

It is early summer. I am on a train in Poland. The train rushes past endless green fields, monotonous colors punctuated by shocks of bright tint. On the disturbed embankments by the train tracks, a fright of blood-red poppies drop their petals.

A few houses appear outside the train window. I see a mail truck in the distance, kicking up dust as it speeds between remote farmhouses. In the adjacent field, a small redheaded boy, dressed only in his underwear, hoes a row determinedly. Another boy, with a buzz cut and high-tops, leads a cow on a leash like an overfed pet.

I feel a bit scattered. Restless. Tired. I find myself waking in a panic too often these days. Something has shifted in me. And with a memory as faulty as mine, it's hard to tell if this feeling is new, or if it has been with me all along and I have merely forgotten it.

The inside of the train darkens. Outside, the fields become forests, become a country of pine. Europe was once covered in forests so immense that the root of the word *wilderness* stems from early Teutonic descriptions of them. It meant land that was self-willed. A kind of wild nature that could never be entirely controlled or conquered by human desire. These forests seemed to possess an element of the unknowable. In the sixth and seventh centuries, spiritual seekers would retreat into these woods to search for God, living off roots and berries and leaves until they experienced a sign of divinity.

The fate of the forest has long been entangled with the fate of its game animals. Ancient kings hunted in these woods and passed some of the first environmental laws to protect the land that supplied their meat. Today, nearly all of Europe's primeval forests are gone, but I've come to Poland to see the last piece, a relic of culinary infatuation, a vestige of royal appetites.

My great-grandmother Esther grew up in a *schetyl,* or small forest village, somewhere near here. The village never stayed in the same place for long—the borders of this land shifted often with the tides of war. Before Esther was born, her village existed within the Prussian Empire. During her childhood it was part of Russia. And after she fled her home for a safer country, it became part of Poland. The village no longer exists.

Esther's home was always under siege. Each new invader tried to convert the Jews to their own religions and beliefs. World War I was a time of ugliness and upheavals. The villages were empty. The trees lay burnt and wasted. Stumps dotted the barren landscape like monstrous cadavers. Those who mapped the borders held mastery over the people.

To escape this violent landscape, countless Jews emigrated to faraway places, carrying their mothers' recipes, something precious to hold onto when everything else had been lost. They gave themselves new names to match the new places they inhabited.

"Being Jewish means having three thousand years of suffering in your blood," my mother joked as we sat around her kitchen island last fall. "Who would want that heritage?" she laughed.

"Your great-grandmother Esther was tall and stern. And quite beautiful," my mother had told me. "She took her tea the Russian way: strong and bitter with a cube of sugar under the tongue."

Esther came to the United States as a teenager around 1919. She took her husband's name, which was likely Hauptman (High Man), although it was changed to Antman to sound more American. As they settled into a new life in a new country, they hid their Judaism, for like their name, it was not something to be proud of. But her faith was kept alive in the food.

"They were always making chicken soup—Jewish penicillin, we called it," my mother remembered. "The apartments always stunk of it. Matzah balls. Borscht—so good. Blintzes. I remember the thick dark bread."

Esther lived most of her adult life in Brooklyn, but in the summers the family would rent a home in the Catskills. My mother remembers her foraging for a wild plant, something she called sour grass, a type of wild spinach with a tangy taste. Esther cooked it into a light-green drink. She called the finished product *schav*. A tonic for the grief of placelessness.

Little else is known about her.

41

———

I visit an ancient oak, more than seven hundred years old, growing on the side of a road. It has been known by many different names. With each new ruler, the tree was rediscovered, and the land was rechristened. Somehow the ancient oak remained standing through centuries of deforestation, perhaps solely because it was already so old. Today, along with six other oak trees in the area of a similar age, it is considered a Polish national monument.

The pedunculate tree is rotting and lightning scarred. The branches are riddled with smaller cavities, and netting has been secured over the holes to stop the birds from nesting inside. There is a large hollow at the base of the trunk. In 1880, a wooden door was fitted across it, and a guard was posted outside. It was claimed that eleven soldiers could fit within the interior.

From the oak, I walk uphill on a path through a small hardwood forest. Over the far-flung horizon, a glimpse of sand rolls into the Baltic Sea. At the top of the rise, there is a humble Gothic church, constructed of whitewashed stone. Just inside the entrance, hanging by a spiral staircase, is a large wooden cross adorned with deer antlers. Next to the cross, a Virgin Mary made of seashells holds her swaddled baby. Her halo is made of pastel-striped macoma clams. Her robe is of mussels, stitched together by seams of periwinkles. A necklace of amber—the dark compressions of time, the potential of a thousand ancient trees and a million sunlit days—garlands her delicate throat.

Outside the church, three foresters stand around in grey-green uniforms. The district manager holds his leather belt at either hip. He wears thick-rimmed glasses with sun-darkening lenses and a dark-green tie with a tiny red deer emblem embroidered near the knot. State foresters were recently voted "the most trusted public servants" in Poland, and these men look proud of their position.

Most of the forests that remain in Poland are highly managed plantation stands, planted according to "normal forestry" in unnaturally straight lines of pine or spruce, all the same age and nearly identical in height. The Polish State Forests was formed in 1924 as a nationalist cause, and from the very beginning, the organization prided itself on its hierarchical and military values. After World War II, the forests became a symbol of a newly reborn nation, and the foresters were the custodians of this national heritage, patiently stewarding trees into revenue. They drained and channeled forest rivers to dry out the land, and planted the most marketable species—Scots pine and Norway spruce—in uniform lines, coniferous trees that grew well in the thin, xeric soils.

Without the competition for light and moisture from hardwood species, the tree crops grew quickly and very straight—ideal for lumber. The understory was cleared of dead trees. Row after row, each tree the same kind and age, all cut down according to an optimized rotation length. After centuries of chaos and confusion, the land was no longer in disarray or rife with mayhem. The forest was finally made rational.

Today, the unfavorable consequences of a century of mono-
culture forestry have become evident. Plantation stands are
more susceptible to blights of invading insects and the gusts
of windstorms. All these trees, the same age, planted in even
rows, has meant that there is less habitat for the birds and
insects who live in rotting fallen logs or nest among broad-
leafed shrubs in the understory. Now the forestry service is
working to make their tree plantations less like machines and
more like networks, mimicking the characteristics of an eco-
logically healthy "wild" forest with the hope of increasing both
biodiversity and resiliency. The repercussions of this approach
are yet to be seen.

In the afternoon, I join the foresters for lunch in the dining
room of a tourist resort. The room is made to look old. Plaster
and brick walls are fitted with wooden ribs. The ceiling pitches
steeply above a lattice of massive beams. Wrought iron chande-
liers hang on thick chains from the polished timber.

We sit at a table that spans the length of the room and seats
twenty-eight. It is covered with a white cloth and set with porcelain and silver. Candles in towering, ornate ironwork holders
cast flickering light on the diners below. In the center, a gaudy
bouquet of cream flowers droops from a tall crystal vase.

I've been told we are having wild boar for lunch, and I am
eagerly awaiting what I imagine to be a sizable portion of
roasted meat. I am hungry.

The earliest humans were not hunters. They were scaven-
gers. When wild packs of dogs and large carnivores tired of their
catch, and night settled in, we humans overcame our fear and
timidly pulled pieces of bloody flesh from the remains. Meat
was a major source of energy, calories, and fat, and a craving
for meat may have been an adaptive strategy in early homi-
nids. The high levels of essential fatty acids found in the bone

marrow and brain tissue of animals, as well as the micronutrients found in the mineral-rich livers and hearts, were essential
building blocks for our expanding brains. As we learned to hunt,
44   we invented feasting to partition the meat from the cooperative
endeavor, to share in the glut before it spoiled.

Wild boar has been eaten for at least ten thousand years. In
the Cova Remígia in Spain, a cave painting dating to the early
Holocene period (8000–6000 BCE) depicts six archers running in pursuit of wild boar. Some of the boar are slashed with
arrows, while others are painted upside down, presumably having succumbed to their wounds.

Stories from the Roman period also document the hunting
of wild boar, often associating it with masculinity and power.
Pliny the Younger (c. 61–115 CE) went boar hunting with nets,
although he just barely put down his pen in time to pick up
a javelin and slay the animal. Marcus Aurelius took them out
from horseback, and because boar are known to fight, he was
careful to keep the horse at a full gallop so as not to be injured
by the wounded beast. There is a story in the *Gesta Romanorum*,
a collection of Latin anecdotes written in the Middle Ages, that
chronicles Emperor Trajan's demand for a boar's heart, as he
"loved the heart best of any beast, and more than all the beast."
But the chef tasked with preparing it was too tempted by the
heart and ate it himself, then told the waiters to inform the dictator "the hog had no heart."[1]

For medieval kings in Europe, the larger the beast, and the
more perilous to hunt, the more noble it was. Wild boar was
one of these dangerous species, and thus classed as "greater
game" and especially coveted. In England, these animals were
of such importance that the *Little Domesday Book* (1086) measured the size of forested land by the number of wild boar that
roamed the woods. Herds of wild boar were called *sounder* in

medieval reports, and the dewclaws, called *argus,* were prized hunting trophies, while boar grease was a medicinal product given to the poor. By the thirteenth century, wild boar were so overhunted in England that they became extinct. Yet their mys- 45 tique lingered on. Four hundred years later, Charles I, wanting to reintroduce them to England, went to considerable expense to procure a pair to mate from Germany.

Today, in Poland—and many other countries around the world—wild boar have become a common and destructive agricultural pest, thriving in the fragmented forest and farmland environment that now exists across Europe. For rich trophy hunters, wild boar are a source of pleasure. For poor farmers, they are a headache.

The Polish government recently passed a law to cull around 90 percent of the population—about 200,000 animals—in an effort to stop the spread of African swine fever, which can infect domestic pigs. This has caused public outrage and protest, primarily from wildlife biologists and conservationists, who are concerned over the adverse ecological impacts—wild boar eat rodents and insects, plus help to regenerate forests by aerating the soil and burying tree seeds—but some hunters' associations have also objected over the extremity of the measure.

A plate is set before me. A delicately carved rack of boar ribs is balanced on a stack of thin potato fritters. This precarious sculpture is surrounded by a pool of forest-berry gravy. A frisée salad decorates the perimeter. The meat tastes like pork but earthier, although it's hard to get the nuance of flavor beneath the cloyingly sweet berry sauce.

The district forest manager sits across from me. His hair is dyed coal black, although the white roots are beginning to show. A manicured mustache angles down from the corners of his mouth and ends in a narrow strip of beard rimming his chin.

In forestry terms, we might call this style a "clearcut surrounded by seed trees."

As we eat, I ask about the history of hunting in the region. The district manager responds in Polish to the translator sitting next to him, but as he speaks, he stares at me as if wishing he could devour me instead of his meal.

The translator, Lucas, blushes and smiles in embarrassment. His lips stick to his glinting braces as he says sheepishly, "I can't translate that. It is not... translatable. Nor polite."

I look down at my empty plate. I'm still hungry.

———

The countryside may appear static at first glance, but seen from the seat of history, it experiences constant flux. The forests surrounding the old Polish fortress towns are certainly in a perpetual state of falling down and up, arrested in simultaneous decay and growth. But it's not just the trees that change. How we see the forest changes as well: the myths we construct; the conclusions we draw; the way we understand ourselves among the stands.

What we know of the lives and rituals of the indigenous cultures in Europe's dense forests is piecemeal and largely based on legend. In Poland, the Old Prussian tribes lived in small, self-sufficient villages that did not penetrate very far into the vast woodlands. They named their settlements after the woods, streams, and lakes that surrounded the places where they lived. Wild game animals—deer, moose, aurochs, forest bison, wild boar—were so abundant that no form of hunting restriction was necessary, and meat was often smoked for preservation.

Along with their game-heavy diets, the tribes also practiced swidden agriculture—slash-and-burn shifting cultivation—to grow barley, millet, wheat, and corn on small patches of cleared forest, and free-pastured pigs on acorns, young shoots, and beechnuts. The pigs—long-legged, yellowish-brown, and bristly—were the hybrid descendants of Roman gilts and wild boars. They used their snouts to break up the ground in search of tubers, insect larvae, or mice, and in doing so, helped to regenerate the forest by loosening the soil and occasionally burying tree seeds. Other than their more pleasant countenance, the domesticated pigs were barely distinguishable from their wild counterparts. Occasionally, a pig would even wander off and breed with a wild partner of its own volition, helping to maintain the overall vigor of the herd.

47

The seasons were worshipped like gods. Each year, after the first seeds were planted, rituals were performed to kill the spring and bring in the summer. When a leader felt he had become too old or weak to govern with the necessary strength and prudence, he made a pile of thorn bushes and straw, then climbed atop this pyre and delivered his last sermon. When the long oration reached its end, he took the flame of perpetual fire that burned in front of the holy oak and lit the pile and himself afire. In the days that followed, the people would erect a stone *baba* to honor his death. They vowed not to be afraid, for in their hearts they knew that everything returns.

To the Romans and Greeks, who were primarily agriculturalists, these people were as barbaric as the beasts they hunted. Civilization and barbarism were associated not only with different kinds of landscapes, but also with the foods they supplied. Ancient Greeks believed it was wine, wheat, and oil that led to civilization. The Romans distinguished between land that was cultivated, and thus cultured—*agri-culture*—and land that was wild, and thus ungovernable.

Romans did hunt, but primarily for sport and military training rather than sustenance, and their hunting laws were some of the first to be written down. These followed the ideas of *ferae naturae* and *res nullius*: wild animals belonged to nobody and anyone was free to kill them as long as the hunter was not trespassing on another man's land. While in theory this gave common access to game, in effect it meant it belonged to wealthy landowners. Enclosed estates were set aside as game preserves for statesmen to hunt stag, wolf, and bear, as well as imported exotic species such as lions, leopards, and elephants. Peasants were only allowed to snare hares and hedgehogs.

Early Medieval Christians carried on the belief that social class mirrored both natural environment and diet. To them, the vast forests of Central Europe were symbols of moral chaos, and the pagan tribes living among the uncultivated stands of trees were savages. Their rituals and ceremonies to thank the earth for good harvests were described as horrid spectacles of demonic devotion. It was said that if a Christian were to be so unlucky as to witness one of their Wild Hunts, he would be pulled into the underworld later that evening while he slept. His spirit would join the cavalcade of elves and fairies, the cloudy roar of heathen goddesses and wood wives, living forever among the unseen dead. During the Crusades, those pagans who refused to submit to the new religious regime were killed, exiled, or most gruesomely, burned alive in their armor in front of the shrines of their gods.

For European kings in the early Middle Ages, though, the forests were not inimical places but symbols of power that served a vital role in their diets. Game meat—generally just called venison, derived from the word *venari* (to hunt)—was an essential element at feasts and a way for kings to display their amassed wealth and status. The meat was often braised with fruit, rose water, and the fragrant spices ambergris and musk. In Italy, it was customary to roast game animals whole, cover them in gold leaf, and bring them to the table in one piece to be ceremoniously carved in front of the salivating dinner guests. Polish kings served meat that was heavily spiced, as condiments from Asia were less expensive here than in the rest of Western Europe.

As early as the eleventh century, the demand for timber began threatening the forestlands where game animals lived. This prompted kings in England to pass some of the earliest environmental conservation laws. These forest laws were based on the Roman idea that the right to hunt lay with the property owner, and they restricted hunting to the nobility. Since the king technically owned the entire domain, he had the right to hunt wherever he pleased, and certain tracts of forest were, as one law put it, "privileged for wild beasts" existing under "the safe protection of the king, for his delight and pleasure."[2]

As the centuries wore on, hunting became increasingly bureaucratic, and nearly every aspect of the endeavor was codified in law and highly controlled. What began as custom to ensure the best-tasting meat—red deer bucks in late summer, when they were "in grease" and fat from browse and nuts, but before they began to rut; does from fall through February—morphed into open and closed seasons for hunting. Under the oversight of the King's Forester, wardens collected rents, handed out hunting licenses, made sure game animals didn't starve in winter or in times of drought by providing them with feed, prepared venison for royal feasts, and meted out punishments against poachers.

Numerous hunting manuals laid out the proper techniques for the venatic arts and formalized the vocabulary used to describe them. A thirteenth-century Welsh manuscript has a section called the Venedotion Code, which elucidates the "Value of Wild and Tame." The "worth of a Hart" could be divided into legal pieces worth three score pence each: "his two chaps as well as his two horn; his tongue; his breast; his heart; his rectum; his liver; his two loin; his haunch; his paunch; and his chine."[3]

50

There was also increasing concern with the ethics of hunting. An anonymous French work, *La Chace dou cerf* (1275) suggests that the aristocracy would find hunting more pleasurable if they did not have to worry about the horridness of killing any mortally wounded animals—this should be the duty of the master of the hunt. Indeed, by the late thirteenth century, much of the venison eaten by the aristocracy was hunted by servants, and large households employed numerous people to acquire this important food.

Game meat was becoming increasingly expensive in Western Europe as hunting preserves were threatened by the demand for timber and arable land. Wood was needed for the seemingly infinite increases in the iron, brick, and tile industries, for building houses and making casks, furniture, carts, wagons, and coaches. There was also enormous economic opportunity in cutting down the forests and growing grain. Europe's population was steadily on the rise—from 36 million in 1000 CE to more than 80 million by the year 1300—and the best soils in Western Europe were already under cultivation.

Unlike their kings, most European peasants rarely ate much meat of any sort, except for ceremonial purposes. In literature from the early medieval period, the word *meat* was often used interchangeably with the word *food*. It is therefore unclear just how much meat was actually eaten—being offered *meat* may have meant any kind of food—but there is evidence that it wasn't until the mid-fourteenth century, after the plague took out huge swaths of the population, and more grain fields were turned into pasture, that domesticated meat became abundant enough for the general population to increase their consumption.

As meat eating became more democratized, kings could no longer define their power by the amount of flesh they con- sumed, and there was a renewed focus on the delicacy and distinguishing quality of wild game. Even the way game was butchered—the unmaking or breaking of the animal, as it was called—became highly ritualized and regulated. The *Boke of St. Albans (1486)*, described how to butcher a stag, instructing that the pelvis must be cast aside at the kill site as an offering to the raven and that the left shoulder should be given to the forest administrator as his fee.

The first Polish forest laws were passed in the mid-fourteenth century, and like the English laws, these declared that certain tracts of woods were reserved for the king and his retinue as exclusive hunting preserves, and therefore could not be cut down. But the rest of the landscape was undergoing rapid transformation. Royal Prussia, as the region was then known, was quickly becoming one of the primary suppliers of both grain and timber to Western Europe. It was here that King Philip of Spain sourced his mast trees to build an armada to sail against Holland and England in the 1580s. Over the next few centuries, old forests were felled and turned into new fields.

By the early seventeenth century, Europe's vast forests covered just 20 percent of their former expanse. The sandy soils, no longer held down by the roots of trees, began to erode. Entire woodland species went extinct or disappeared. The aurochs—large wild oxen that were the ancestors of modern cattle—suffered miserably. The last one died in 1627 in Poland's Jaktorów Forest. Squirrels vanished as the trees in which they lived were denuded. The fur-bearing pine marten fled. Rabbits multiplied in the spaces left behind.

In the nineteenth century, large areas of Poland's forest-land were taken over by Russian administrators. Landowning families, previously embroiled in feuds with each other, took up arms and united in opposition to their new rulers. The remaining forests were no longer places of gods or demons, but landscapes of politics and insurrection. The wolves proliferated, feasting on the bodies of slain men and their horses. The sandy soils whipped up and stung the air. Blind cupidity had left its mark on the land.

By the dawn of the twentieth century, empires and individuals had cut down nearly all of Europe's old-growth forests, which had once seemed so intractable. The bits and pieces that remain survive in part because of the meaty cravings of dead kings. The stories we tell about the forests may have changed, but the fate of the game animals and the fate of the trees continue to be intertwined.

———————

One evening at sunset, I watch a herd of wild forest bison graze from a perch by the side of a farm road. I lean against some hay bales and peer through binoculars at the creatures, silhouettes against the pines at the far edge of the tolerant fields. They seem dimwitted and overbred. Only in the steam puffs from their jet-black nostrils, and within their sad, searching eyes, rimmed in curls of black fur, is there a hint of their prehistoric nature.

My guide receives text messages from his farmer friends telling him where he can find the bison. But he made a game of the search by first taking our small group on a hunt to find the tracks. "The other group didn't see any," he says, as if our sighting was rare and mystical. "There are no more cows here. The bison are our cows," he says with a smile.

These bison roam Poland's Białowieża Forest, a tiny remnant of the lowland old-growth forest that used to cover nearly the entire continent. Declared Poland's first national park in 1932, it's as close to "natural" as is left in Europe. The European bison, also called wisent (*Bison bonasus*) exist today because of this forest, and yet this forest also survives because of long-standing protection of the bison. It has been a pervasive and variable relationship.

53

Beginning at the end of the fourteenth century, and lasting for six hundred years, this forest was the private hunting grounds of those in power. If a commoner was caught poaching animals, they could be given the death penalty. But even as Białowieża Forest was protected from major deforestation, the surrounding trees fell to wars and commerce, often one and the same. The bison, once found across the continent, were reduced to a remnant population in eastern Europe. Even so, kings still found great pleasure in hunting them. In 1752, Augustus III, King of Poland, killed forty-two bison in a single hunt. He employed hundreds of beaters to flush the animals out of the woods and drive them to where he sat and waited. Legend has it that his wife killed twenty bison herself, reading novels while she waited for the animals to appear.

Like in other protected woodlands, the local peasants continued to have the right to graze their pigs, make hay, occasionally harvest timber, and tap honey from tree bees. Honey had been collected from wild hives in these forests for at least three thousand years. Wild bees lived in the cavities of tree trunks, about twenty to thirty feet above the ground, and people tended particular trees and the hives they contained.

Sometimes the beekeepers' torches lit inadvertent fires in the forest, as did careless travelers passing through. The peasants also used fire deliberately to steward the land, encourage new grass growth for animal browse, and to back-burn areas near habitations to prevent uncontrollable wildfires from destroying the village.

With each fire, the tree composition of the forest shifted. Some trees, like pines, thrived: the flames burned away hardwood seedlings that grew in the understory, which would otherwise compete with the evergreen trees for light. When the fires became less frequent, the hardwoods started to grow back.

Poland was partitioned again in the nineteenth century, this time among the three great powers of Prussia, the Austro-Hungarian Empire, and Russia. Loyalties changed so frequently it was difficult to know if an insurrection would have the support of the local people. Occasionally, the lines of demarcation ran straight through the middle of a village.

The Russians plundered Polish libraries, the spoils of war carefully taken back to the Imperial Library in St. Petersburg, which at one time contained nearly 500,000 volumes and manuscripts, including the love letters of ancient kings and queens. Białowieża became the hunting grounds of the Russian czar, who only ever visited once or twice, but kept the bison under royal protection just in case he wished to someday shoot them. Despite their imperial protections, the bison population dwindled, victims to hungry men in the midst of battle.

By World War I, there were only about eight hundred free-living bison left, and many soldiers survived by eating these animals. The last European bison living in the wild was shot in 1919 here in Białowieża by a poacher. Only twelve remained alive in captivity—those that had been sent abroad as royal gifts—scattered across Europe's zoos and menageries. In the interwar period, field biologists bred these lonely beasts in the confines of research institutions and slowly reintroduced their offspring to the forests. Nearly 80 percent of today's current population can be traced to just one pair.

The State Forests follows a long tradition of feeding these animals in winter, and has set up stations piled with hay to dissuade the bison from eating the buds of young trees in man-aged commercial forests or destroying the crops of local farms. The animals are monitored and treated for disease. Each year, about twenty are culled to prevent overpopulation. Their lean 55 flesh is sold to restaurants. In winter, the bison wander into town. Recently, one walked all the way through the park and visited the museum.

Some areas of the national park are strictly protected, and one cannot visit them without a guide. My guide tells me that Białowieża Forest belongs to the earliest era of life on earth. The primeval. It has incredible biodiversity—more than eleven hundred species of flora and an estimated twenty-five thou-sand species of fauna—and is the last remaining refuge for numerous species that once existed across Europe. As we walk through the forest on elevated walkways, past some of the tall-est oak trees in the world, we pause to peer at a middle spotted woodpecker hammering into a dead standing tree. He wears a red feather headdress with a cape of dusky white pixels on black silk.

We come to a boggy wetland and watch a marsh harrier swoop low. The landscape changes from silver birch, black alder, and ash trees to stands of hornbeam, Norway maple, and small-leaved lime. A few spruce, slender at the crowns, peek through the foliage. The ground is blanketed in boreal feather mosses. We pass an open meadow, a former hayfield, now royal with the heavy blooms of Siberian iris and purple foxglove. The wolves walk the forest roads at night, and at a crossroads, we find a mark of their territory: claw scratches two feet long.

This forest is a hotspot for fungi (more than 4,000 species), particularly macro fungi (1,850 known species), making it one of the most diverse places in the world. Many of these mushrooms glow with phosphorescence through the darkest nights.

If meat was a masculine pursuit, and the forests were defined by the desire of kings to control their territory, then for country women these woods had long been a place to gather mush-
56   rooms. During the Enlightenment, as a great many foreign plants were being imported from abroad, people in England and Western Europe were still suspicious of eating mushrooms, perhaps partially due to a lingering distrust of forests in general. In 1620, one Somerset physician declared that only "fantastical people" ate mushrooms. Still, at least one British adventurer brought news home that indeed mushrooms were "wholesome and toothsome."[4]

But the village women of the Polish forests knew mushrooms to be not only a delicious delight, but also an important source of remedies: larch bracket was used to treat bleeding, festering wounds, vomiting, and hemorrhoids. The hoof bracket mushroom fought toothaches. Judas's ear could cure ear and eye infections. Puffballs had antiseptic powers and stinkhorns were aphrodisiacs.

There is no way to draw a line between the trees and the mushrooms. They grow in symbiosis, each fungus associated with a particular bark or root. There are no individuals here. There is only a multi-species network, sharing resources, making plans, stochastic soulmates defined by their connections rather than their differences, obliged to coexist. In mast years, when the trees need tremendous resources to produce their huge quantities of nuts and acorns, they borrow nutrients from the extensive networks of fungi that exist both above and below ground. In other years, the trees store the captured energy of the sun by transferring it to the mushrooms. There is no border, no solid line between territories and definitions.

Many wild mushrooms have high concentrations of heavy metals such as mercury. Yet the desire to eat them has only grown in recent years. Strangers move through the woods, ripping up edible and inedible species indiscriminately, extracting their flesh for a global market. In some areas of the world, the commercial harvesting of wild mushrooms has gotten so intense that the practice threatens the health of the forests.

Białowieża Forest is a mosaic landscape. Pockets of Douglas fir, plantations of Scots pine and Norway spruce, stands dominated by hardwoods, rivulets of dead fire-scarred logs, open wetlands, and hayfields. The variation in trees mirrors not only the variations in topography and water supply, but, more importantly, the past and present actions of people on the land. Only in satellite images is it obvious that the human presence has long been entangled with the character of this ancient forest. Geometrical forms show the influence of men. Straight lines and squares that are unfamiliar to nature.

This "wild" place is heavily managed. The majority of the Białowieża Forest is still actively logged. The average age of trees at harvest is a hundred years. In the strictly protected areas, where logging is not allowed, diseased trees are removed so that they will not infect their neighbors. The amount of dead wood left on the forest floor is meticulously counted and enforced, as many of the diverse fungi rely on it to survive. In a few areas, the scientists have decided to leave nature completely alone, to see how it will experience bark beetle blight and fires all on its own. "We think on the scale of eternity," the guide tells me.

Meanwhile, even the natural cycles are no longer so pure. Invasive plants creep into protected areas, undeterred by the human desire to keep them pristine. The wildflowers bloom earlier in the spring due to climate change. The deer no longer concentrate in the valleys as they once might have, but instead gather around wooden huts that contain overwintering fodder of salt and potatoes, put out by the hunters who will kill them in their season.

In the past, when diplomats and wealthy men visited Poland, they would sometimes bring an exotic tree specimen as a gift and a sign of friendship. Many of these trees were American species such as red oak, and today the forests are sprinkled with these foreign aberrations, splashes of color on grids of green, whispered reminders of the past, adumbrations cast by the future.

As I watch the bison at sunset, I think of these kings who exchanged gifts of trees. Of the kings who, after a successful hunt, would anoint each other with bison blood. And now, in the last relic of primeval forest, the tourists hunt bison and old oaks too, their worship in the form of photos, the beasts as domesticated as cows. The local farmers and herders rarely find time to go gather in the forest. They have become entrepreneurs catering to the influx of visitors, leading sightseers around like savvy nature guides, too busy to search for mushrooms from the soils of the dead. How easily we forget the quantity of blood that has been spilled. These former hunting lands hold a kind of memory, a fragile archive of the wealth of the past, now mere echoes, hidden in the rings of trees, waiting to be heard.

———

"Poland's forests hold many secrets," my translator Lucas says, as we stand on a wooden watchtower at the edge of a pasture, gazing at a red deer disappearing into the woods.

Perhaps these Polish forests hold some key to my unruly instincts, my appetite for gathering. *I want to see everything, go everywhere*, I think. Perhaps that sense of wild restlessness is my heritage. *But at the same time, I want to stay in one place, build a life.* I stare into the distance hoping for one more glance of the wild animal, its elegant rack melting into the tall grass.

The oasis I grew up in did not last. I left my home carrying with me the nostalgia for what magic could have been. Perhaps I have been searching for it ever since. That simple curiosity. That authentic blood-filled existence.

My great-grandmother Esther's home was destroyed by war. The only picture I have ever seen of her is in a carved frame in my mother's house. The photo is from her wedding day: she wears a delicate tiara on top of a simple veil, the white gauze spilling over her thick hair, which has been woven into intricate braids on either side of her head. She has thick, close-set eyebrows, and dark, heavy-lidded eyes. Her thin lips turn down into a slight frown. I do not know if she was in love with the man she has just married. Her resigned expression seems to embody the Hebrew saying, *If there's a doubt, there's no doubt.*

I imagine the contours of Esther's childhood.

Spring was for nettle soup and linden-flower tea.

In May, when the poppies bloomed, the villagers crushed the seeds to make oil or cooked them into gruel. With hands dusted in pollen, they boiled poppy petals with dark honey from the wild bees found in the cavities of trees, and made a thick syrup for young children with coughs and colds who could not get to sleep.

In late summer, at reaping time, the last sheaf of wheat brought down by the last threshing stroke was adorned with flowers, tied with ribbons, and carried through the village on the last harvest-wagon.

The fall was busy with the gathering of berries and dead wood before winter set in, and it became so cold even the quicksilver froze.

And of course, all throughout the year, but most abundant in early fall, on nearly every stump and base, the fruiting bodies of mushrooms, each with a name like poetry: bare-toothed russula (handsome and white-stemmed, along the forest floor), copper brittlegills, yellow-cracking boletes, cloudy clitocybe, and sandy knight caps (purple-topped and sprouting from rotting logs); sulfur tuft, scaber stalks, and horse mushroom (large and sessile, glossy and red); king boletes, bay boletes, brown birch, and pestle-shagged puffballs (growing from the sides of a standing giant); woolly milk caps, orange slime cort, and parasols. Each with their own dark smell, like the musk of an animal. To procreate, these mushrooms released their invisible spores into the air, musty rich explosions, winging on the wind, buoyant and weightless, like silent wishes for a prosperous future.

The villagers ate fresh mushrooms, and dried and pickled and stored even more, holding on to them like treasure for uncertain times ahead.

All told, these forest rituals and traditions bound together a culture that was always under siege. A way to map a forest of invasions and retreats, where boundary lines were only ever a mirage. The armies and borders may have moved, but the people and their loyalties remained in place. They were *from here.*

Did Esther stand at the edge of a pasture, gazing at a red deer disappearing into the woods, its elegant rack melting into the tall grass, and think of escaping somewhere else? Perhaps she pocketed the gloomy tips of spruce when she was meant to be gathering firewood, or couldn't stop herself from eating the miraculous blueberries she was supposed to collect. I imagine she picked the swollen white stems of *borowiki* mushrooms with purple-stained fingertips, each movement a small revolt. Perhaps she lived her life according to the Russian/Polish proverb: *Ciszej jedziesz, dalej będziesz*—"One can go further if they remain quiet."

3

FISH, FIN, SHELL, AND CLAW

The Devouring Sea—Driftwood Oysters—A Touristic Appetite—Afflicted with Madness—A Suffering Subject—Tastes Sublime

M Y FRIEND MARY has invited me to visit her in Maine for a traditional lobster bake, a yearly get-together with friends and relatives, followed by the annual Lobster Boat Races the next day. I've been to Maine before, and eaten lobster on many occasions, but I've never experienced a lobster meal with those whose lives are so entwined with the sea. As a child of the desert, I have always had a deep fascination with the ocean. It seems so utterly immense. So full and yet so hidden. It is for me an inevitable attraction.

Mary and I take a boat out to Middle Tide Island. Along the coast, the land juts into the sea in spits and skewers. Here and there, the consistency of earth is broken apart, and islands that formed long ago retain their solitude. There are three thousand such islands in total off the coast of Maine. Some inhabited. Others only drowning rocks that peep above the water at low tide. All of them navigable hazards in one way or another.

Inhabiting an island means always thinking about the sea. On Middle Tide Island, the tide drops fifteen feet in just six hours. Since property rights are determined by the tide line, sea-level rise means this island will legally shrink, until it no longer exists at all.

On the shore, a small wooden cabin and an outhouse are situated under tall pines. There are shells among the forest litter, relics of storms and seagulls. Thin soils cover old, pale rocks. Fir trees grow twisted and gnarled from decades of salt spray. Their roots hold back the precious earth from the devouring sea.

In the beginning of the seventeenth century, during the earliest years of European colonization, this area was some of the most contested land in the Northeast. European demand for timber was steadily increasing, particularly large old-growth trees for ship masts, which needed to be a minimum of 120 feet long and forty inches in diameter. Trees of this size were nearly gone from Europe's forests. The towering white pines of New England promised a solution. Maine's islands served as trading posts for inland exploration, and the bountiful seafood on the coasts provided the necessary sustenance for conquest.

As merchant colonialism spread across the oceans like spider's silk, it was not uncommon for news about one colony to arrive at another colony via an intermediate stop in Europe, a ship journey that took six weeks to three months. The temporal distances between these correspondences meant men wrote of pressing matters that had been resolved by the time the recipient became aware of such turmoil. It was through such letters that, piece by piece, a picture of a new world was recorded, imagined, dreamt up, and believed.

Back in Europe, those left behind sat by meek fires and read reports detailing the fantastical and profuse beasts of this other world. The seafood was so abounding it was difficult to believe. Oysters a foot long and clams as large as bread loaves. Codfish that weighed a hundred pounds. Mussels and quahogs by the millions—so numerous, they were used to fatten pigs at low tide. The lobsters were said to be five and six feet long, so large and full of meat that just ten would feed forty laboring men. Because these reports were intended in part to encourage further colonization, and many were written in spring and summer, the vision of perpetual abundance may have been somewhat exaggerated. The plenty of one season could not predict the poverty of the next.

History permits only a crack of light onto the lives of the people who lived here before European colonization. The region that ranged from maritime Canada westward into Vermont and New Hampshire was occupied by a number of distinct tribes who all spoke languages within the Algonquian family. These include the Passamaquoddy, Penobscot, Maliseet (Wəlastəkwiyik), Mi'kmaq, and Abenaki nations, who shared a loose alliance since the first half of the 1700s known as the Wabanaki Confederacy, or "People of the Dawn."

The first European account of Maine's Indigenous people was by the Italian Giovanni da Verrazzano in 1524, but most of our written sources come from French colonists and Jesuit priests in the seventeenth century. By the time many of these accounts were recorded, the Wabanaki had already been impacted by European colonization and the fur trade: coastal settlements prevented use of some former fishing areas, and diseases brought by the newcomers led to a series of epidemics that killed between two-thirds and three-quarters of the Wabanaki.

The narratives of Wabanaki food traditions are thus inherently fragmentary, a world described by outsiders, filtered through their own prejudices. The knowledge they translated had previously been passed down by oral histories and the doing of the thing. In writing it down, the lived wisdom was transmuted into dead words.

The tribes moved between the coast and inland forests throughout the year, following the greatest concentrations of foods. Light and dark, high and low tides, waxing and waning moons, long and short days, hot and cold seasons. The waterways were their roads and often delineated territorial boundaries, which shifted when the rivers did.

The Wabanaki named their lunar months after the foods that were most abundant. In spring, with the Moon of the Smelts, came infinite schools of alewives, arriving in such multitudes it seemed possible to cross the water upon their silver backs.

Long summers were spent in coastal villages. The Wabanaki caught lobsters with two flexible prongs of hardwood lashed to a shaft and steamed them in seaweed over hot rocks—supposedly the inspiration for the traditional New England lobster bake—or dried them over low fires to eat in the coming winter. Men took birchbark canoes out into the ocean to spear sturgeon by torchlight. Women gathered sea urchins, scallops, mussels, clams, oysters, whelks, periwinkles, crabs, and squid by hand in the shallows.

In late summer, during the Moon of Fall Fish, there were herring, capelin, shad, mackerel, plaice, white and squirrel hake, sardines, sculpin, striped bass, sea perch, skates, anchovies, flounders, and brook trout. This was followed by great hordes of salmon migrating upstream into the forests to spawn. After fulfilling this task, many salmon died among the trees. Their bodies fed the forest with the nutrients they had brought from the sea. The forests and the ocean were not separate entities, and the enormous trees depended on the marine ecosystem to grow. When the winds came up, the woods smelled like salt.

With the Moon of Eels, a first chill hit the air, and tremendous eels rushed downstream toward their reproduction rites at sea, preparing for futures as creatures of salt water. Under the Moon When Ice Forms on the Margins of Streams, it was time to head inland to hunt, until the Old Moon rose and game animals became scarce. The coast produced swordfish, walruses, seals, whales, and porpoises. They shared the icy waters with masses of tomcod. Everyone collected mussels through holes in the river ice.

The Moon That Provides Little Food Grudgingly was precarious. The men smoked tobacco in pipes of lobster claw. When they moved to a new camp, it was the mothers who carried the fire. A hot coal was nestled in powdery wood and covered in moss. This was placed in a clamshell and secured in a leather bag at her waist.

By international law, the first English and French settlers were required to have deeds or treaties to acquire land from the Wabanaki, although these were often signed under force and deception. There was also a great deal of misunderstanding between the groups. To the Wabanaki, ownership meant to be given a share of use of the land, and did not restrict their right to continue hunting, fishing, and gathering there. To the Europeans, these property rights gave them exclusive possession.

As colonialism deepened, larger settlements on the coast prevented the Wabanaki from accessing their former fishing and gathering grounds, and the dams built on rivers to power the grist and sawmills blocked the spring and fall spawning runs of fish. The Wabanaki began to rely less and less on seafood.

Tribes took to salting their fish to preserve it like the Europeans did and spent their hours hunting beavers for the fur trade.

66 The detrimental effects of colonialism have a long arc. Many traditions were forgotten during the following centuries, when men and women suffered the poverty of reservation life and were taught their culture was inferior. Children were taken from homes in a state-sponsored act of forced assimilation. The Wabanaki Confederacy was forcibly required to disband in 1862. It was revived again in 1993, and in 2015 the Wabanaki Confederacy passed the Grandmothers' Declaration, outlining future steps to protect their wild foods and the lands and waters where these are sourced. Tribes across Maine continue to fight for their sovereign rights to fish in the rivers and on the coasts. They gather among familiar ghosts.

———————

The dock on Middle Tide Island lies in a shallow bay on the opposite coastline from the open seas. Reaching the dock requires edging one's boat through a narrow spillway surrounded by rocks. When the tide is ripping out toward the ocean, it's nearly impossible to enter the bay. Mary's cousin, a buxom woman in a trucker hat named Persephone, arrives late and just barely makes it through the funnel of sea foam. She revs her powerboat forward. The tide pushes back. It takes several attempts, but finally she catches the wake of a larger boat passing out at sea and swoops past the jagged hazards, into the shallow bay, and around to the dock.

Persephone unloads stacks of beer and hot dogs and wood, piles of camping gear, bags of snacks. As she steps out of her craft, she is carrying a white plastic bucket of oysters. She gathered them from the Damariscotta River estuary, where shell middens have been accumulating along the banks for thousands of years. There is one such mound of shells in Maine estimated to contain 7 million bushels. (The earliest evidence of the extent of past lobster consumption is gone—lobster shells degrade too quickly to be preserved in the archaeological record.) As these shell wastes decompose, the soil becomes more alkaline and calcium-rich. The resulting anthropogenic environments often have a higher biodiversity of native plants than the surrounding landscape.

Oysters have been popular delicacies for generations, and are some of the oldest creatures to be intentionally managed by the people who gathered them: Indigenous Americans generally harvested oysters from shallow waters by hand or with small tools, which left behind those in the deeper waters to regenerate the larger reef. Tribes also only ate oysters seasonally, which allowed the source colony to recover for significant periods of the year.

Today most of the oysters we eat are cultivated, but rogue wild ones still exist, usually the descendants of oysters that escaped from the cages where we grow them. The difference is subtle, since they all live in the same water, but it can be discerned in their shape, texture, color, and structural attachments. The wild ones are more irregular.

I sit on the beach with Persephone and her bucket. The next day, at the annual Lobster Boat Races, she will tow an inflatable party lounge with built-in seats behind her boat and drink wine coolers in the sun in a neon bikini, but tonight, she teaches me the art of opening gathered oysters.

She holds an oyster firmly in her gloved hand and delicately angles the tip of a small blue-handled knife into the slight depression where the two shells come together.

"You want to poke the tip in... here... for leverage... like opening a beer with a lighter... it's all about the leverage."

The oyster splits in two with a slight cracking sound. She hands me the knife.

The work is difficult but satisfying. I get most of my oysters apart, although I fracture the shell into razor-thin bits on more than one occasion. We shuck for a time, placing the open oysters on a plate of weathered driftwood. Persephone's oysters look appetizing. Mine do not. They look a mess. I can't quite muster the necessary choreography: edge the knife below the pale, glistening mucus mass, loosen the muscular footing, then turn it over with a quick flip to expose the creamy belly while simultaneously tucking the purple lacy edging neatly underneath. Slivers of shell dot the disheveled surface.

Technically, this whole time, the oyster is still alive.

It is alive, too, when I tip it into my mouth and swallow. Alive, just as every time we eat raw oysters. I've had them plenty of times before, in restaurants, but never like this, with a golden summer breeze from the south and the sound of a radio coming from a boat across the bay, echoing off the granite rocks.

For most people, seafood remains the only wild food in their diets. This likely won't be the case for long. Nearly half of all seafood is already farmed, often with negative impacts on the remaining wild stocks. It remains unclear whether eating wild or farmed fish is better for the environment. The issue is complex, as "wild caught" can mean the fish are scooped up by industrial trawlers that completely alter ocean ecosystems. It is estimated that more than a third of the world's fisheries are overharvested beyond sustaining levels.[1] There is also the issue of "seafood fraud," whereby endangered species are labeled as something else, or farm-raised fish is marketed as "wild caught" to capture the premium price associated with eating wild.

In the United States, nearly 90 percent of our seafood is imported. We know very little about where the fish is coming from or what effects its harvest has on fishing communities and ecosystems. While estimates vary, it is likely that globally more than a fifth of all seafood caught annually is a result of "pirate fishing", illegal practices, or indentured slave labor.

Lobster remains one of the few species still primarily harvested in the United States. There is a common misconception that lobster used to be despised, fed only to servants and prisoners, who according to legends demanded it not be given more than twice a week and on occasion even rioted against the diet. Other stories suggest that they were used for fertilizer, or if eaten, the shells were buried in the backyard to hide the desperation. This may have been true in certain parts of colonial America—in Plymouth, it was said they washed up on the beach in piles two feet tall—but generally lobsters were not detested. Indeed, lobster from the eastern Atlantic and Mediterranean coasts was served at many fancy banquets in Europe. As such, European colonists would have been familiar with the creatures, although American lobsters were much larger in size, and their abundance meant they were widely eaten.

Like lobster in New England, green turtles in the Caribbean colonies were so plentiful as to be a common food. The colossal number of these creatures that existed just a few centuries ago is hard to imagine. When Columbus first arrived, the ocean was so thick with turtles that they looked like little rocks. It seemed the ships would run aground. The beaches were plastered in even more. There were so many turtles that if a vessel lost its bearings in murky weather, sailors could navigate by steering to the sounds of the reptiles swimming. If Columbus had taken an age to make the count, he would have found more than 91 million individuals.

For pirates who sailed the Caribbean beginning in the sixteenth century, the location of green turtle breeding grounds determined, in part, where they would pillage next. Green turtles were particularly sought after, as they were said to be "the best food the Sea affords... none more delicate in taste, and more nourishing,"[2] and the immense amount of fat could be rendered into butter and used to fry fish. Father Labat, a Dominican monk, ate turtle meat the buccaneer way—minced and cooked in its own belly shell in a trench covered in coals—and wrote that he had "never eaten anything more appetizing or better flavored."[3] The English privateer and slave trader John Hawkins said the meat tasted "much like veal."[4] It was also rumored that turtle prevented scurvy and was a restorative against the highly infectious Caribbean climate.

The beasts were big enough to carry five men on their backs, and one or two would sustain a hundred men. Because they breathed air, and could live off their incredible fat stores, green turtles could be kept alive onboard a ship as fresh meat for up to a year. They were flipped upside down, so as not to be suffocated by their own weight, and had to be regularly wetted down with seawater to stay cool.

Without the flesh of turtles, it is likely that the plantation economy would not have been possible. Green turtles migrated along a similar route to the slave trade, following the same currents and winds from West Africa to the Caribbean. The French, who were some of the first to enter the transatlantic slave trade, fed enslaved people turtle meat during the Middle Passage. For the English, it was the Cayman Island green turtle rookery, and the massive quantities of protein it provided, that allowed them to make Jamaica their most important colony. One sea captain in 1657 reported stocking up on twenty-five tons of salted turtle meat before a voyage.

Turtle flesh was so important to the economy of the Caribbean and the success of colonialism that as early as 1620, the
Bermuda Assembly passed what could be considered the first
endangered-species legislation. The law, "an Act Agaynst the
Killinge of Ouer Young Tortoyes," prohibited the killing of any
turtle fewer than eighteen inches in diameter. Its aim was to
stop those who would "snatch & catch up indifferentlye all
kinds of Tortoyses both yonge and old little and great and soe
carrye awaye and devoure them to the much decay of so excellent a fishe..."[5]

Another attempt at management occurred during the Treaty
of Whitehall (1686) between England and France, which included a section to regulate green turtle fishing in the Cayman
Islands. Still, by 1688, there were forty cedar sloops turtling
there. Each day, 120 to 150 men reaped turtles with wide
mesh nets. Over the next five years, nearly thirteen thousand
turtles were brought from the Caymans to Jamaica each year.

Despite the attempts to limit the harvest, the Bermuda turtle
colony was one of the first to disappear, and within a hundred
years, the Cayman fishery was also entirely decimated. The
fleets moved on to other islands.

It is not exactly known when the first green turtle arrived
in England or who decided to turn it into soup. Every day a
hurricane of extraordinary things arrived at Europe's docks and
customhouses. At first, the new foods brought back from the
colonies were considered suspicious—an attitude rooted in
long-standing beliefs about the relationship between food, identity, and the environment. When colonialism was first proposed
in the fifteenth and sixteenth centuries, the merits of the project were debated in letters and pamphlets. It was a literature of
worry: What would happen to Europeans if they were exposed
to warmer climates? Would they be adversely altered by the

New World's environment, so full of unknown wild animals and disorderly plants? Any person living in such undomesticated environments would surely become uncivilized, too. And how would the food affect their character?

There was particular concern that the farther the British traveled from their homeland, exposed to different climates and eating unfamiliar foods along the way, the more they risked "creolean degeneracy" and lusty behavior.[6] Foods from warmer climates were thought to enliven the blood and cause "animal spirits" in Northern bodies—so chefs were tasked with toning down the supposedly sexual and vibrant nature of these ingredients. By the act of cooking, wild food could be cleansed of "the heart of barbarism" and provide "a greater abundance of purer and freer spirits."[7] It was a contradictory appetite. The spirit of these foods was both desired and required taming.

The culinary origins of turtle soup are not precisely known, but there are many myths about it. In one story, a ship-owning alderman in Bristol, one of the oldest slaving ports in England, was given a gift by his captain of a keg of limes and a green turtle. He happened to be giving a civic banquet that evening and knew he would impress his guests with a novel dish, so he ordered the turtle to be stewed. The guests were so delighted, they re-elected him nine times. Other accounts say the inventor was a confectioner. The candy maker spent much of his time at the docks, buying barrels of molasses and bags of raw sugar from the Caribbean. Perhaps on one of these market excursions, he decided to take home a green turtle.

We do know that the first written instructions for cooking green turtle were penned in 1732 by Richard Bradley, a botanist and the founder of Britain's first horticultural periodical. While collecting specimens in the Caribbean, he acquired recipes for roasted turtle and turtle pie, "From a Barbados *Lady*," and describes the flesh as "between that of veal, and that of a Lobster."[8]

As green turtles became increasingly scarce in the Caribbean, the English upper class became enticed by this exotic—and expensive—new food. By the mid-eighteenth century, green turtle had become popular enough that ships were built with special tubs of seawater to bring them over from the West Indies. (One newspaper reported that a two-hundred-pound turtle was seen floating in the Thames, evidently having fallen off a ship during transport). The London Tavern served green turtle in its Great Dining Room, and supposedly kept live turtles in large vats in the cellar, where they would live up to three months "in excellent condition if kept in the same water in which they were brought to this country."[9] In 1755, the *London Magazine* published a satirical story describing a turtle-eating fanatic who had an enormous oven, seventeen kinds of utensils, and a special pair of expandable pants that he wore when he ate. The green turtle was cooked with the "generous spirit and benevolent zeal of the West Indians," and by the end of the meal, the author is predicting that men will soon be trading "shares in turtle, as any other kind of stock."[10]

Hannah Glasse included nose-to-tail instructions for cooking green turtle "The West Indian way" in the fifth edition of her bestselling cookbook, *The Art of Cookery Made Plain and Easy* (1755). It must have been a frightful and rather awkward act to butcher a live turtle in the manner described by Glasse. The spectacle of dismemberment begins by taking the beast out of the water the night before and laying it on its back. The next morning, cut off the head and bleed the turtle well. Remove the lower shell, then slash the belly before baking. Remove the meat and entrails from the upper shell, leaving the green fat on for baking. Boil the fins, head, and bones together to make a broth. To make the soup: split open the guts, scrape clean, cut into two-inch-long pieces, and stew together with chunks of meat, a half-pound of butter, spices (cayenne, white pepper, and cloves), Madeira, and the broth. After four or five hours of cooking, put the stew into the upper shell and brown it in the oven. The resulting soup, served in a tureen or china bowl, had little hint of its unsavory origins.

Turtle soup quickly became a must-have for any civic banquet, and the menus upon which it appeared can be read like economic history or genealogies of wealth. Eating green turtle was no longer about subsistence but about the superfluous. But it was not only its rarity and expense that made it popular. There was something about the wild nature of its flesh. At the time, philosophers were debating the idea of the sublime. It was an experience of being in Wild Nature where one felt passion, mesmerization, terror, awe, and reverence simultaneously. In trying to make sense of these fragmentary and contradictory feelings, the mind would transcend its own limits of understanding, and the self was mystically absorbed into the experience. To submit yourself to the sublime was to be threatened with a pleasant obliteration. It was a dual metaphysics that tried to hold our domination of and deference to Wild Nature simultaneously.

Turtle soup, like rugged and dramatic natural landscapes, allowed one to experience a feeling that was quite absent from daily life. It was a touristic appetite. With each dripping bite, did the diner imagine distant sunshine, pirates, and palm trees? Did the royal scientist or alderman hope that by ingesting the long-living green turtle—a lifetime rumored to be more than 150 years—he might gain that longevity for himself? The flavor transported him into the torpid violence of the waves, without the ill effects of dislocation.

By the time turtle became an upper-class staple, there was no longer worry over the effects of wild colonial environments on white bodies, as there had been a few centuries earlier. Now it was the excesses of civilization and the increasingly destructive effects of colonialism that started to become of concern. Political satire increasingly drew a connection between the violence of slavery, the obscene wealth of the merchant class, and their fatal attraction to turtle. Numerous political cartoons in magazines and newspapers equated a taste for turtle with greed and a lack of self-control: a man in an elongated chancellor's wig eats from a bowl labeled "Royal Turtle Soup" while outside a hungry mob protests the high price of staple crops as a result of protectionist tariffs; a very rotund Lord Mayor is fed turtle soup by a chef with a long spoon; a gout patient sits in front of a map of the Caribbean. The physical symptoms of gluttony seemed to be a visible manifestation of immoral character. It was as if the turtle eater was humbled by his perversion, repressed madness refined as taste.

Turtle soup became increasingly democratized as more and more turtles of all kinds were harvested globally. It lost its association with wealth and was eaten well into the nineteenth century. Cans of turtle soup can still be found in some distant outposts, artifacts of another age. The population of green turtles in the Caribbean today is merely 300,000 individuals, the remnants of a vanished society.

The ocean has experienced centuries of plunder. It is a dying wilderness, coughing up plastic. But because the destruction is mostly out of sight, in far-off places or on early mornings when no one but commercial fishers are awake, we do not react to it the same way we might to a clearcut forest. We think this depleted ocean is normal. We fall prey to shifting baselines and forget the abundance that once existed, which seems so unfathomable it might as well be fiction. We do not understand our own poverty.

———————————

When viewed over the distance of time, our ability to harvest the sea has grown in a steady arc of improvement. But in the day-to-day experience, this occurred in fits and starts, by accident and necessity in equal measure.

The New England lobsterman, holding a long familiarity with the untrustworthy disposition of the ocean, would hide away in winter. The lobster, too, migrated south or farther away from the coasts to deeper water. The lobsterman worked at the pace of the winds and the movement of his own hands. He knew the call of the seabirds and the timing of the fish runs.

Then someone made a more powerful boat that could head farther out to sea, and in doing so, extended the season into winter. And another discovered that the coolant lines from the boat's diesel motor could be run through fifty-gallon barrels of seawater. And so the lobstermen began to plunge their trap ropes into this hot water to clean them, and the work became more efficient. Mary spent much of her childhood on her father's lobster boat. On the chilliest days, when the sleet drove sideways, they'd heat up cans of soup by dropping them into the hot barrels.

How does it feel to eat wild seafood caught that morning, adjacent to the waters in which it lived? To examine the hands of the man who caught my dinner?

On the pebble beach, a bleached-white carcass rests among lilac sea heather and the corpses of shipwrecked trees. Blue worms orgy in the tide pools.

Three men prepare the kitchen. They nestle a massive steel drum pan in the crook of two large boulders and build up a pile of rocks to stabilize the free-hanging side. Firewood, brought from the mainland, is pushed underneath. Other people haul buckets of rust-green seaweed from the tideline, a few little crabs hidden in the tangles, and dump the contents into the cooking pan. This is covered with wet paper bags and a layer of food—raw black lobsters, tinfoil packets of half-onion half-potato, corn on the cob in their husks—followed by more wet seaweed. Someone lights the blaze. The lobsters turn orange in the infernal seaweed.

It is a dry summer and thunderheads tease in the distance.

As we eat, piano riffs float from somewhere across the shallow bay. I think of stories about heroic lobsters, five feet long, forty pounds, blue and speckled, as old as a century. The rough incrustations upon their backs were like the bark of a tree, marking their decades of growth.

We eat with our hands. We eat as if afflicted with madness. It is the best lobster I've ever had.

Over the course of the meal, the seagulls flare their courage and grow closer. Like beggars at a coronation feast, they seem to think of themselves as wrongfully uninvited guests. It's illegal to throw lobster trash on the beach, and so the birds are denied even our scraps.

"I think I forgot to breathe while I devoured that," I say, surveying the ruins of our meal.

Picked-over crustaceans crowd our paper plates, piled at odd angles like the fallen tombs of a ransacked kingdom. My hands are sticky.

As the sky darkens, we light a bonfire on the beach. Someone tosses brightly colored glowing bocce balls like they are at a rave. A boombox plays pop music nearby, although it's been turned down.

Fragments of conversation gather around me.

"You want another insect?" the fisherman who brought the lobsters says. "I sure don't. I don't care for 'em."

"We've all got Maine privilege," another answers, with the surety of a well-used phrase.

Two men pass a joint. "Sure, we've got that special *terroir* up here," he jokes in a pitched tone as smoke slowly escapes his mouth.

"... The land we've got ... we call it Poison Ivy island ... I'd love to plant some weed there," the other man says, taking the joint. "That would give it some serious *terroir*!"

Athena's voice is husky and scratched by cigarettes. She has a cursive name tattooed on each foot, the calligraphy sharp and luminescent like fish scales. She likes to eat lobster "unadulterated"—without butter or sauce, barely steamed, fresh. She's been around lobster a lot these last ten years, drove a truck full of them, up and down the Eastern Seaboard. It wasn't the work that she disliked; it was always being held accountable for greater forces.

"I got sick of it. They was always blaming me when prices went down. 'Why the prices go down?' I'd get from both lobstermen and middlemen. Like I knew?" Athena says casually, as if her little history is just a coincidence.

"You know what I told my boss when I quit? I said, 'Go get yourself a facial! You look old!'" she laughs through a cigarette atmosphere. "Now I buy clams from the local guys and sell them to wholesalers, you know, for restaurants. Treats me much better."

She's older than most of us, pushing fifty, but wears the uniform of a teenage girl—cheap flip-flops, jean shorts, a baggy black tank top, lacy with rips, and a glimpse of her bright bikini strings peeking through. Her hair is greying with a bad dye job, but it suits her, this rebellion against time. Like an aged groupie following the music of her youth, she keeps adjusting her base-lines, accommodating her vision of how life seemed to be until she forgot how good it once was. Later that night she will fall asleep with rocks in her pockets.

"So rare to be on a beach at night these days," the man sitting next to me says. "When I was a kid, beach bonfires happened a lot. They were crowded. Hot ash blowing in our faces. That was how we experienced childhood."

"I'd say we've got another twenty years before it's all gone. The lobsters, this beach, this kind of life...," a woman replies.

A few couples lean into each other around the fire. I feel lonely and also content in my solitude. A paradox I've wrestled with most of my life.

Sometimes, I wonder if it is possible to be romantically in love with a moment and everyone in it. I've often felt a sort of intimacy with existence that I could never find with any individual person.

A shooting star falls across the sky. We call out our delight and a boat in the dark horns a response.

As I make my way to my tent, a soft wind blows through the old and dull hills, hunkering down, patiently saving its sharp fury for the coming winter. A sliver of moon rises, darkly, as if to summon the dead.

It was perhaps in the eighteenth century—when turtle soup was all the rage—that we first broke from earth's time and tunings, and began creating the conditions for an accelerated future. As if in hidden recognition of a shift we were scarcely aware of, we invented natural history as a language to describe what we were destroying—like a eulogy at a funeral, which circumscribes a life already past.

One of the most distinguishing features of Enlightenment thought was the belief in a *natural* course of events. Wild Nature was thought to be as predictable as any other experimental endeavor. Like a well-regulated state, every part supported the rest, performing some function in subservience to the whole, and the world was only stocked with the exact number of animals it could support. Natural scientists merely sought to uncover God's divine order, which brought the drift of mysterious forces into balance and benevolence.

But these studies were based on a nature already quite unnatural. The seas and specimens had already been deeply impacted for at least two hundred years—they were a mere adumbration of a much more crowded past. Yet to Enlightenment natural scientists, the past was not a problem. The truth of Wild Nature was unchanging and the rational was always retrospective. They didn't realize that the normal baseline they sought was dismal and anthropomorphic. It shifted under their feet like sand.

Like a volcanic eruption or an asteroid hit, the ecological impacts of colonial appetites had far-reaching effects. Green turtles are a keystone species, and, like the ruminants that graze on dry grasslands, are a transformative force of trophic ecology. Just by eating seagrass, they cause the plants to temporarily increase their nutritional value and coax forth new shoots, further increasing the food supply of the ecosystem that supports bivalves, mollusks, polychaete worms, amphipods, crabs, shrimp, herbivorous parrotfish, surgeonfish, sea urchins, small invertebrates, and many kinds of juvenile fish. Green turtles also have enzyme-producing microflora in their guts, so when they defecate, nitrogen is released into the sea currents and deposited over a wide area, helping to fertilize coral reefs.

Green turtles live long lives, and it takes forty to sixty years before they are mature enough to reproduce. What wisdom must be gained before passing on their genetics to the next generation! What a sense of accomplishment to thrust themselves out of the ocean and lay one hundred amniotic eggs after such a long wait. A significant number of these do not hatch but decay into the beach, providing nutrients for vegetation on the shoreline that then prevents the sand from washing away.

As the green turtles were decimated, epiphytic algae exploded into growth. This suppressed seagrass productivity and led to the widespread mortality of the long-spined sea urchin, the most abundant sea urchin in the Caribbean for the past 125,000 years. The coral reefs were no longer fertilized as they had been and began to die back. The beaches started to erode.

How would the green turtle understand its own history, not as a product of human will and desire, but as a species regulating the environment in which it lived? And what of those turtles that were destined to become a cartilaginous broth, starved for the months-long journey on a windswept cutter, as silent and stoic as weathered mountains—did they enter a sort of spiritual hibernation on the ship crossing, a liminal existence in quiet contemplation of the doomed future? The turtles were both themselves and something else. Their greenish fat both sacred and profane. Abundant, ancient bodies decimated and dissected by our violent appetites.

The creatures of the sea cannot be removed from their context without consequences. They are never discrete objects. They exist because of an ecosystem, and the ecosystem exists because of them. What ecological harmony is missing from New England's rivers and forests without the ample runs of spawning fish that once existed? What ecological changes occur today when we eat lobster?

Lobster fisheries are some of the most sustainably managed: fishers are required to throw back both the big lobsters, which are the best breeders, and the smaller lobsters, which haven't had a chance to propagate yet. There's also a law in Maine that requires fishermen to notch a *V* on the back of any egg-bearing females they catch, which signals to other fishermen that she is fertile and should be thrown back.

Although there are lobster aquaculture attempts underway, so far they haven't been economically successful. But due to heavy management, wild lobster fisheries are slowly becoming domesticated. The traps are baited with a pound of herring or other small fish, and since most lobsters are too small to keep, they are thrown back having eaten this meal. With nearly four million traps in Maine, it is estimated that the baited traps contribute nearly half of the lobsters' diets. By overfishing larger predator species like cod, we've also inadvertently given juvenile lobsters a better chance of surviving.

Maine has been experiencing a lobster boom for the past few decades, but scientists warn that due to a number of factors, including climate change, it won't last. The sea surface temperature is rising, particularly in the Gulf of Maine, where warming is happening at a rate 99 percent faster than on the rest of the planet's sea surface. This warm water causes problems for lobsters, interfering with their respiration, lowering their immune response, and increasing the likelihood of shell diseases, but most importantly making reproduction more difficult. As a result, the populations of lobsters that are thriving are increasingly found in cooler waters to the north, off the coast of Canada.

Wild fish stocks in general are threatened by climate change. Scientists predict that by the end of this century, the oceans will be 150 percent more acidic than they were in the eighteenth century. The seas are souring ten times faster than they did during any previous periods of marine extinction. Even 55 million years ago, during the last major marine extinction, the rate of change was ten times slower than it is today.

The current shift has come so quickly that species do not have time to adapt. Species with exoskeletons such as mussels, clams, and oysters are particularly vulnerable to acidification. It is unclear how this will affect lobsters, but there is evidence that acidification interferes with their sense of smell and their heart rate. As native seafood dies off, coastal ecosystems are increasingly becoming invaded by foreign snails. We face the loss of a very long maritime heritage.

———

In the morning, we eat squares of blueberry cake on paper towels and drink coffee from a Coleman coffee pot. Athena rips butts and drinks coffee from a mug with the words *Florida Greetings*. The wastes of our excursion are strewn across the picnic table. Bendy straws and stale glow sticks. Chips, Cheez-Its, and gluten-free crackers. Empty Natural Light beer cans and Jack Daniel's bottles. Eggs from someone's chickens. There's a backlog of the meatlog, and moist cheese mingles with glistening deli meats. iPhones charge from a bank of solar panels set up near a folded air mattress and a pair of Merrell shoes.

I eat leftover lobster, cold and delicious.

We had come to Middle Tide Island to remember time, to overcome our self-control, to engorge ourselves with wild food and experience the liberty it entails, to eat because we were hungry, because lobster tastes sublime. Perhaps this kind of feasting is not so different from the pre-enlightened sort. Along the way, pieces are gathered and understood, but we can never quite grasp the plentitude of the whole.

SALMIS OF ROASTED FOWL

A Domesticated Wild—Cartographic Erasure—
A Market Phenomenon—Restrained Violence—Collapse
and Renewal—The Factory Ecosystem

O N A HOT summer day in New Haven, Connecticut, I sneak into the abandoned Winchester gun factory. I crawl through an opening in the chain-link fence surrounding the factory and walk into a central courtyard. Behemoth buildings enclose it on three sides like ragged, groaning mountains.

In the open space, a meadow has erupted in summer bloom. Tiny, lovely pale-yellow flowers of sulfur cinquefoil keep company with the upturned faces of oxeye daisies. Bursts of wild carrot (Queen Anne's lace) grow between clusters of common tansy and bushes of purple-stemmed mugwort. Knotweed, barberry, bittersweet, and multiflora rose spread in the rubble. Wild grape and mile-a-minute vines mantle over defenseless walls.

In the center of the courtyard, a catalpa tree, with wide, flat leaves and cigar beans, grows adjacent to a tree of heaven. They are still in the breezeless afternoon and illuminated by sunrays. Beneath them, a rash of cottonwood-leafed aspen, Norway maple, and autumn olive thrive in the poor polluted soil.

Many of these species are naturalized invasives, first brought here by early European settlers as medicines, famine foods, or ornamental plants. Over time they have fitted themselves into the ecosystem. Today, these plants define our wastelands.

The air is noisy with a symphony of insect worries. A red-winged blackbird, dressed like a little soldier with red epaulets, whoops across the courtyard and disappears into industrial wreckage. The melody of a brown-headed cowbird in a high tree is eerie, like dripping water. She scans the courtyard looking for other birds to raise her young. Once a suitable host is found, she'll deposit one of her own eggs in the warm nest. The alien hatchling will have a relentless appetite.

There are only a few birds here, but that is "normal" to us. What was it like before, with so many more in the sky?

Where today stands a decaying factory, there was once a wilderness. Some of the earliest written environmental descriptions of this region, dating to the late sixteenth and early seventeenth century, are contained within colonial reports of "merchantable commodities."[1] Descriptions of places were like lists of goods. Wild Nature seemed raw and untouched. It was possible to walk from the top of a hill to the valley below and pass through a dozen different ecosystems. In some locations, one could ride at a full gallop through the open parks of massive hardwoods. There were no fenced fields or private enclosures, no cities overflowing with steam and refuse and labor.

The wild bird populations were so immense when the first colonists arrived, it seemed they might survive on "nothing but roast meat of divers fowls."[2] The skies were demented with wings. Endless flocks of geese and doves and pigeons. Partridges the size of hens. Wild turkeys—sweet and fleshy and weighing nearly forty pounds—were found in groups of a hundred. They were so calm as to be nearly tame, and it was possible to kill a dozen in half a day. The heath hen was so abundant on the Hempstead Plains of Long Island that it had the reputation of being a poor man's food. In 1634, William Wood wrote, "If I should tell you how some have killed a hundred geese in a week, fifty ducks at a shot, forty teals at another, it may be counted impossible though nothing more certain."[3]

Still, many early colonists didn't hunt—having come from places with restrictive hunting laws that barred anyone but the nobility from taking game birds, they simply didn't know how. For other settlers, particularly Puritans and Germans, centuries of folklore about ungodly wild men had cast hunting as barbaric precisely because it required living in the dangerous forests to master.

But, for the majority of people, wild birds filled in the contours of survival, and eating fowl became symbolic of independence and self-reliance. One simply had to pick up a gun and enter the woods just beyond the homestead to find dinner.

The earliest guns in America were English muskets, heavy and unwieldy things that didn't take well to wet weather. They could only be fired once before forty motions were required to reload and shoot again. Unlike arrows, lead balls could shatter bone, but the muskets were so inaccurate that a clear shot was as much a consequence of chance as of skill. But it hardly seemed to matter. There were so many birds, they harrowed the azure sky.

Of course, what appeared to be a wilderness to the colonists was in fact land that had been inhabited for thousands of years by Indigenous Americans, whose land management practices were partially responsible for the abundance of edible wild birds. There is evidence that the Indigenous peoples of the region—including the Pequot, Mohegan Niantic, Quinnipiac, Paugussett, and many other distinct bands belonging to the Algonquian language family—regularly burned the Eastern forest to improve hunting. These annual low-temperature fires disturbed the stability of the forest, but they were as much an act of creation as of destruction. They promoted a diverse woodland, in many states of ecological succession, of many ages, densities, sizes, and species of trees providing habitat for a great many wild edible birds.

After a fire, tender young rushes and sedges burst forth in renewed quantities, a favorite forage of game animals. Sunlight bathed the newly opened forest patches, and wild strawberries, blackberries, and raspberries flourished in the warm, dry soils. One settler remarked that there were so many strawberries, the woods were dyed red, and another wrote it was possible to gather enough to "fill a good ship within a few miles compasse."[4] These copious berries fed finches, orioles, robins, and waxwings, which made their homes in the liminal spaces between fire-scarred meadows and protective forests.

The fires thinned out the smaller trees and non-woody plants. Over the course of many cycles, the woodlands became open and parklike, which favored the growth of nut trees—chestnut, hickory, walnut, and oak. After the shallow blazes, these fire-resistant species regenerated, sprouting new stems from their charred bases, which caused an increase in nut crops in the following years, food for humans and birdlife alike.

The large oak trees made perfect nesting sites for the abundant passenger pigeons, which lived in these forests for tens of thousands of years. A million in one flock was not uncommon.

They crowded out the sun for days. Their flapping wings sounded like the onrush of thunder. When they landed to roost, these convulsions of nature broke as many branches as a tornado.

Passenger pigeons' nesting sites were a boon to predator species, which ate the babies that fell to the forest floor. Their roosting created an immense amount of guano, which fertilized the soil, creating beneficial effects throughout the food chain. For local tribes, a roosting site signaled the occasion for a feast, and the tender squabs were cooked in stews.

Fire was also used to clear land for crops in a swidden system. The nutrients of the trees were returned to the soil in the form of ash. The fires burned away vermin and pests, kept the weeds down, and destroyed plant diseases. Throughout the Indigenous Americas, women were primarily responsible for agricultural management, and many used a highly dynamic form of cultivation that mimicked wild ecosystems. Stalks of maize collected water and acted as the scaffolding for the runners of beans—so many varieties that, according to one colonist, they were "too tedious" to list.[5] The beans dispersed nitrogen into the soil, nourishing the tangles of squash, pumpkin, and bottle gourds, which in turn shaded the ground, helping to retain soil moisture and crowd out noxious plants. It was an ingenious system that strengthened crop roots and reduced soil erosion. By some estimates, it yielded over two hundred bushels of food per acre—five times the amount grown in English fields. After some years, when the soil lost its fertility, the fields were abandoned and regrew into forests.

Indigenous farmers also practiced a kind of feral husbandry, feeding wild turkeys with corn in the summer and catching them in baited traps when they were fat in the fall. At the edges of fields, with the forest for cover and crops for food, the turkeys flourished in the company of humans.

90

In the coastal salt marshes, the Quinnipiac built weirs from brushwood to capture fish at low tide. These temporary pools were lush with insects and seafood that attracted flocks of waterfowl. Over time, parts of the trap would fill in with sediment, and then grow over with marsh hay and cordgrass. This helped to accelerate the formation of the salt marsh, which provided nesting sites for edible snipe, terns, heath hen, long-billed dowitchers, and pectoral sandpipers, among others. Women and children gathered the eggs of waterfowl—treasures on the shoreline. In April and May, common eider, large sea ducks twice the size of European hens, were captured with snares or clubs. In fall, tribes ate a decadence of roasted migratory birds—brants, mourning doves, terns, canvasback duck, and green-winged teal.

Many of these coastal birds migrated through the Great Plains, where evidence shows that the recurrent low-grade fires set by early Indigenous peoples thousands of years ago extended the prairie habitat beyond its natural range: the burns prevented trees from encroaching the land, recycled nutrients back into the ground, and helped to germinate certain grass seeds that required heat. In spring, generations of flowers tinted the flatlands in successive waves of carmine, gold, violet, and peachblow. Among these flowers were millions of wild birds. Some of the most delicious were prairie chicken, or sage grouse, which the Sioux, Shoshone, and Blackfoot honored with dances inspired by the birds' elaborate mating rites. Game birds were baked inside jackets of clay, and when the dressing was removed, it stripped away the feathers, leaving behind succulent steamed meat.

Every culture has an impact on nature, and the Indigenous American relationship with the land was not always one of harmony. Some tribes stripped hillsides of trees for blazing bonfires that raged through the night. Sometimes they lost control of ground fires and a whole mountainside would be mislaid to flame. Some years the game birds were so overhunted, they remained scarce the following year. But the wilderness in which the Indigenous American groups lived was a domesticated wild. They were aware of their disturbances to the land. They knew that their presence would shift its trajectory. Some impacts were a revitalizing force, increasing biodiversity and abundance. Others required giving nature a period of rest to recover. Managing land in this way was a form of politics, culture, and technology that allowed for long-term coexistence.

From the central courtyard, I walk up a rusted staircase covered in vines, stepping over the tree trunks and spirals of leaves that flush through the metal slats and wind around the railings. On the second floor, I find a busted window and duck inside.

Each room of the factory is like a different ecosystem. The wood floors buckle like the substrate ridges of the deep ocean. Tidy eddies of dead leaves push against the moraine wrinkles. The courtyard-facing windows are painted with vine maple and Virginia creeper, in delicate tendrils and sprites of fresh leaves, hazy in their exactitude, as if watercolored. Many windows bear holes from rocks or bullets or bricks. The leaves of climbing ivy push through the gaps. The opposite bank of windows is shedding like paper birch.

A long hallway terminates in a room that is impassable and darkened. The ceiling has collapsed into a pile of senescent beams, floorboards, and wooden benches, like the chasms created by tree blowdowns during alpine microbursts. The materials are pitched up into such odd cascades that they seem to double back on each other, as if still in the throes of impact.

The fallen wood is shredded at the edges by the handiwork of termites and fungus. Trees felled first by chainsaw, then again by neglect.

To the earliest European colonists, the New World was *terra nullius*—wasteland. The word *waste* had been used for many centuries interchangeably with the word *wilderness* to denote undeveloped lands. (The Latin root, *vastus*, meant empty or desolate.) John Locke, who believed that improving land was a natural right, used the word *waste* to connote territory not yet turned into property. This reflected a long-standing European concern about idleness in both people and nature. As early as the sixteenth century, the British government discouraged farmers from returning existing agricultural fields to meadow, which was seen as a "turning of the earth to sloth and idleness," and letting a field lie fallow was considered "the greatest and most dangerous nuisance and damage to the common people."[6]

To many colonists, possession of the land was therefore determined by use and occupancy, and Indigenous American hunting, gathering, burning, and agricultural practices weren't qualifying improvement activities. The settler-colonialists practiced a form of agriculture based on Roman ideals: fields were laid out in geometric patterns, and lined by ditches and fences. With this mindset, the Indigenous fields looked unkempt—they lacked the straight lines of a settler's plow.

By the late seventeenth century, maps of New England legitimized the presence of settlers by leaving the "wastelands" occupied by Indigenous peoples blank. There was a widespread belief that the Indigenous Americans would "naturally" go extinct anyway—they simply weren't meant to survive modernity. Indeed, one of the main tactics to encourage this "natural extinction" was the destruction of the wild food sources they relied on. While many of the original land deeds promised Indigenous Americans continued use of the land for sourcing food, this was contingent on the territory being unenclosed. As soon as a fence was erected—that is, the land was "visibly improved"—the wild birds that lived there were no longer considered open access.

This seemingly simple idea of ownership led to large ecological transformations. The Europeans imported an agricultural system based on commodity crops, which depended on large draft animals like cattle that were evolutionarily absent in North America. Their heavy hooves troubled the soil, compacting it, making it less fertile, and reducing its ability to absorb water. The homesteaders overgrazed meadows and drained salt marshes. The plow was a recurring catastrophe, a cyclical disturbance to the skin of the earth. Bluegrass and white clover invaded, pushing out the native grasses that were home to numerous game birds. Ragweed and dandelions floated out of the fields and invaded the surrounding woods.

There were bounties on carnivorous eagles, hawks, lynxes, foxes, and wolves. These predators were so well exterminated, they no longer kept the mice in check. The loathsome vermin returned in force. With wood a precious commodity, fire was seen as a threat and suppressed. But without the Indigenous art of firing the woods, the composition of the forests changed. Smaller trees, bushes, and brambles crowded in. The pests erupted. Rats—which had arrived on ships—sprawled out over the forestland.

Nearly every last tree was put to some use. Without the tall trees, which had moderated the weather, temperatures fluctuated widely. The surface of the land became colder in winter and hotter in summer. The winds picked up. The soil blew away. Rains turned to floods more easily. The soil washed off.

The rivers ran drier in summer. Lakes filled in with sediment and disappeared.

By 1790, the ground of the Eastern Seaboard was increasingly barren, windblown, and exhausted. So many unanticipated consequences had become monumental in their accumulation. In the course of just a few centuries, the colonizers transformed the wide-open forests teeming with game birds into a legacy of pasture and scrublands.

The wild turkey became scarce as early as 1672. The heath hen became a rare and expensive bird, highly sought after by those with taste. The farmers abandoned their fields, gave up their rocky pastures. They saddled their horses, shouldered their rifles, and swarmed west toward the frontier and unexplored country. The long, unbroken string of wagons formed such an exodus, it was as if they were chained together. Still, the brightness of the morning was eclipsed by passenger pigeons, which shadowed the sky with their river of tangled wings and bodies, though perhaps not as thickly as they once had.

Meanwhile, civilization was rising upon the prairies. Horse-drawn plows became archaic. Steam combines churned up the soil. Crops of wheat and corn extended many miles, in every direction. The roads improved. The railroads came. "You look around and whisper," one guidebook for western settlers proclaimed, "I vanquished this wilderness and made the chaos pregnant with order and civilization, alone I did it."[7]

On the third floor of the northeast wing of the factory is an immense room. *CAUTION*, a yellow sign reads at the entrance, *EYE PROTECTION ~ REQUIRED ~ IN THIS AREA*. There are scratching noises just ahead, and as I walk down the cavernous space, an animal scurries away through the pipe above me.

Halfway down the great room, a message is stenciled on a central column.

NEW HAVEN

MURDER RATE

THERMOMETER

The bottom of *thermometer* is half obscured, sinking into chipped blood-red paint. Nearby, a dead raccoon lies curled in a fetal position, a victim of noxious factory taxidermy. His paw and tail point in the direction I am walking, like a rigor mortis signpost. The smell of chemical rot is so pervasive it seems to interfere with my sight. It reminds me that I am an intruder here. I cover my nose and mouth, stymie my breath, and hurry on.

In the stairwell to the fourth floor, the walls are screaming with a thousand identical messages... *RA. RA. RA. RA. RA...* in bright spray-paint blues and reds and lavender-purples. The shouts overlap, as if they had been made by many voices and all at once and for days at a time. *RA RA RA* scream the risers and treads as I ascend another flight. The handrail, once shined by the busy palms of a thousand workers, timidly ekes out its own single *RA*. I leave them all behind, to continue their manic conversation without me.

At its peak in the 1940s, the Winchester factory employed more than forty thousand people. It stretched over eighty-one acres and took up nine city blocks. Railroad tracks and roads ran between the outlying sections. There was an electric shop, janitor service, salvage department, sheet-metal department, pipe shop, box shop, transportation department, warehouse, eleven drying kilns, and a finishing shop. Powder ammunition for making bullets was stored in five large ponds on a 216-acre pine swamp just down the road. American black walnut for the gunstocks had to be sourced from a particular five-hundred-mile belt in Missouri and Kansas: wood from too far north had frost cracks, and wood from too far south was soft and sappy.

But when this factory was established—in 1798 by Eli Whitney, the inventor of the cotton gin—the first contract was for just ten thousand muskets, to be delivered to the government in two years. Whitney hoped to create a gun that was not only more accurate, durable, and easily repairable than those that currently existed, but also to do so quickly and cheaply. This would require making standardized and interchangeable parts by precision machine and organizing the factory along strict divisions of labor—a fairly novel idea at the time, when gun making was still a craft-based industry.

As Whitney developed his factory, he wrote, "One of my primary objectives is to form the tools so that the tools themselves shall fashion the work... which once accomplished, will give exceptional uniformity to the whole."[8] I wonder if he knew the prophecy in his words. As the creation of guns became more efficient, the ability to slaughter the birds did, too.

Whitney was part of the burgeoning market economy dominated by industrial capitalists. This new economic configuration relied not only on standardization, but also on increasing the distance between production and consumption. The early nineteenth century "market-place" existed because of a change in time and circumstances unlike anything the world had seen before. The sparsely populated hinterlands, dense forests, cultivated fields, and growing cities were becoming linked together by networks of roads, canals, and railroads. Products from a thousand miles in one direction were on offer, purchased by consumers hundreds of miles in another direction.

The market was at the center of all this activity, a blood-and-feathers manifestation of distant frontiers. It teemed with strange breeds and rare varieties from the forest-regions to the north, the prairies of the west, and the gulfs and coasts to the south. By the mid-nineteenth century, consumers in the eastern metropolitan centers could purchase a variety of wildfowl from all over the country. Looking at the available options reveals the paucity of our own choices today. One writer, in 1867, cataloged a staggering 119 kinds of wild birds for sale in the public food markets of New York, Boston, and Philadelphia.

Whistling swan, trumpeter swan, mud goose, hell-divers. Birds humble and elevated, birds alive in wooden cages, birds dead, full-feathered and eyes intact, as if their carcasses were merely in a different state of living. Willow grouse, long-legged sandpiper, yellow-legged snipe, solitary tattler, and clapper rail. Millions of years of evolution were on display. Forty varieties of ducks: golden-eyed, sprig-tailed, hairy-headed, and dusky. Nighthawks with flesh of very delicate eating. Robins and blue jays tied up in strings. Bobolinks, cedar-birds, plovers, curlews, rails, thrashers, and thrushes. Even an eagle, caged alive, destined for the taxidermist.

With the rise of so many available birds for purchase, cookbooks for the burgeoning middle-class housewife began including recipes for wildfowl. Geese or duck or woodcock, seasoned with onions, sage, and a little pepper. A pretty sauce for boiled fowl: bruise the liver of the bird with a little of the liquor, add lemon peel and butter, then boil all together and pour into a dish. And remember not to overcook the wigeons or teals. Just fifteen minutes under a very good and brisk fire, or they will lose their gravy and you will eat hard. Luckily an overcooked bird can easily become a salmis—a highly seasoned, wine-based ragout of mushrooms, game birds, and, if you can afford them, truffles. The dark flesh of one large prairie hen will make a meal for the entire family, unless you are large eaters, and then it's best to get two. Stuff a grouse with a lovely dough made of cornmeal and brandy, and it will come out of the oven with real epicurean style. But do please beware of dishonest men selling unwholesome birds mixed in with the birds of good character. If you pull the feathers around the vent, and they give easily, the bird is unfit to eat. One's nose, too, can be employed to detect the unpleasant smell of unsound flesh.

Fowl were no longer a mark of homespun self-sufficiency. They had become a consumer phenomenon. Wild birds were heaped upon tables, in simple but plentiful condition. At one particularly ambitious hotel in New York you could order heron, bald eagle, vulture, and owl. Any bird was fit for a meal but the buzzard. At Delmonico's, perhaps the most famous of New York's high-end dining establishments, the menu stretched beyond ten pages; the entrees numbered 346 and included ten kinds of wild duck.

The canvasback duck was considered the finest choice for the table, and the best ones came from Chesapeake Bay, where they got their delicious flavor from eating celery grass. Like the eighteenth-century turtle eaters, canvasback gourmands were ridiculed for their food of choice, and particularly for their inability to taste authentic difference. At least a few kitchens were known to embellish plates of lesser duck breeds with canvasback heads, and when the empty dish returned, the diners satisfied and none the wiser, the heads were made ready for the next order.

As demand for authentic canvasback rose, the price increased to three dollars a pair. Six barrels cost $1,000. By 1885, canvasback reached five to six dollars a pair. With the increase in cost, there was an even further frenzy to bring down the feathered game.

The first market hunters had been backwoodsmen—men who had grown up in the Adirondacks or Great Lakes and known the streams and valleys since childhood—and birds were so abundant that there was little concern about waste. But as demand for wildfowl grew, every man with a rifle wanted a piece of the profits.

Market hunters used whatever means had the most efficient slaughter: sink boats and baited sneak nets, swivel guns, breechloaders, poison, and birdlime. Dull-toned bells and whistles called the birds in. Wooden decoys littered the lakes. Live passenger pigeons were tethered and trained, then hoisted in the air to call in a flock. Over six hundred birds could be taken alive in one haul of the net. More than seventy-five thousand passenger pigeons might be brought to market in a single day.

The largest-caliber guns were capable of tremendous extraction. The punt gun—a custom-built shotgun with a barrel up to two inches in diameter—discharged a pound of shot at a time. The recoil was so strong it would knock two men down, so it was usually mounted onto a boat. One pull of the trigger killed upward of fifty birds. Often there were eight to ten boats lined up, ready with coordinated firing. Five hundred waterfowl dead in a single afternoon. The harvest of an entire flock, a mass execution.

Despite all the hunting, some wild birds—like today's deer and raccoons—briefly thrived in the nineteenth century's environments of progress. The farms that dotted the Great Plains were still sparse, surrounded by wayside sections of undeveloped grasslands. During seasons of migration, immense flocks of prairie chickens—feathered down to the ankles, "clothed to his toes," tender and fine-flavored—settled in the fields.[9] With the crops as a source of food, and grassy hills nearby to nest, the broods grew and spread. Hens everywhere on the land laying twelve to fifteen eggs at a sitting. Their hideous squawking could be heard for miles. The males looking for mates poured forth booming notes, grand and elastic, soft continuous exhilarating vibrations that sounded like they were calling in the rain. The birds perched on fence posts, morning and evening, made a circuit of the farms. They gathered round the unpicked cornfields as emperors prepare for a feast, and acres of crops were ruined by the destructive character of a thousand prairie chickens.

The prairie felt almost more desolate with these wild birds roaming the crops, not only ignoring man's attempts at civilization, but, like barbarians on plunder, actually benefiting from them. Everyone wondered why the birds had become so plentiful, more so than ever before. Questions arose among the market hunters: Is the prairie chicken even native to this country? How did it support itself before the fields of corn settled in?

The market hunters were offered free food for themselves and their horses in exchange for their extermination services. And splendid hunting it was! In one forty-acre field there were more birds than all the Union cities could hope to eat in a month. You could kill a hundred in a day. The local markets were so sick with glut, you could not give them away.

But with the spread of the railroads westward, birds in the prairies could be shot in the morning, iced in the afternoon, and in New York a few days later as a "thing in season."[10] Plovers and snipes, prairie chickens and quails, ducks and even dow birds in their short season were laid away in abundance. The dead birds were cooled off on ice, then packed so tightly together in wooden boxes that they carried the cold through two or three days on the train. It was not uncommon to open a box crammed with the bodies of eight hundred birds retaining the full chill of winter. It was as if the railroads ran on ice instead of steam.

The wild duck trade was particularly big business. One dealer on Long Island employed twenty men, who used twenty-three kegs of gunpowder over the course of a season. The birds were packed into barrels and shipped to New York by steamship. On average, fifteen to twenty-five barrels shipped each week, although during one particularly devastating week, the dealer shipped thirty-one.

Fowl speculation crisscrossed the country, and game birds were traded as readily as cash or government bonds. Birds would be killed when their numbers were highest and kept in canvas bags in underground cold rooms. When the market supply went down in the off-season, these birds, thawed out sweet, would fetch a hefty price. Still, such an excessive volume of birds arrived to the East Coast markets every day that many went sour.

For a time, the city was a cocoon, wrapping her inhabitants in obliviousness as to the violence of their hunger. The abundance of a city market masked the local bird extinctions, and consumers were hardly aware that a slight rise in the price meant an overall decrease in quantity. It seemed the wildfowl had neither beginning nor end. And yet these dying birds, like ill omens, predicted something of the irrationality of human appetites. In our attempts to avoid the randomness of living, we became greedy for stability. *Waste* came to mean something else—an overabundance of human industriousness.

The country poured forth her wildfowl by the millions of pounds.

———

One bright section of the factory is filled with standing water underlain with colonies of mottled algae. Vine-covered windows cast a grid of shadows over the chaotic mass of plant life. The walls have turned a marbled green, stained with pale blues and the muted orange-maroons of reptile skin. A red concrete fountain where workers once crowded to wash their hands is full of cobwebs. The room has the affect of a carefully planned neoclassical water garden, adorning the grounds of a faraway European villa, the baroness tearfully admitting she can no longer afford the upkeep.

As I walk through these factory rooms, I feel invisible, elated, unwatched. It is the same sense of freedom I feel when thrashing through an empty woods.

Freedom, like the word *waste* was also redefined with the rise of the market economy. For centuries, the concept of freedom was based on political sovereignty, but in the mid-nineteenth century, it was increasingly applied to an individual's ability to buy a diversity of goods. The expansion of gastronomic culture in urban centers contributed to a rising sense of individualism. You could define yourself by what you ate. The market, in turn, relied on this sense of "individual freedom" to diversify and grow.

But for transcendentalist philosophers of the time, the highest freedom was the ability to know oneself, and they believed this was best achieved in Wild Nature. Engaging with this primal source allowed one to find truth within. In the midst of all this fowl frenzy, nature tourism became the highest form of individual liberation.

Wealthy industrialists went on excursions into the wild. In the Adirondacks and the White Mountains, they stayed at hotels kept intentionally primitive—the bar was a barrel of whiskey in the corner. After an exhilarating day out in the forest, seated in the hotel dining room in front of a plate of wild duck, one experienced a perfect digestion and a sense of liberty.

Still, it was not wise to take the bracing tonic of wilderness with too great a frequency. Temporary adventures were necessary to build health and stamina, cultivate self-reflection, and take pleasure in the pristine—but only so that you could return to your art, writing, and industry with renewed vigor.

Nostalgia for the past mingled with pure techno-optimism for the future. The machine and the mountain man collided in the collective imagination. In one breath, these high-tech Romantics quoted Thoreau, and in the next, they claimed the merits of the steam combine. And so the wealthy came to believe in both an idyllic view of Wild Nature and in perpetual technological growth.

But for the poor, particularly in the less developed South, nature was not a place for tranquility—it remained a place to find basic nourishment. Before the Civil War, the majority of Southerners who were not slave owners supplemented their diets with hunting and gathering. Wild foods occupied the margins between sustenance and hunger.

This was even more true for enslaved people. To the thousands who ran away, swamps were places of refuge and wildfowl were a source of survival. They fashioned pyramid-shaped traps from cane to capture partridges, worshipped in the hollows, and wore pathways along the waterways to remind themselves they retained an identity beyond their enslavement. Wild Nature occupied the margins between freedom and the violence of white power.

During the Civil War, hunger was nearly universal among the troops. It was forbidden to waste cartridges on killing wild birds, but many soldiers did. There was still a great abundance of waterfowl in the southern wetlands, as these had not yet been decimated by market hunters. Soldiers took to cooking birds over the fire on their bayonets. The butcher for the 101st New York Volunteers, posted near Stafford, Virginia, brought in nice fat robins, and if the colonel would supply him with shot, he promised a mess of snipe. Though wild turkeys were sparse outside the canebrakes, they made the best meal. Soldiers wrote letters home describing battle smoke and famished stomachs with turkey-feather quill pens.

After the war, thousands of weary veterans returned home to their farms, impoverished and haunted by memories of the prolific waterfowl down south. Before the Civil War there were fewer sportsmen, but something about 250,000 dead had made men susceptible to nervous exhaustion. Perhaps they longed to experience the wilderness—with all its drama of life and death—in a manner that felt controlled.

Sport hunting was a restrained kind of violence, a structured form of leisure steeped in style, rules, and technical vocabulary. The Civil War had led to better gun technology, allowing the sportsman to drop a single bird from a chaotic flock of hundreds. Every action was a test of both his skill and his ethics. He made fair chase. There was no necessity to the killing, and that made it something even more pure. Nothing could beat the glowing feeling inside that resulted from reckoning with fear and fresh air, with the thrill of the hunt and sore muscles around a campfire, recounting the particular challenges and prizes that had been won.

For sportsmen, the adventure of bird hunting was a commodity in its own right. Men traded advice, read stories about hunting, and learned about the necessary accouterments in popular magazines and books—ivory-buttoned shooting jackets, broad-brimmed palmetto hats, short double-barreled fowling-pieces, small powder flasks, and first-rate ammunition.

Railroads began advertising sport hunting trips down South to unimproved lands where the birds were stronger of wing and better for shooting. These trips relied on the labor of recently freed slaves. The freedmen skilled the boats past bending willows, acquainted the out-of-towner with the habits and peculiarities of the local fowl, handled the dogs, made camp, cooked dinner, built up the fire, performed, entertained, were sociable, and generally provided the expected spectacle of a "genuine Southern negro."[11]

Many sportsmen encouraged women to take up shooting, as a way to legitimize the sport as a respectable form of upper-class recreation. For centuries women had been hidden. Among the garden crops with kid on hip and corn in hand, hidden in the kitchen, hidden in their own separate rooms in restaurants, hidden behind bonnets and miles of fabric in long, trailing skirts with layers of lace and silk and flounces and trimmings. Their freedoms were constricted as tightly as their waists. The women who took up sport hunting were motivated by the chance to be equal, if only for the briefness of the excursion. In wild country, with fewer material goods all around, a woman was also relieved of her role to serve merely as property. To be out on the hunt meant to enjoy the liberties that wealthy white men were given so generously in civilized life.

I walk into the remains of a laboratory. The decay feels more ominous in this room than in other parts of the factory. Its artifacts are within our lifetimes. Electric burners and rusting machines sit on lab benches, the cords disconnected and coiled at the floor like dead snakes. Tempered steel worktables warp in an excruciating attempt to defy abandonment. White plastic blinds conceal some windows. Others have been torn off. A rubber hose leaks water. The linoleum tiles no longer fully adhere. Drawers and cupboards lay open. It must have been a hasty retreat. What would have been the point of shutting them?

By the end of the nineteenth century, Wild Nature was no longer for the freedom of self-provision. It had become a place for the freedom of transcendence. It was sportsmen, lamenting they had to go farther and farther afield in search of game, who were among the first to notice signs of plummeting wildfowl populations. To the sport hunters, market hunters were a threat to Wild Nature. They tore it up, drank too much, worked too little, shot the flapping air for the fun of it. The sportsmen and market hunters followed the birds from Wisconsin to Texas and along every coast. Violent threats and bullet-laden skirmishes between the two became as common as competing for the same take.

The ideology of protectionism spread from the North first, traveled westward, and finally settled in the South. Although game laws were meant to protect wildfowl, in most cases they were written in such a way as to benefit the sportsmen. Still, game wardens were generally sympathetic to market hunters—they saw themselves as coming from the same community rather than the sporting elites—and frequently took bribes from dealers. The "poachers" and "pot hunters" smuggled birds banned for sale in one state into adjacent states with less stringent laws. They sold pheasant under the name of owl, and shipped ruffed grouse and quail in boxes marked "ducks." Large amounts of game were seized from shippers, and sometimes the wardens made a profit from the confiscated goods.

The destruction of habitat likely killed just as many birds as the hunting did. Between 1850 and 1910, forests fell at an astonishing rate—almost 10 percent of all the land in the United States was clearcut. The Central Valley of California had been a vast riparian ecosystem supporting huge numbers of wild birds. By the 1890s, it had been transformed into agricultural fields. The prairie grasslands were shrinking as more and more farms spread over the land.

Conservationists obsessed over renewal and purity. There was some kind of pleasure connected to cleaning up the mess their ancestors had made of the forests and prairies, and returning them to the "pristine" environments they once were. According to the emerging conservation ethic, the solution to our relentless appetites was to remove us from the wilderness altogether. Industry could continue to destroy some parts of the country as long as others were kept in a state of supposed purity.

When the country's first national parks were created, it was often by the forcible removal of Indigenous Americans living on the land. Poaching crimes, which increased during recessions, were seen as acts against the "public good" and "national commons." There was little concern for those living at the far fringes of the cash economy. Increasingly confined to isolated and resource-poor reservations, Indigenous Americans were brutally encouraged to eliminate their traditional practices. Because buying a state hunting license was a big expense, and access to open land was so restricted, tribes began relying on subsistence hunting and fishing less and less, even as many became hunting and fishing guides for American, European, and Canadian tourists.

The wealth created by an industrializing nation had erected a distinct line between the appetites of self-sufficiency and those of touristic pleasure. Wild Nature, in its own right, had become a valuable commodity, and game birds seemed more valuable alive to the economy of nature than as dead bodies on the table. In 1900, the Lacey Act banned the transportation of wild game across state lines, although by that point, the populations of many game birds were so reduced that their pursuit was no longer profitable. Market hunting was outlawed altogether with a series of federal laws by 1918.

In many ways, it was changing tastes that saved the remaining birds. The newest fad in the markets was rare and spectacular breeds of domesticated chickens.

Today, the pleasure of eating wildfowl is unfamiliar to most of us. Canvasback ducks are hanging in, but they no longer migrate through Chesapeake Bay much. The prairie chickens are endangered. The passenger pigeons were eaten to extinction (as were the heath hen, Labrador duck, and the great auk). Wild turkeys were reintroduced in the 1950s, and now they are timid beasts, wandering suburban streets, looking for the fields of their ancestors.

Sport hunters continue to work to protect wetlands and waterfowl habitat, although many have taken to shooting at private reserves, where birds are raised in confinement before being released into the wild air to meet the bullets that carry their deaths.

I have friends back home in New Mexico who still hunt fowl. I remember one evening, a friend cooked up "buffalo" duck wings. I bit down through the chewy, sweet skin and hit something hard. A piece of shot was lodged in the flesh.

In many ways, the conservation laws worked. A lot of birds have recovered, some to the point that we now call them a nuisance. But we are also left with a conservation ethic that views wild lands as pristine places without people, existing purely for moments of brief tourism and spiritual renewal. Meanwhile, outside these preserves, development continues to threaten avian life—in just the last fifty years, it is estimated we've lost nearly three billion birds, mostly common species like finches, blackbirds, and sparrows.

When Indigenous Americans were erased from their homelands, we forgot not only their culinary language—and their ingenious methods of cooking wildfowl—but, more importantly, we severed a relationship with nature. We are just beginning to acknowledge the many ways Indigenous American tribes *maintained* the wilderness through their cultural practices. In recent years, tribes from across the country have begun remaking their food traditions. The Sioux are involved with projects to restore the prairies in the hope of bringing back its birds. They're burning the grasslands once again.

―――――――――――――

I ascend to the northern roof on a delicate rusting ladder. The iron strip anchoring the ladder to the wall no longer carries its bolt, and a number of the structural holds at the top and bottom are corroded, eaten away by unseen but ever-present forces. I hold the thin handrails lightly and climb past pale-green walls toward a small square of bright light. The ladder vibrates the whole way up.

I sit on the eaves, spray-painted with *OM*, the sacred sound that represents the entire universe, and stare south at the city. Post-industrial. 1970s gothic. Concrete and bricks gleam in the five-o'clock light. Police sirens echo in the distance. Above and beyond, an accelerating sky.

In the opposite direction, I can see the blue-green shapes of distant forested hills. Our well-managed Eastern forest is a saved forest. It is growing back faster now than it has in centuries. But it is not the same kind of forest that once supported so many birds. These forests are missing the passenger pigeons, whose effects on tree ecology were immense and are still not entirely understood. These forests are missing the fires, too. Without them, multiflora rose and bittersweet vines take down entire trees. Ticks have proliferated with the increase in wet, dark spaces. Asian longhorn beetles are attacking the maple trees. Blights have nearly wiped out the chestnuts. The wolf trees—enormous, solitary white oaks growing here and there— are the only reminders of a precolonial legacy we've lost.

There is something beautiful about this decrepit factory, but all I can think of is the incredible violence that led to its creation and eventual decline. I imagine the glow of a forest at dusk, a sweep of ducks landing on a lake trailing white sparks. Then each bird transmogrifies, and I see the men in bloody aprons, the women toting heavy baskets, and the twisted bodies of wild birds. The trains, the ice, the guns bringing an end to their flight. Hidden among the feathers of so many dead birds is an entire history of chasing wild frontiers.

The wild frontiers of the future are likely to be these neglected spaces that capital has forsaken. The abandoned factory is a hybrid landscape possessed, inhabited, and occupied by nature, each room with a history of collapse and renewal. These rooms transmit the cataclysms of the past. Rather than a snapshot of a violent instance, each disturbance is layered into strata of melancholy. It is a raw, feral undoing of uniformity. Nature is not making progress. It is decaying progress.

Just as the factory's buildings exist in a state of being forgotten, so too the plants and animals figure out their own fates without our action. The wild birds have a way of life among the ruins that differs from their cousins in the forest. They return here with each cycle of the breeding seasons, like a ritual, dropping seeds in new irregular chinks, to watch the rattail fescue, marestail, spike trisetum, and green foxtail grasses sprout through crumbling manufactured substrate. The ivy that flames the factory walls is like velvet graffiti escaped from management. Indifferent. Deliberately uncontrollable. Thriving in the annihilated spaces of lost economies. Is this not the definition of a wild place? It has the independence of self-willed land.

With time, I have become the object in the factory's ecosystem. Wild Nature is the subject here. It has been an afternoon well spent in exploring. The light is fading. I continue through the factory until I can go no further.

PART 2

SUBJECTS OF DESIRE

· 5 ·

FOREST FLESH
WITH ROOTS AND TUBERS

*The Hunter Among Them—Refugia—Spy Games—The Power of
Ancient Kings—The Tired Eyes of Men—Two Frogs Sing a
Love Song—A New York Nightclub—The Poacher's Jail—A Wordless
Lesson—Overlooking the Congo River—Ancient Habits*

T IS MIDSUMMER. I am flying above a dense tropical forest in the Congo River basin. The single-engine Cessna is steeped in clouds. The pilot is a Protestant missionary named Garth. As we gain altitude, he tells me of the things he has transported: fourteen bicycles, four motorcycles, seven goats, innumerable vials of blood and medicine. His eyebrows droop, looking as if they want to migrate to his mouth. Below us, rivers bleed through the forest in slow, velvety meanders.

I have come here to follow the trade in wild meat from the forests of the Democratic Republic of Congo (DRC) to the streets of Paris. Bushmeat consumption in the Congo Basin has concerned conservationists for nearly four decades and has come to be seen as an intractable problem rife with military conflict and entangled with the small-arms trade. Once a subsistence food for the rural poor, wild meat is increasingly an urban luxury.

We land on a bright grassy field at the edge of Africa's largest tropical rainforest reserve. I descend the steps of the plane with my hands full of thin-skinned avocados. I had bought them for a few dollars when we touched down to refuel in a slightly less remote settlement along the route.

We had picked up a small boy then, too. He had never left his village before. He is dressed in pressed blue slacks and a white button-up shirt. When he boarded the plane, he seemed alone in his terror and excitement, but as we gained altitude, he unwrapped a white roll and offered me some. We chewed the plain bread and watched the clouds convene around us.

When I disembark, the boy stays on the plane. He will be returning with the pilot to the capital city, with only a small suitcase and his mute bravery.

A crowd gathers around, and as hands are outstretched to help unload mail and supplies, I too am swept up by this procession of strangers. It is easy to notice the Hunter among them. He wears a faded Ramones T-shirt and a wide-brimmed, waxed-canvas bush hat, so well broken-in that it gleams like leather. Around his neck is a leopard tooth strung on black cord. But before I have a chance to fully take him in, I'm loaded onto the back of a motorcycle with all my belongings and driven away in a cloud of dust.

In the late afternoon, I settle into my accommodations, provided by an international conservation organization that helps to manage the adjacent national park as part of a larger consortium. The Hunter stops by and offers to take me on a walk through the hamlet. He helps to coordinate anti-poaching patrols in the national park for another conservation organization—working with both park guards and the military—and has extensive knowledge of the bushmeat trade.

As soon as we leave the gated compound, a group of children surrounds us. "They want to know if you are my wife," the Hunter translates as they giggle. He smiles at their teasing, revealing a lovely set of crooked teeth. The Hunter is older than me, although not much taller. His shoulder-length wavy hair is a deep honey brown, sparkling with sparse grey. He has a robust chin, balanced and not too heavy, roughly shaded by stubble. His narrow lips arch into two perfect mountains at the center, surrounded by deep smile lines, like the walls of a canyon valley. There is a kindness in his blue eyes, and something sad, but I do not notice this at first.

The hamlet is a *grand petit ville*—a big little village—with a school and a medical clinic. We walk toward the center, where a soccer game is underway, and then down a dirt road away from the gathering. The air quiets. Under the shade of a massive bokungu tree, military men sit in plastic chairs arranged in a semicircle. They have just finished eating, and a few women clean up the leftover food from the feast, swaying slowly, as if they are dancing underwater.

The road becomes a meandering overgrown path down to a tributary of the Congo River. The water is shadowed by overhanging foliage. Electric-indigo butterflies congregate on the shoreline. A dilapidated cargo boat, flat-bottomed and rectangular, rests in the mud at a skewed angle, like the carcass of a beached whale. It looks much too big to have navigated up this stream. A few slender dugout canoes, called pirogues, are pulled up on the sand next to it. These are made by hollowing out a single tree. The rot-resistant hardwood is strong, and such boats typically last thirty years, although some of the biggest ones are nearly a hundred years old, grey with time.

"This is the only river out of the village, and the main way people come and go from here, so sometimes the park guards will set up river checkpoints," the Hunter says. "Ivory smugglers have been known to cut the tusks of elephants into six-inch pieces and put them in wooden boxes built under the bottom of a pirogue. So the guards will take a rope and scrape it along the bottom of the boats as they pass by to feel for any irregularities."

We walk back uphill a short distance to where the Hunter lives—a rambling, elevated house, providing offices and accommodations for the conservation staff—and sit in the front yard on hand-carved wooden-plank chairs.

"Here, have a slightly cool Primus," he says, handing me a large brown bottle of beer, the label worn away from reuse. The Hunter has built a small garden in a corner of the yard, in an attempt to grow enough food for the staff. We drink the warm beer and watch the chickens scratch for insects in the sinking sunlight.

The Hunter grew up in the Democratic Republic of Congo, the son of Swedish missionaries. His parents were as unmatched in height as they were compatible in their sternness. Later in life, as a graduate student, he spent years observing the behavior of bonobos in the wild, those great apes that resemble us in their perpetual desire to make love. But when he saw how threatened they had become by poachers and wildlife pet traders, he left behind his academic work, compelled by a sense of urgency.

"Most people can't conceive of conservation," he says, taking a sip of beer. "They wake up in the morning, wash, and want to eat. To them, the forest is for survival. You can't care about conservation with an empty stomach."

His voice has a smooth, throaty quality, although it is not particularly deep.

"But here conservation is good business. It is one of the few industries that is growing. It's one of the few ways that people who live here, so remotely, have access to the modern world. International conservation organizations bring money, generators, motorcycles. They bring satellite internet."

The air is filled with the flashes of fireflies slowly winking awake.

"But at some point, your money *becomes your message*," he continues. "It's no longer about conservation for the animals. It's about what conservation can do, what kind of *material wealth* it can bring to the village. Conservation brings the desire for more material goods."

He turns toward me, his brow furrowed. "And it's so corrupt, everywhere is corrupt. Lots of money not going where it is supposed to be. The bigger the budget, the less efficient," he says gloomily. "Meanwhile, the forests are still emptying of all their animals. Every week, tons of bushmeat leaves the country's national parks."

"Where is all this meat going?" I ask.

"A lot goes to the eastern part of the country, where there are informal small-scale mining and logging camps. Logging roads open up new parts of the forest that weren't easily accessible before. These places spring up overnight—people leave their villages and move into the forest, where they require food—so there is very high demand. The middleman buys meat from hunters and makes ten times the amount selling it to diamond camps.

"But there is also a luxury market emerging in the cities," the Hunter continues. "Other countries in Africa are already to the point where they've eaten all their animals and have to import bushmeat. We aren't there yet in DRC, partially because we have such a huge amount of forest."

Even though the national park here is just a small portion of the massive Congo Basin rainforest, it is still enormous—at nearly 8 million acres, it is larger than Belgium—and likely holds 40 percent of the world's bonobo population. Much of it is relatively difficult to access, and there are not enough guards to cover the entire territory. The Hunter goes on four patrol rounds a year, into the most remote areas.

He points to the well-worn Chaco sandals on his feet.

"These are my preferred footwear for walking around the forest. All the guards in their boots think I'm crazy to wear sandals, because of the snakes. But I find it so much easier going this way."

"You must have seen a lot of wildlife, spending so much time in the forest," I say.

"It's actually quite hard to see animals in the rainforest. Many are small, solitary, and nocturnal. They evolved to be elusive. Mostly, I've just seen dead animals, or animals captured in snares that are waiting to be dead." He sets his beer down in the dirt. "All this poaching threatens the trees, too. The whole ecology of the forest changes."

For many tree species—especially those that grow best spread out from each other—animals, birds, and bats are the primary seed-dispersal agents. They eat the tree's nuts or fruits and then pass them elsewhere, where they grow into new seedlings. Or they might bury them in caches to go back to later but then never return. Sometimes the animals pick up sticky or barbed seeds in their fur and accidentally transport them. Without these processes, certain trees don't reproduce.

Forest elephants in particular eat a lot of fruit and defecate the seeds over large areas, helping to increase forest diversity.

There is also evidence that the elephants' eating and stomping patterns help promote forests with larger, slow-growing hardwood trees, which store more carbon than smaller softwood trees. The loss of elephants could drastically affect how much carbon is sequestered in the Congo Basin's forests.

"The scientists call it 'Empty Forest Syndrome.' A forest without its music," the Hunter says with a note of sadness.

We are both quiet for a moment. I am thinking about his life, an existence where time is measured by the hunting seasons. I notice a pockmark scar below his right eye, like a fallen tear. It is the most delicate cartographic feature on the rugged landscape of his face.

The sky is darkening. An exquisite lightning storm gathers in the clouds to the west. The intermittent flashes reveal trees like apparitions.

"I feel most at home here," he says, "but I will always be out of place. When I go home to Sweden, I am out of place there too."

"I feel this, too," I say. "It seems difficult to find a place that feels like home these days. The world has become a giant mall. Everything is for sale. Everything has become tourism. How do you live an authentic life in that sort of existence? What does authentic even mean?"

"It is sometimes possible here," he replies. "My favorite time of day is just before dawn, when the nocturnal animals are going to sleep and the others have yet to awaken. The forest is so still and silent. It's amazing. You don't notice how loud the forest is until it becomes quiet. I'll make my coffee over a small kindling fire, and as the sun rises, the forest comes alive again. Those few moments in between are very special. A landscape of momentary hush. Listening to a day beginning."

The storm grows bigger, seems to be all around us, although there is still no rain. Only a searching breeze. "In the forest there is still lots of magic. There isn't a separation between the spiritual realm and everyday life," he says, as if speaking to the sky.

There is something so completely present about the Hunter that I do not notice the time passing. We are content to listen and speak with each other. There is no need for anything else. Across the river, the ripe rainforest makes love to itself.

The end is sudden. A motorcycle pulls up into the yard. The headlight beams into the dark like a kind of violence. Someone has come to collect me and take me home.

Some of the creatures that live in the dense tropical forests of the Congo Basin are near-mythical. There are forest buffalo and striped bongo antelope, monkeys (endless varieties) and red river hogs. There are duikers of many colors—blue, black-striped, yellow-backed, and red. There are slender-nosed crocodiles, cane rats, mud turtles, and pangolins with medicinal scales worth millions on the black market. Bonobos, our lust-bound relatives. The forest elephant, so tormented for the wealth of its tusks. The swamp-haunting sitatunga antelope, with its elegant twisted horns. The elusive Congo peacock. The silky clawless otter. The blind cave-dwelling river fish.

On the forest floor, more life abounds. Termites in monstrous nests that rise like stone monoliths. Saprophytic fungi that live on the dead. Armies of polished driver ants that hunt in groups by spreading themselves over the ground and up the sides of the vegetation, marching forward together, catching whatever prey crosses their path. There are irascible snakes so dangerous that even uttering their names sparks fear. *Black mamba* is whispered to children, like a ghost story meant to provoke nightmares.

A species cannot exist in isolation—the boundaries between one and another are illusory—and so it is not enough to name each animal. We must describe the tapestry in which each is woven. In the forest, sedimentary rocks deposited millennia ago are overlain with sandy soils and a thin layer of microbe-rich humus. The plants that grow in these soils produce chemicals called secondary metabolites—tannins, flavonoids, carotenes, phenolic acids, and alkaloids—which serve a variety of functions. It is an incredibly complex system that we don't fully understand. Humans have long used plants that contain secondary metabolites to treat disease, flavor foods, color cloth, or protect food crops. The animals that eat these plants use the chemicals, too, as a cure for intestinal parasites or to increase fertility. They are an essential part of what gives game meat its distinct flavor.

The forest ecosystem of the Congo Basin has always been in flux. It has experienced long cycles of contraction and expansion, each with new opportunities for evolution. Beginning about 800,000 years ago, the region was subjected to recurrent arid periods, which came and went about every 100,000 years. During cool climatic intervals, glaciers in the northern latitudes grew and the rainforest dried out and died off in pieces. Open grasslands spread. The remaining islands of forest became refugia for non-grassland species. When the climate warmed, the northern glaciers shrank, and the wet forest expanded again. This long history of fragmentation created one of the most biologically rich and diverse places on earth, with many species that do not live anywhere else in the world.

Around eleven thousand years ago, with the beginning of a warm period called the Holocene, the forest expanded even further. With the decline of the grasslands, nearly fifteen genera of large herbivores went extinct. Without these animals to help maintain the remaining open grasslands—by grazing down new trees, thus preventing seedlings from maturing—the forest grew wetter and denser, favoring the evolution of insects, fish, and small mammals.

Streams veined through the trees, merged to become rivers, mixed further to become arteries. These braided waterways turned the land to marsh and swamp. For some land animals, the waterways were a barrier to movement. For others, like us, the rivers became a transport network through overpowering foliage too thick to traverse on foot.

The indigenous groups in these rainforests were short-statured forager-hunters generally referred to as the Twa, although this name was imposed by outsiders onto a varied group of distinct tribes. These groups lived in the Congo Basin since at least the Middle Stone Age Period, around 100,000 years ago.

For thousands of years, customary land rights dictated which community could hunt when and where, shifting over time and space to account for semi-nomadic lifestyles. This strategy was also a form of game management that prevented any one area of forest from becoming depleted. Game was captured with spears or poison-tipped bows and arrows. Hunting occurred all year, although it was in the wet season when game was most plentiful. The rains flooded the lowlands, and the animals crowded into the highlands. In the dry season, the rivers pulled back from their banks and fish swarmed in the shallows, easy prey for sharp-tipped spears.

Because all life was communal then, eating was too, and meat was the glue that bound society together. A forest buffalo would feed the entire community. Diets were protein rich and carbohydrate poor. Game meat is very lean, so the fattiest parts were prized most of all. Women had customary rights to certain portions of the meat, with chiefs often dividing the catch.

Between 2000 BCE and 500 CE, a series of migrations brought the Bantu people—a general label that describes hundreds of different ethnic groups who speak the Bantu languages—into the Congo Basin from northwest Africa. They practiced slash-and-burn agriculture: a portion of the forest was burned, and then planted with low-intensity and shade-tolerant crops such as oil palm, wild rice, and wild yams. After a period of time, new areas were cleared, and the old agricultural land that had been abandoned regrew into forest again.

There is evidence that the Bantu enslaved, displaced, or killed much of the Twa population, although extensive trade networks also existed to exchange weapons, pottery, and agricultural provisions for smoked game meat. One historic reference describes this relationship as a patronage whereby a Twa hunter would attach himself to a specific powerful Bantu man, who in turn would gain some prestige in having this hunter associated with him.

Elephant was eaten widely, as it provided an immense amount of meat, although some communities believed that if you weren't careful, a witch doctor could cast your soul into an elephant, and you would be bound to it in both life and death. Killing one of these animals was thus a profoundly sacred act. Other groups prohibited eating bonobos because they were seen as having a direct link to the ancestral spirit world. These cultural beliefs had an ecological basis, helping to conserve animals with complex social groupings that were slow-growing and thus particularly vulnerable to overhunting.

There is no longer such a thing as a virgin tropical rainforest untouched by humanity—and there hasn't been for a very long time. Even in areas of old, mature forest, as remote and fierce as anything left in this world, there are relics of lost human societies: old fruit trees still bearing fruit; coconut and palm trees, growing as silent reminders of previous inhabitants; charcoal fragments in the soil; grave sites, hand-axes, projectile points, and the wastes of stone tools, all echoes of past conflicts. The forest holds these memories even after we have forgotten them.

124

———

Virtue, a Congolese man with a master's degree from an Ivy League school in the United States, is the project director for the conservation organization that is hosting me. Every morning, he drinks his tea with honey from the forest, dark amber liquid stored in a plastic bottle. Forest honey is thought to counteract poison—an old Congolese remedy from the days political enemies were frequently poisoning each other—and Virtue has equal enthusiasm for paranoia and simple habit.

"You must not stay out at night like this," Virtue scolds me over breakfast, the day after my visit with the Hunter. "We are responsible for you." He laughs lethargically, then stops abruptly and sucks in a long intake of air, as if he has been running and needs to catch his breath.

After we eat, he takes me to meet the village chief, who is drinking Tiger beer and smoking filterless cigarettes on the porch of a brick building, crumbling in the sunshine. The chief wears a black sleeveless shirt and a pagne, a patterned swath of fabric wrapped around him like a sarong. His long, elegant fingers and smooth nails are stained orange at the tips. Sitting next to him is his wife, wearing a headscarf and pagne in matching fabric. She looks uninterested and does not acknowledge me. In a third chair is an army commander. His brown-and-green socks are pulled up to his knees.

Virtue addresses the group in Lingala, one of the primary languages spoken in this linguistically complex country. French is the official language in DRC, but Lingala is the main language of the Congolese armed forces. It was already widely spoken before the arrival of Europeans—having originated as a trade language between the many different groups living along the Congo River—but after both Catholic missionaries and the Belgian colonial government adopted it for administrative purposes, its usage spread. Today, Lingala is spoken by more than 70 million people throughout the central African region.

I introduce myself and then watch their conversation quietly, unsure of what is being said. While they talk, a tiny orange kitten winds among the chair legs. As we leave, Virtue turns to me with a slight grin and a tidy explanation of the conversation. "They want to make sure we aren't using you as a spy."

If a white man kills a wild animal and eats it, we call it *hunting game*. Sometimes the animal is called venison. Other times it is named—deer, elk, moose. If a black man kills a wild animal and eats it, we call it *bushmeat poaching*. The animals are too numerous to name and so it is merely called flesh, protein, meat.

The story of how hunting became poaching, and game meat became illegal bushmeat, begins with the power of ancient kings.

Beginning in the eleventh century, when kings in Europe passed the earliest forest laws to protect the animals they hunted, ignoring or disobeying those laws could have terrible consequences. William the Conqueror deemed that "Whoever shall kill a stag, a wild boar, or even a hare, shall have his eyes torn out."[1] Under Henry II, innocence was established by ordeal or trial by hot iron. Convicted poachers were either blinded or castrated.

These kinds of proscriptions were passed down over centuries, appearing in various forms, in woven tapestries and paintings, described throughout numerous manuals and laws, twisted together from one king to the next, as if they all amounted to an ever-evolving book, echoes of blood and desire ricocheting through time.

But to the landless poor, poaching was an act of resistance against an unequal system. By the fifteenth century, with the spread of firearms, illegal hunting rose significantly and became increasingly organized. Poachers joined together in bands that fought each other for the best hunting areas, and game administrators were often threatened with open warfare if they dared to enforce the king's law. In 1417, England's Parliament debated whether these poaching gangs were part of a conspiracy that was organizing an insurrection. Forest laws became increasingly entwined with fears of revolution—that hunting skills would breed disorder among the common tradesmen and servants, or that rebels might disguise themselves as hunters—and the laws became stricter. Punishments against poachers included removal from the country or death.

Despite all the restrictions set forth in these laws, they were difficult to enforce—many wardens engaged in corrupt activities and took bribes. But the laws certainly made the lives of peasants more difficult, and as such, were passed not only to protect game animals but also as a form of social control. Over time, a great suspicion of forests became commonplace among the general population.

When the first European missionaries arrived in the Congo Basin forests in the eighteenth century, they carried with them this long-standing belief that the forest was an inimical and dark place. Myths arose to justify the outsiders' sense of unease: the French priest Liévain-Bonaventure Proyart reported in 1776 that some missionaries had come across the claw marks of a monstrous creature, a yard in diameter.

Beginning in 1874, the Welsh journalist Henry Morton Stanley—famous for searching for the source of the Nile and finding
Dr. Livingstone—undertook a violent exploratory expedition
through Congo's forests, which he described as "suffocating
wilderness."[2] After returning to Europe, Stanley was recruited
by King Leopold II of Belgium, who aimed to make a vast
stretch of central Africa his private colony. Stanley's explorations and trade deals would help Leopold to gain a foothold in
the region.

In May of 1885, the "international" community (England,
France, Germany, Belgium, and Italy) recognized King Leopold II as having a sovereign claim over the extensive area that
came to be known as Congo Free State. Leopold II divided his
new territory without consideration for the preexisting divisions made by the people who already lived there. Villages,
once dispersed along riverbanks, were brutally relocated and
concentrated along newly built roads. Such compulsory reset-
tlement, and the restriction of movement, became key tactics
in controlling a previously scattered and semi-nomadic rural
population.

The land and its people came to be viewed scientifically—a
methodology both driven by neutral curiosity and in service
of colonial power. Mustachioed men mounted expeditions on
river steamers. They wrote extensive reports of waterway nav-
igability. Exotic plants and animals were amassed, labeled, and
sent back to collections. The many ethnic groups in the region
were treated similarly; everything from their social structure
to their inheritance customs to their physical appearance was
painstakingly described and cataloged.

Leopold II had a railway line built between the Atlantic coast
and Léopoldville (present-day Kinshasa), where a port was constructed. An extensive upstream riverboat network was put

into place to export resources. Brussels busied itself preparing agricultural bulletins. More roads were hacked into the forests. Large tracts were cleared for plantations of cash crops like coffee, cotton, rubber, and palm oil, which caused the thin layer of nutrient-rich humus soil to erode—it too could not live in isolation from the whole. The Congolese were forced into agricultural labor and the ivory trade under increasingly appalling conditions. Failure to comply led to the loss of hands.

In 1900, one of the first international conservation treaties was signed: the Convention for the Preservation of Wild Animals, Birds and Fish in Africa. The treaty had very little to do with the basic intrinsic value of wildlife and much to do with protecting African landscapes for European exploitation. In Europe, forest laws had restricted hunting to rich landowners for centuries, so it was with little thought that such laws were implemented in Africa as well. The local inhabitants were told they could not use the forests as they once had. With their access to forests restricted, and plantation agriculture replacing food crops, meat became scarce. The Congolese relied on famine roots and tubers, peanuts, and palm oil. The people became starch eaters. Meat came to symbolize power and potency more than ever before. The Belgians took to sport hunting on horseback.

King Leopold II amassed a personal fortune worth well over $1.1 billion in today's currency. His reign resulted in the massacre of more than 10 million Congolese between 1885 and 1908. As the Belgian administration transformed the country into a model colony, they began to envision it as a new touristic playground for Westerners. Travelogues recast "Darkest Africa" as a "travellers' happy hunting ground."[3] At the time, national parks and preservation initiatives were happening in numerous countries around the world, and conservationists recommended setting up game reserves as a way to attract visitors who would spend money. King Albert I, Leopold's successor, toured the national parks in the American West and decided to declare a similar protected area in eastern Congo in 1926—the first in Africa. More protected areas were declared in 1938 and 1956.

129

By the 1950s, independence movements were beginning all over Africa, and one of the biggest concerns among the colonists was what would happen to the wildlife with the change in government. In 1961, a pan-African conservation symposium was organized to discuss the problem, aiming to convince the new African leaders that wild animals were a part of the collective beauty and wealth of all humankind. The military dictator who came to power after DRC's independence revolution in 1965, Mobutu Sese Seko, enacted many wilderness conservation laws that were strikingly similar to the laws instituted by the Belgians. He expanded park boundaries and used the national parks as private hunting grounds.

In 1994, genocide began in neighboring Rwanda. Thousands of people fled westward, and the forests were overrun by rebel soldiers and armed refugees. They took hostages to make sure local villagers supplied food and shelter. Then in 1996, civil war broke out in DRC. Everywhere there was crisis, starvation, and desperation. Hunger was so rampant that previously held taboos against eating bonobos disappeared. Local militia groups hid out in the forests, stockpiling smoked game, ivory, and drugs to be traded for supplies and small arms.

Any attempts to curb hunting were futile in such a violent landscape. Renegade military leaders stripped national park guards of their uniforms and weapons. Forest protections collapsed. The incursion of automatic rifles into the forests increased potential hunting returns by up to twenty-five-fold. Roving poacher gangs made strongholds deeper within the forest.

Cash streamed into remote areas. The conflict had irrevocably changed the pace of wildlife extraction.

Today, the land has been recolonized by conservation non-governmental organizations (NGOs), which bring the new noise of generators and motorcycles to an ecosystem they are worried is becoming silent. Meanwhile, people living in or near protected areas are seen as a disturbance to the natural order and a threat to wildlife.

The forest is haunted by many ghosts of power. We must not forget to speak of them for fear of awakening spirits, or offending the ancestors who kept their lives but lost their hands.

───────────

My host organization has assembled a group of local hunters to speak to me. Fifteen men sit in an open-air thatch building waiting. They will be paid 5,000 Congolese francs (about US$3) for their time. For some, it will be quick money. For others, they will have to sit and wait all day until it is their turn. In either case, the cash is welcome in a place where paid work is rare.

Most have come on foot, walking here from their villages bordering the national park. Nearly 180,000 people live either in or next to the forest reserve, residing in 716 villages and four towns. Two populations reside entirely or partly within the limits of the national park: the Kitawalists, a religious sect, and the Iyaelima people, semi-nomadic forager-hunters who until recently relied on traditional methods of hunting and agriculture.

While killing and eating bushmeat is in many regards a legal activity, there are various aspects that are illegal. One of the most difficult problems is that each province determines its own hunting laws. These incongruent legal frameworks mixed with long-standing customary laws of land access have created a complicated tangle of regulations. Many of the hunting laws are colonial relics. All hunters are required to have a *permis de chasse* (hunting permit), although few of them actually obtain one. It is illegal to hunt out of season or own a gun without a permit. Animals protected under the Convention on International Trade in Endangered Species of Wild Fauna and Flora (CITES)—such as chimpanzee, gorilla, bonobo, and elephant—cannot be killed, although they garner the highest prices on the illicit market.

While hunting within the national park is strictly prohibited, some villages on the border of the park are granted access to a strip of corridor land. Much of this is in the form of either mixed cultivation or secondary forest—forest that has regrown after the old-growth trees are cut down. Unlike old-growth forests—where the dense canopy shades out small bushes and tracks are opened up by large animals like elephants—secondary forest is difficult to walk through. The village hunters follow narrow paths tunneled through the vegetation over many years, or hack their way through nearly impenetrable thickets.

As they walk through the forest, the hunters will place snares—digging a small hole, setting a loop of bike cable or nylon cord on a trip stick, and covering it in leaves—to capture small- to medium-sized mammals such as duiker (antelope) and cane rat. Snares are often put in areas where animals are known to migrate. When the animal stumbles into the hole, it is caught either by the leg or neck. These traps can be very wasteful: the hunter may not return for a week or two, and many animals suffer to death in the interim and are no longer edible.

There is very little, if any, large game found in the corridor forests, though people do use them to gather edible insects, wild honey, and medicinal plants. To kill the big animals, the villagers hunt in the national park. To them it is not illegal—these forests were the homes of their ancestors.

The men are of various ages and in various states of dress, although most seem to have put on their best outfits for me. When they address me, they stand. My translator is a language teacher named Blaze. He wears a calculator watch.

As I interview the men, word spreads, and more show up to talk to me.

Most of these men have been hunting since they were small boys. Most don't own guns, but will borrow a *calibre douze*, a twelve-gauge shotgun, from someone in their village, in exchange for a share of their catch. The ammunition, *cartouche 00,* is supplied by traders from the cities who visit the villages a few times a year.

After an animal has been killed, the hunter disembowels it. The skin is left on. The body is splayed dorsally by a frame made of two crossed branches. Fresh meat rots quickly in the equatorial rainforest, so the animal is warm-smoked for many hours. Over time, the meat develops a thick, strong crust on the outside. Because of the humidity of the forest, the meat is re-dried over small fires every four to five days. All this slow roasting means that when it is finally reconstituted, in rich stews of tomato and spice, the game is delicate and tender. It falls to pieces in your mouth.

Smoked game prepared this way is often called *boucané*. The French word originally derives from the Caribbean Taíno word *buccan*, which described a wooden frame that was used for slow-cooking and preserving meat. French privateers would break from attacking Spanish trade ships to hunt the abundant sea turtles, as well as feral pigs, and adopted the local method of smoking the meat. It was stored in the bowels of their boats like treasure, and their food came to define them as *boucaniers*. English colonists in Jamaica knew these men as buccaneers.

The hunters speak softly. Their faces are delicate and beautiful. One man has a twitch that is enlivened by talking. I write down what Blaze translates. *The price of game meat is increasing.* One man wears a Harley-Davidson button-down shirt. *I do not see the elephant or forest buffalo so often any more.* Another man wears formal dress shoes and pants, contrasted with a T-shirt depicting palm trees, a sailboat, and the sun setting into the ocean. As he speaks, his gold chain and gold watch flash. *I hunt monkey, rat, and antelope.*

If a village hunter manages to kill game, he will sometimes give it to family or other village members, but more and more frequently the meat is stockpiled until a trader comes to town. These *commerçants* come to the rural areas from large cities far away. Sometimes the trader will hang around for a few weeks, negotiating for the best game. Sometimes the people in these villages are his relatives, and he has come home.

Wild meat is traded for soap, salt, cups, clothes, cigarettes, and bullets. If the village hunter happens to get cash for his game, it is used to pay school fees and hospital bills. He will feed his family the leftover parts of the animal that cannot be traded. *People are suffering so they hunt more*, a pastor dressed in an oversized brown shirt tells me. *To hunt has no real benefit. It is only a way to keep living. We have no other opportunity.*

Another man, part of the Kitawalists religious sect, wears all white, with Nike flip-flops and a laminated picture of his religious leader around his neck. When he was a child, there were one or two hunters in the village, he says. But with the rise in market demand, *now every boy, every man, has become a hunter.* Another man is in fashionable jeans that have been pre-cut to look distressed and a green shirt edged in embroidery. *The animals can't be wiped out by overhunting—they are always able to reproduce. It's just that with so many more hunters in the forest, the animals have been scared away.*

A hunter in a soccer jersey and green pants tells me *there is conflict in our forests.* Sometimes it is between local men but usually it is with strangers from elsewhere—migrants, refugees and smugglers, transient loggers, and unemployed miners. But the outsiders who are most violent are the market hunters—highly organized groups of poachers, armed with AK-47s.

While the village hunters will go home after a few days in the forest, bearing only as many animals as they can carry, the market hunters set up camps deep in the forest. They shoot down whole troops of monkeys and herds of bush pigs. The smoked meat is stockpiled into large baskets made from slender bent saplings. Then the heavy loads are carried out by foot to a more accessible part of the forest. As payment, the porters are given a monkey for every five they carry.

If a suitable river is found, the game will be loaded onto pirogues. Otherwise, it is balanced on modified bicycles—saddle removed, chain and pedal off, strings tied from the handlebars to the baskets—and pushed for many more miles over rutted, single-track dirt lanes and across log bridges. Poachers push these bikes (sometimes weighing over one hundred pounds) up to five hundred miles, a distance that takes two to three weeks to cover.

A man with reading glasses perched on the tip of his nose tells me: *Before the military came, there were lots of animals and lots of meat.* Prior to the arrival of the international conservation NGOs in the early 2000s, the national park guards weren't paid regularly. They might go months without their salaries, so to get by they might hunt, take bribes from poachers, or let their friends in the villages hunt in exchange for some game meat.

Until the late 2000s, there were still rebels hiding out in vast stretches of the national park, arresting local people, extorting and torturing, confiscating goods, amassing weapons, and using bushmeat and ivory sales to fund their anti-government activities. In 2010, a paramilitary group left the forest and took over the town of Mbandaka. It is hard to know where they got their munitions from, but it is very likely they were helped by military defectors, or park rangers willing to look the other way.

To address the problem, and prevent future insurrections, 135 the country's president started "Project Bonobo" and committed three hundred members of the Congolese National Army (FARDC) as eco-guards to patrol the forest preserve, seize illegal weapons, and arrest suspected poachers. Since then, the military has confiscated thousands of pounds of meat, along with more than 120 high-powered firearms, including assault rifles. Scores of suspected poachers have been arrested. Although overall elephant circulation appears to have significantly increased since the arrival of the military, it's possible hunting has just moved to less policed areas.

The FARDC military presence entangles both market and subsistence hunters, despite them having very different impacts on the wildlife. Soldiers commandeer the village shotguns because most people don't have permits to own them legally. They impose arbitrary and exorbitant fines. There have been accusations of rape, torture, and murder. Bushmeat was once sold out in the open but is no longer so easily available. Now there are secret codes required for buying and selling it. The military burns confiscated meat in big fires so that everyone will see. People go to sleep hungry.

Every village hunter I interview tells me that conservation is a good thing. But could they say anything else when it is the conservation organization paying them for their time? Were these men truly just subsistence hunters trying to survive, or did they have ties to larger-scale market hunting? I wade through layers of deception and misunderstanding trying to locate the truth. As we talk, it is as if the words materialize in the air between us, turn electric blue, float into the palm leaf ceiling, and dissolve into a smoky haze. As if none of us has heard anything at all.

"These people grew up with wild meat. It was all they had," Blaze, my translator, says. "Now they eat more domesticated meat—pigs and chickens they raise themselves. They would prefer to eat wild meat, but since that is no longer possible, they want domestic animals, which are like money in the bank. Perhaps the conservationists could give them some? Perhaps there are jobs for them as park guards?"

The tired eyes of these men implore me, *Please help us.* With my white skin, my ability to come and go. *Please help us.* They believe I have that power. Perhaps I do. But in the wilting afternoon light, I feel as much a pawn of history as these men feel powerless to their fates. *People don't have much trust in the future. There is always concern that things will descend into instability.*

The last of the hunters has left. A short man stands at the wooden table where I have conducted my interviews. The declining sun streams through the small, high windows, casting aquatic shadows on the whitewashed mud walls. He is pressing a shirt for Virtue, with an old cast-metal iron, an artifact from the colonial era. The belly of the implement is filled with glowing coals. He does his work slowly and with great attention. His back is to me and as he smooths out the creases, he hums softly. He does not notice me watching. For a moment, we are equally invisible.

―――――――――

That evening, I am left alone at the compound. I want to visit the Hunter, to talk to him about the men I've spent all day interviewing, but I am not allowed to wander outside these walls without someone to escort me. I feel imprisoned by my gender and by my status as a foreigner. It is a frustrating feeling of otherness that I have rarely experienced. I am something worth guarding, both for what I might do and for what might be done to me.

I hear gospel hymns floating through the night sky from somewhere across the village. The beats of drums are sparks among the gentle harmonies of unseen voices. I walk out into the backyard. A towering cactus-like tree elegantly caresses the crescent moon. Two frogs sing a love song from a wet corner. There's a chill in the air I never would have expected at the equator.

The next morning, the Hunter comes to visit. We are like two nocturnal creatures, startled to see each other in the illuminating flush of day.

"I was hoping to see you last night," I say.

"I thought about coming," he replies.

I have barely known him two days, and I already feel enchained. Pulled toward him by an inward impulse, an instinctual desire that I cannot repress by rational thought, a search for some kind of freedom. It is not so much a strong attraction as it is a deep sense of familiarity. Like a treasure hunt, it is as if he has been showing up in my life in little clues all along. A stranger's smile here, a former lover's caress, a half-remembered character from a dream, a breezy spring day when everything felt eternal. Each instance a piecemeal reflection of his total future manifestation. It is as if we have always been in the ordinary company of each other.

In the days that follow, he is increasingly by my side. Inevitable.

Even in the rainforest, there is a certain kind of excess that is only possible as the sun sets. One evening, I walk with the Hunter and Virtue down a sandy lane to the village nightclub, a new addition to the hamlet following the increased military presence. The hamlet has grown only very recently. The inrush of conservation organizations created numerous new jobs, mostly for men, although there are a few female park guards.

138

Technicolored lights have been strung around the perimeter of a dirt yard enclosed by palm-thatch walls. A disco ball throws lasers of light around a section meant to be the dance floor. A large diesel generator, hidden behind another palm-thatch wall, is nearly as loud as the beats of the Congolese pop music it powers.

We sit at a simple wood table with two members of the military eco-guards. Captain Jacques is short, with long eye-lashes and an affable smile. In contrast, Le Capitain is tall and handsome, with a powerful sobriety underneath his boyish confidence, as if he has enjoyed both the privileges and respon-sibilities of having been his mother's favorite son.

Neither man wears his uniform, although a few lower-ranked guards stand around the nightclub in their military attire, pinned with decorations. A few have assault rifles slung over their backs.

"Just like New York!" Captain Jacques says to me, batting his long lashes and smiling sweetly. The group laughs at this absur-dity. The air is soft and humid.

Virtue brings over beers for everyone and opens them in front of us, either a Congolese custom or a result of Virtue's paranoia, so we can see that the drinks haven't been poisoned or otherwise adulterated.

"There was no beer here fifteen years ago, only locally made palm wine," the Hunter says, and takes a sip of his Primus.

"Yes, yes, we are growing," replies Virtue.

"I guess we aren't doing a good job, then," the Hunter responds derisively. "There used to be so many elephants here. Rare white elephants, even. Now we have … beer."

"You have come here at a very interesting time," Virtue says to me. "As bushmeat is transitioning to a luxury market. Of course, not all Congolese eat game. Here in the west of Congo, people are meat eaters because their ancestors were for- 139 est-dwelling hunters. I come from eastern DRC. Traditionally, we do not hunt. We eat fish there.

"I would like to go into politics," he continues, his eyes bulging slightly. "My father is a teacher, but I have more ambition. Right now there are sixteen people working for our organization here. I want to expand it to twenty-eight. And eventually run for a national office. The current head of the ICCN [L'Institut Congolais pour la Conservation de la Nature] is not strong."

"Last year the regional governor tried to make any kind of hunting completely illegal," the Hunter interjects, "but the former chief of the ICCN was a huge hunter, so it didn't go through."

"It's unfortunate," Virtue says. "The national park guards are paid very little and very irregularly."

"The military eco-guards are not paid much more, but at least they are paid consistently," the Hunter says. "They are much better trained than the park guards, but the guards can bust military game poaching. So there is definitely some tension between the two groups."

"Yes, there are *rumors* that the military is actively involved in the bushmeat trade," Virtue says tentatively, "but they support the current president, so it's not politically feasible for him to really crack down."

"It is the same with timber and ivory," the Hunter replies. "People illegally harvesting resources are protected by generals and rebel groups. It's very difficult to stop these bribe networks. Two years ago, the head of the military operation here was smuggling so many machine guns that he blew up a munitions storage facility to hide it. The state is the ultimate predator here—and has been for a long time."

The Hunter takes a sip of beer and continues. "The dictator Mobutu came to power when I was a kid. I remember in his speeches he would say, 'You take some. You leave some.' He made it very clear that corruption wasn't a moral issue—bribes were just another way of distributing money. At the same time, the worst thing you could do was to get in the way of another's gain. As a result, everything became a transaction. Everything here is to be negotiated."

The Hunter looks at me, and I briefly wonder at the negotiation happening between us.

"I remember when Mobutu first came to power, no one was putting money in the banks," he says, turning his attention back to Virtue, "so he changed the color of all the paper money— the blue ones became green, green became blue—and required everyone to exchange their old bills. My father organized a missionary plane to fly the cash to Kinshasa. It was absolutely amazing how much these old *Papas* had hidden in their huts and under mattresses! In the remote areas, it took a year and half for the money to be returned. In the meantime, Mobutu had this surplus of cash, and he could control how much it was worth. He truly created this ethic that remains today—if you don't take the chances you are given, you are an idiot."

The men continue their conversation. I suppose it's for my benefit, to teach me about the poaching situation, but as they speak, it seems they are talking across each other—not so much a debate as it is two monologues, broken into pieces, the men taking turns to orate, as if a prize will be given at the end of the evening.

The colored lights spin. Le Capitain stands in a dark corner over a woman dressed in a short skirt. I drink my warm beer. I think about lions, predators that drive an ecosystem forward, pushing their prey toward strength and speed and keener senses to avoid their sharp claws.

═══════════════

There is no rarity of tragedies here. Many layers of violence are associated with these forests, and women, who are considered second-class citizens, experience an unfair share. Their bodies have repeatedly borne the brunt of domestic violence, rebel upheavals, and civil wars. I see hushed evidence of it every-where. Like the black eye on the woman who cooks for the conservation organization, which she tried to camouflage with a smear of violet eyeshadow. The fate of these women is the fate of the forest. The plea of both is embarrassed with too many inconveniences.

One day, I visit two men who have been caught with ele-phant meat. They are housed in a temporary military jail, a mess of wood thrown together into a shack next to the barracks that houses the soldiers. Guards stand around in their green uni-forms holding guns under the heat of the midday sun.

The men claim the elephant died naturally in the forest, and that they were given the meat as a gift from a village chief for helping him to smoke and transport it. The poachers look sullen and disheveled. They stare at me without hope.

The smoked elephant meat lies on an oil-stained wooden table. Four gnarled lumps, like fossilized amber, with cracked striations of flaking muscle. It is impossible to imagine this brown, thick-crusted meat was once an elephant. Le Capitain stands over it like it's a trophy, the edges of his mouth curling into an inscrutable smile.

The Hunter and I return to these same barracks the follow-ing night to watch the World Cup, beamed down by satellite.

Men crowd around a tiny TV under a bare lightbulb. Their faces are distorted by the harsh light. On the mini-square of green, the players look like ants. I wonder if the prisoners are still sitting outside in their thatched confinement. I wonder if they are thirsty.

The next morning, I find a small sand-colored scorpion in my boot. Its skin is thin and translucent, a clear and sinister threat, and yet, it is too small to really be all that frightening.

Supposedly an MSF (Médecins Sans Frontières—Doctors Without Borders) plane will make a brief stop here this morning, with room for me. There are no direct flights scheduled to go back to the capital city of Kinshasa, where I will continue my research in the urban markets, so I will have to stop over for a few days in Mbandaka, a medium-sized port town on the Congo River. Virtue is also returning to Kinshasa and will travel with me.

I sit on the edge of the airfield waiting for the plane next to three little boys. They are peeling off the thick outer stalks of a palm-like plant in long strips and piling the delicate, pale inner cores on two large leaves. Without words, they give me a lesson. They do not seem to mind their task and giggle as they work. Occasionally, one of them devours the sweet treat they are meant to be collecting, and the other two laugh their approval.

The Hunter roars up on a motorcycle, wild hair licking behind him underneath his ubiquitous waxed-canvas hat. An army-green duffel bag is slung on his back, a beat-up grey Fjällräven backpack rests on his front, and a camera hangs off his neck. A large hunting knife in a leather sheath is fastened to his waist by a simple brown belt.

I didn't realize he was returning to Kinshasa, too. I do not know how to feel. There is something intoxicating about him, even if it is not entirely appealing. He scares me a little. And how clichéd it feels, a young woman who falls for an older man in a steamy, foreign locale. But I smile to myself at the terrible excitement that he is here.

The plane was meant to arrive a half hour ago, but there is no real time frame. Everything here is relative—*ça dépend, ça dépend*—it all depends on other factors. When the plane does arrive, the flight takes less than an hour. If I had done the trip by pirogue, as most people do it, the journey would have taken three days.

The stream below us winds slowly through pockets of dense forest, widens as it meets a larger tributary, breaks apart into swampland, flows past little villages built on stilts in the flood plains. Then the tributary reaches the deepest watercourse in the world, locally known as *Le Fleuve*—simply, The River.

––––––––––––

At the Mbandaka airport, we hire motorcycle taxis to take us to the center of town. I sit on the back of one, and the Hunter sits close behind me. As the driver accelerates, we press into each other for balance. It is the first time we are touching. His chest is warm against my back. A soft wind is in my ears.

As we circle a wide roundabout, he tells me of his hiking trips to Nepal and India. As we pick up speed past flat fields, of spending weeks in the high mountains helping a farmer plant his crops, and as we bounce into town, with its narrow streets and little wooden houses, he speaks of nights sleeping on the floor of a house built of stone. When we take a sharp turn into the courtyard of the guesthouse where we will be staying that evening, we press into each other once more to maintain our balance on the bike.

We are staying at a colonial-era convent run by nuns. In the late afternoon, after we have all settled into our separate rooms, the Hunter and I walk to a hotel overlooking the Congo River for a drink. We sit outside facing the water on a rutty concrete deck. Rebar juts out of half-finished columns, stark silhouettes against a grey undercast sky. The deck will be completed in an unknown future when there are enough guests to pay for the construction.

Below us, a dozen or so large pirogues, each twenty feet long and three feet wide, are tied up on the bank. People are busy loading and unloading the boats. They walk over wooden planks set between the vessels. The simultaneous labors become a blur of colors and patterns. People in red and orange T-shirts carry tan rolls of foam and mattresses tied up into long tubes, pile them next to cardboard boxes and white woven sacks of rice bulging at the seams, wooden bowls and bundles of fresh leaves for steaming food, handmade traps of flapping fish, gasping at the dry air. People stand on the bank with bags of red peanuts and snug rolls of tapioca bread displayed on their heads on large metal trays. A woman sits surrounded by children, braiding a girl's hair. A woman in a mustard-yellow kerchief bends over. Two men lean against bamboo fencing. One holds a piece of paper and throws his head back in laughter. Nearby, a woman walks with a baby on her back, wrapped in luminous cloth. The boy's head, black hair muted in the somber light, rests above the edge of the fabric.

"It wasn't always so difficult or expensive to transport goods here," the Hunter says, noticing that I am entranced by the scene below. "Congo used to work very well. During the Mobutu era, the roads were well-maintained. There was a state-managed ferry system to transport people and vehicles across the major river crossings. But all that changed after the civil wars in the 1990s, when the whole economy collapsed. There was very little gas. The roads and bridges fell apart. A lot of the ferries were destroyed or left to decompose. Today, pirogues are often the only way to get across a river, which limits the traffic to bicycles, motorcycles, and pedestrians."

Two men standing in a small pirogue propel themselves   145
swiftly between the larger boats with long, thin carved paddles made of dark wood.

"I was once out on patrol, in the deep, deep forest, and I met a game poacher who had been a banker in Kinshasa in the 1970s. He used to take the bus to work every day. Thirty years later, he was trying to survive by snaring rats in the jungle," he says, shaking his head. "DRC is sometimes called *the richest, poorest country on earth*. So much wealth in its forests and mines, but concentrated in just a few hands. The people remain in poverty. So many live hand-to-mouth. Things are not sold here. They are sold and resold for as many times as a profit can be made, no matter how small the increase. 'Informal' is a misnomer, though. The trade networks are highly organized. Especially for bushmeat."

An enormous, flat-bottomed steel barge is slowly making its way downriver. It is difficult to grasp just how large a craft it is. This section of river is as wide as a delta, and the boat is far out in the middle, where the current is swiftest. The boat looks like a carnival camp, hung with fabric tents, colored tarps, and striped umbrellas. A group of passengers stand on a pile of goods, high above the heads of the other travelers, surveying the lively scene below.

"These boats are like floating villages. People live and die onboard. Get married. Give birth. After some time, the people living on these boats even begin to *think* like the river," the Hunter explains. "They are very savvy, trading products the whole way, up and down. They go upstream with manufactured goods—plastics, razor blades, hair weaves, bullets, clothes— and then return bearing the goods of the forest—caterpillars and grubs, salted river fish, burlap-wrapped bundles of charcoal, and baskets of smoked game. Live animals are also transported. It is an exchange of the industrial for the natural. They bring the city to the country, then turn around and bring the country back downstream."

He turns toward me.

"When you are poor, you covet the goods of civilization. When you are rich, you have met your needs, you covet the goods of nature." He smiles goofily, as if he has just summed up my research and there is really very little need for me to keep conducting it, so we might as well talk about other things.

"Very true." I smile. "This is what interests me about wild food. Eating it is an act of nostalgia, for both the natural abundance and the material poverty of the past. It's like we want to re-experience a time when being human meant something different than it does today, but with the benefit of being able to escape back into the comforts of domesticated civilization whenever we like."

"The past always seems simpler than the present," he replies.

"That's its charm," I say, staring at the water. "But people in the past had to contend with the unknown just as we do."

We both fall quiet for a time and continue watching the people down below. As the evening light casts protean shadows on the water, the scene becomes a trompe l'oeil, tricking the eye into seeing something that isn't there. The light compresses the focus toward the horizon until all that remains is a flat representation. The blur of patterns and colors becomes golden with sadness and a sense of loss.

The Hunter turns toward me again with a look of gleeful admiration, as if he is witnessing a surprise. Grateful that I am indeed sitting next to him in this moment. And then a flicker of doubt passes over his face, as if questioning whether he is anything more than a source in my quest, a conduit of information, an experience I will later write about.

There is something so vulnerable about his expression, I feel a sudden urge to kiss him. Instead, I look into his doubtful eyes, reassuring him with my own that even when I write about this moment many years later, it will feel like a small fiction of the immense reality we are sharing, sitting there above the lovely river, an experience made together and ever fleeting.

147

———————

The next day, the Hunter and I walk to the wholesale food markets that line the riverbank. Bicycle taxis—called *toplka*—"Let's go!"—rush past us with well-dressed men and women riding side-saddle on colorful knitted cushions strapped to the back racks.

Many traders will buy bushmeat here for further transport downriver on wooden freight boats called *baleinières* (whale boats). The goods they carry must be worth a certain price in Kinshasa to justify the long, arduous trip and the many middlemen. Smoked game meat, which garners four to five times the price in Kinshasa as it does in the villages where it originates, is a particularly high-value product because it is relatively compact and lightweight, and does not rot quickly like vegetables.

Still, vast quantities of wild meat turn rancid during transport. People are increasingly bypassing this river network and moving goods by plane. Restaurants that sell game meat typically have a *fournisseur*, a buyer, located here to source meat on a regular basis and send it by freight or passenger plane. Commercial passenger flights from Mbandaka to Kinshasa often smell quite distinctly of game meat and fish.

At the main port market, a wild baby bush pig, the color of caramel, rests in a plastic tub. Its tiny legs have been tied together at the feet. It is subdued and breathing shallowly as customers consider it. We walk past a woman with a live pangolin tied to a round perch. The woman next to her is selling a whole family of Allen's swamp monkey, dead and smoked, their deformed bodies crucified on a cross of delicate branches.

"Smoked monkeys are often only identifiable by their paws," the Hunter says, squatting down to examine the meat. "You can tell the health of the forest based on the species found for sale in a bushmeat market. For example, red colobus monkeys are one of the first species to be decimated by market hunters, so when you see a lot of them, you know they come from a relatively intact and healthy forest, which means a national park or a protected area where there has been active patrolling in the past."

He picks up a section of smoked antelope. "You can test how old bushmeat is by pressing into it. If it is hard and dry, then it is likely many months old."

Men unload crates of smoked game. We see monitor lizards, forest turtles, and piles of river fish. A live river crocodile is strapped to the back of a motorcycle, its mouth bound shut by thick twine. A man in green flip-flops and a Central Michigan Football Champions T-shirt carries a pair of freshly killed monkeys with rust-red and grey fur. Their long tails have been tied to their necks, making for a sort of handle. The man holds them in one hand and his cell phone in the other as he walks through the market. Monkey arms and legs and hands and feet dangle downward and swing slightly in the air.

In the afternoon, we go back to the mission guesthouse, and the Hunter invites me to his room. Mosquito netting hangs over the twin bed like gossamer. Above it, a stark wooden crucifix is nailed to the chipped, pale-blue walls. A sallow breeze, too warm and sticky to be refreshing, limps through the open window, delicately caressing the insubstantial cotton curtains.

We sit on the bed side by side as there are no chairs, and I wonder if we will continue talking about the wild meat trade. But I can feel our unruly attraction, and it makes me momentarily self-conscious. Is it wise to fall for one of my research informants? To open my heart to this wild man?

The Hunter kisses me. Outside his room, the hushed black nuns in their ancient habits walk beneath the covered balconies, potted pelagic plants hanging from the carved wooden eaves, and I am a tree branch bending in floodwaters.

Suddenly, there is a knock on the door. We freeze like two animals caught in artificial light. Another knock, this time more insistent. I scramble to my feet and try to hide. But Virtue has already opened the door uninvited and is peering inside.

"I am looking for my phone charger," he says as some sort of excuse. I cannot tell if the look in his eye is one of embarrassment or cruel pleasure at having caught me here.

The Hunter is large in his anger and concern, and soon the room is dark again, cast in the blue-green glow of a dying afternoon.

I move in with him as soon as we arrive in Kinshasa. Inevitable.

STEWED ANTELOPE IN TOMATOES AND SPICES

*The Bel Vue—Changing Tastes—A Bout of Malaria—
Authentic Women—Stalking the Stalls—The Gritty Port Market—
Mothers and Sisters—Unbounded—Friday Night—
A Paranoia of Outsiders—Nostalgia Is a Tricky Beast—A Necessary
Pessimism—A Symbol of Power—Terrors—Eating the Past*

I HAVE BEEN STAYING with the Hunter at the Bel Vue Residential Compound in Kinshasa for nearly a week. We are crashing at his colleague's condo because she is currently out of the country. Each night, we fall asleep surrounded by her things. Toiletry products crowd the bathroom counter. Clothes burst beyond the closet door. Her carved artwork decorates the nightstands and her wax cloth *liputa* tapestry, patterned with a colorful geometric maze, hangs over the bed.

The Bel Vue has 101 condos, in generic pastels, like any American suburb, a sports center complete with steam room and sauna, two swimming pools, a restaurant, a bar, and a hookah lounge. Men in blue jumpsuits with flashy yellow rubber boots sweep the sidewalks in the afternoon. They sweep up the fallen leaves, waxy yellow like their boots, before they even begin to wilt. Outside these walls is a mass of anonymous people, writhing about their lives, smashed into cars, lichening the sidewalks, the branching streets dysmorphic with people, the concrete cityscape undulating and animated by so many heraldic desires. Inside, Congo has been manicured and nature is controllable.

The guards at the entry gates complain they are not paid well, but at least it is a regular paycheck in a city where irregularity is the norm. At US$100 a month, it's as good as the average salary for a teacher or a policeman, for whom getting paid is never guaranteed. For lunch, the guards eat thick slabs of smoked pork, red-tinged, flecked with green herbs, and topped with *pili pili*—an orange-colored mix of ground chilis and salt. It is an easy meal for under a dollar. They buy it from a woman who walks around town selling it. They'd eat game meat if they had more money, but it costs six times as much, and nobody walks around town selling bushmeat.

The people who live at the Bel Vue work for the United Nations, for NGOs, diamond mines, resource companies, banks, and charity organizations. They are Chinese construction bosses, Lebanese money launderers, foreign diplomats, and Congolese ministers, plus all of their bored housewives and internally marred children. It is a parade of nations. They drive luxury SUVs in shiny obsidians or pearly whites, inching judiciously out of the compound and onto roads with enormous potholes and dusty traffic, necessarily cautious despite fantasies of getting lost and going fast on empty expanses of gleaming asphalt that don't exist here.

In the mornings and late at night, three rotund Chinese men walk around the compound together. They are here to bring the future. One night I see them watching the World Cup at the bar, eating ice cream sundaes out of crystal bowls while the boss sits in the middle, chain-smoking and squinting at the scorecard.

On Wednesday evenings, the men in blue jumpsuits and waxy yellow boots gas the place. They lug noisy whirring machines up and down the cobbled roads and stone walkways, obscured by a billow of mosquito poison that wafts opaquely into backyards and through screen doors. The condo windows are coated with a gold reflective material, so the residents can feel a sense of visual privacy. Even if they can't block the urban sensory excretions of a city of over 11 million people, at least the walls and gates and guards and mirrored windows keep them hidden from the thieves and beggars and common humanity outside. Such measures are less about keeping out and more about keeping in.

The Stop N Shop just down the street from the Bel Vue is brightly lit and air-conditioned. It offers an abundance of food: pâté covered in herbs and white asparagus in elegant glass bottles, pork and chicken wrapped in plastic, beer from Belgium, wine from South Africa, candy from the United States, an entire aisle dedicated to margarine and pork products, Weetabix cereal and juicy pink grapefruits, two for five dollars, rise-and-shine Tropicana style.

If you have enough money, Congo begins to resemble any other place in the world.

Justine is a slight American woman who works for the conservation NGO that has been hosting me. One evening, she invites me over for a glass of wine. She lives in a posh part of town, and two guards are posted at the gated entrance to her house. Her home was built by the Belgians sometime during the 1930s or 1940s to house colonial officers. After independence, it was gifted to a Congolese military leader who later remodeled it.

"This was the *Dictator Style*," she says, gesturing to the decorative Romanesque columns with gold trim and the ceiling's intricate plaster molding. "Mobutu had a palace somewhere that looked like this, so it was copied by his military officers. Today, all these false ceilings are just great places for the rats to hide."

We sit in her living room and discuss *the bushmeat crisis*. Justine speaks in a high, nasally drawl, slightly holding back the last syllables, as if the effort of speech might not be worth the value of her words. She sits on a low couch opposite mine, with her legs bent and feet curled under her bottom, reminding me of a reclining cat, relaxed but ready to spring into action if something catches her fancy.

"When I did Peace Corps, I had to wait in line four hours to collect-call my mom. Kids these days can email home every day," she says, taking a sip of cold white wine.

Justine has been working in various parts of Africa for a long time. She's been caught in gunfire and uprisings and cattle wars. On the wall behind her are objects she has collected over the years: a decorative cow harness made of AK-47 bullet shells; a simple hunting bow; a woven grass basket. I look at them as she talks.

"We'd like to think these forests are empty. Without people. The scientists just want to count animals, and where there are animals, they want to create a protected area. But there have always been users of the land. Take the Serengeti, for instance. People used to follow the animal migration. In the dry season, it's not a great place to live, and in the wet season, it's difficult to travel there. But in semi-dry seasons, the animals go there for water and people followed. We try to ignore the people, even though they've been living there for thousands of years. At the same time, where there are people, there are pressures. Everyone wants modernity, wants a radio and a TV. So we have to draw some lines. Otherwise we have no wildlife left."

Her face turns pallid, and she shifts slightly toward me.

"Are we facing the end of the world? Yes, the world as we know it. We are facing a crisis of ecological collapse. The elephants are gone. I mean they are pretty much all gone, totally done. And conservation organizations just don't have enough money to make much of a difference. Not when we are up against so many destructive forces threatening the forests— gold, diamonds, oil, rare minerals, and logging for timber and charcoal. The commercial charcoal industry is huge and run by mafia and terrorist groups."

She leans forward to pour more wine into my glass, then refills her own.

"Climate change can already be felt here quite strongly," she says, pinching her mouth, as if the taste of this information itself is bitter. "There is more rain in the dry season and less in the wet season. So the water levels don't change much seasonally. Fisherman use long lances when the water goes down to get these eel-like mudfish that slither along the bottoms of the shallow puddles. But when the water stays high, they can't catch fish. And then what do they do? They eat more bushmeat. And then support for conservation goes down. People say to us, 'You have all these animals and we are starving!' So depleted resources mean tensions get high, things become unsettled."

She leans heavily into the back of the couch, slightly exasperated by the weight of what she has just been saying. But it is a brief deflation, and she sits up again brightly, relit by the next thought.

"There are whole villages where nobody eats protein. Just bread and margarine. All the meat is exported. In the old days, getting enough starch in your diet was the problem. Today it is protein that is deficient. So we are working on creating protein sources to offset bushmeat consumption. Chicken factories that can produce nearly 180,000 pounds of meat a year, and at a price point that is about a third less than bushmeat. But to get domesticated protein you need animal feed. You need soybean and maize production to produce chicken feed, and there isn't any industrial-scale agriculture up in the little forest villages. So we are starting a whole soybean sector in the neighboring Republic of Congo, but until that gets going we have to import all our soybeans from Brazil."

She pauses to take a sip.

"However, if we ignore the cities, we are going to lose the battle of commercial poaching. For a long time, all that conservationists were doing was focusing on stopping the supply side of the bushmeat trade. But it's not working. We need to start looking at the demand," she explains. "So we have to ask: Why are people eating bushmeat in Kinshasa? Out of poverty or luxury?"

She sits up slightly. "Well, we do know that the market is differentiated and certain species are worth more. Monkey is less expensive than antelope or buffalo. Fresh bushmeat is always a luxury because there are no more big animals left around Kinshasa, so it must be flown in. So then the question becomes: Why are rich people eating bushmeat? Is it because there is nothing else? In a way, yes. But really it is a matter of taste. Bushmeat is a status marker. If you want to impress your in-laws, you prepare it for them. It's what you serve at celebrations and weddings and holidays. It's the flavor of home. Like we serve turkey in the U.S. at Thanksgiving. Although the preference for bushmeat is illegal. Just like cocaine!"

Her voice rises as her words rush out, and she speaks with a sense of determination.

"We have to make sure people don't go hungry, but we don't have to give them that option of luxury choice. We have two ways of looking at this problem. We can do it by law enforcement or by changing people's minds and behaviors. For a second-generation urban dweller, perhaps we can interrupt the tradition. American culture is still highly revered here. People loved George W. Bush. He gave Africa a lot of aid money. And the new middle class here, they want to emulate Westerners. Think about Julia Child. She told American women: even *you* can cook fancy French food. Now television cooking shows in the States are über-popular. We could do something similar here.

"After we bring fresh chicken to the market, we could potentially have cooking contests, or shows on TV: how to cook chicken differently; how to cook omelets. You know, work with women vendors to create a new market. Give out tastes, like in a grocery store. Film people doing it. People eat bushmeat to vary their diet, to eat something different. But you can cook chicken many different ways. 'Chicken doesn't have to be boring!' Show the super-rich eating chicken. Show the range of different ways people eat food. And eat food legally. Don't eat elephants; don't eat gorillas. It's the pride of the Congo! That's what your grandparents did. But it's not cool. It's cool to eat chicken. Teach people not to eat chimp or gorilla meat because of the diseases they carry. And we can work with the private sector. Like the 'Where's the beef?' campaigns. The egg campaigns. The pork campaigns. Do similar things here in central Africa. Make it cool to eat domestic meats. With a little bit of prodding and awareness about the state of the forests, maybe we can make big changes."

She slumps back on the love seat, pulls her feet up again, and balances her glass on her knee.

157

"In the U.S., the environmental ethic only arose when everything was gone. That hasn't happened here. People here falsely believe there is tons of wildlife left. Does Africa need an awareness of the environmental crisis before they decide they want to keep it? On the other hand, you need some level of development before you have the luxury to want to save these animals. What matters is money. If you don't fix the money problem for local people, you can't do conservation. You have to get local villagers to support the parks. Give them jobs."

I think back to the national park village I have just come from.

"Seems like such a difficult balance between development and conservation," I say. "Plus isn't a lot of the destruction a result of market hunters, not locals?"

"Yes, of course outsiders are still a problem. How do you stop the leader of a militia from another country killing all your monkeys?" she replies. "And there isn't anybody enforcing the wildlife and hunting laws in cities. Judges don't even know what the wildlife laws are. In Uganda, they recently let go a massive trafficker. Powerful people protected by powerful military keep things status quo. The only way a government is going to have an ethic of conservation is if there is economic motivation. Like tourism. Valuing these animals more alive than dead. In Rwanda, gorilla conservation is now part of the national identity. Tourism lodges in Kenya are a big part of livelihoods there. In East Africa, wildlife tourism employs millions of people. Whereas here, if you are white, you have to be in your house by 4 PM with guards posted outside to stay safe."

Justine seems younger than her actual age and experience, as if she is fighting an internal struggle between the child she was and the woman she has become. I wonder if this split in her character developed over many years working in Africa, her skin always wearing the mask of the colonial oppressor. She's no longer quite sure if she is savior or captive.

"But really there is no conservation ethic in central Africa. Not the same here as it is in the States, anyway. Here you have do-gooders, and then they just get shot."

I think about the many reports I've read of park rangers and conservationists killed in the field all over the world. DRC seems to be a particularly dangerous place. In Virunga National Park, in the eastern part of the country, nearly 160 rangers have been shot during the past twenty years.

The room is quiet a moment. A few mosquitoes buzz around like whimpering puppies.

"Really, it is so rare for researchers to come here," she says as she stands and turns toward the kitchen to search for more wine. "You are the first one in a really long time."

As she leaves the room, she looks back at me, and there is a startling strength in her eyes. It's as if she is attempting to defy a sudden feeling of inadequacy in the face of the tragedies she has just spoken about.

Then, just as quickly, her face relaxes again. "At the moment, our biggest problem is the butter crisis!" She laughs, amused that this is the trouble she will end the conversation on. "There's some import problem and the city is running out. You can't find it anywhere! By the way, would you like some dinner? I've cooked too much, and I don't like eating leftovers."

———

A few nights later, Lucian, my driver from the conservation organization, takes me to a spontaneous after-work happy hour. Lucian is a rotund man with an equable face and a wide smile. He's dressed in a grey imitation Louis Vuitton suit. He is almost always dressed this well, as if his fashion is a form of resistance against the mundane realities of his life. Even when he is just taking me around to the bushmeat markets in the old white Land Rover with the dented passenger door, he arrives buttoned up and busting out of his seams, attired as if he is going out on a date and not about to fix a car that is always breaking down.

160   In fact, the only time I saw him out of his fancies was the morning he escorted me on a walk along the Congo River. He was dressed in a red tracksuit, like a jogger. As we strolled, Lucian confessed to me that he was having marriage problems. He was very much in love, but he worked a lot and when he wasn't working he was often sick.

Lucian has two daughters and a son. He had been studying to become an electrical engineer, but life happened, and then he no longer had the money to pay for his own education. He took great pride in his job, knowing that in Congo the work could always be harder, and that despite his small two-room house and his meager salary, his children had the opportunity for lives bigger than the one he had lived.

On this evening, I sit with Lucian and four other Congolese men from the office on a dimly lit concrete porch. Moths and beetles flutter around us like bursts of tinsel.

"Raphael's neighbor will buy a monkey, or a small piece of antelope, and cut it into tiny pieces to sell to others in the neighborhood," Jasper says, translating for Raphael, an older man who seems to do whatever extra tasks are needed around the office. "He makes just enough money selling it to pay for his own small consumption. An occasional morsel, a tiny snack."

Jasper grew up in Kinshasa but went to Belgium for his university studies and is a master of languages, GIS spatial analysis, and witticisms. He has an easy charm and a generous laugh.

"Underneath the skin, our blood runs the same red color," he says, pointing to his arm, and then mine.

"Yes, of course," I reply.

"Precisely! And so you and I are the same," he says heartily.

We smile at each other, acknowledging this shared feature, perhaps in the hopes that we might blow apart the patriarchal and racist structures that have kept men like him and women like me separate and considered different. But this phrase is sticking to my guts, because it seems both true and false. On purely mechanical terms, it is utterly honest. Human blood is human blood. But oppression is a long game. Despite both our wishes, his statement cannot erase history.

161

As I finish my beer, my thoughts turn to the Hunter.

"Well, Lucian, I'd better be getting home," I say. "It is later than I meant to stay out."

"No! We insist you stay for another," Jasper says as he gets up to retrieve more beers. Lucian shrugs and smiles kindly.

When I eventually get home, the Hunter is in bed, sweating and subdued. His face looks distorted. He has come down with malaria. He lies there with the sickness, dissolving into his fevers, shivering as the parasite spirals through his bloodstream, and his body mounts its defenses against the familiar ailment.

He's fought this disease many times before. Once he was sick with it alone in the middle of the rainforest, camped next to the tinkle of a small stream, with nothing more than a royal-blue mosquito net for shelter, and only the company of the monkeys in the tall trees, shouting down their well-wishes. His body is partially immune to the disease after so much repeated exposure, and the symptoms are relatively mild. But that does not ease my worry.

"Where have you been?" he says softly, pleadingly, without opening his eyes. I sit at his side, holding his hand in mine. "I was gone. But now, I am right here." The words tumble out of my mouth like boulders. The Hunter falls asleep holding my upper thigh in his hand like a prize, like a security blanket.

The next day, to my great relief, he wakes up much improved. From then on, the Hunter starts calling me *Älskling*, "darling" in Swedish. *Puss*, kiss, he says playfully, a nickname and an invitation, *Pussar all over your beautiful body, and then I will hold you tight tight, my love.*

———

Kinshasa is located on a wide bend in the Congo River and has been an international trading community since at least the 1400s. It became the capital and administrative center of Belgian Congo in 1923, and was known as Léopoldville. The only Congolese population that the colonial administration allowed to settle there were young male workers. They needed a work permit to live in town, were not allowed to own property, and had to reside in special districts. A deeply segregated city emerged, surrounded by European-owned cattle and agricultural farms.

Because women comprised the majority of the village labor force, particularly in all stages of food production and child rearing, they were actively dissuaded from moving to urban areas, which were stigmatized as depraved. If a woman did express interest in moving to the city, rumors spread that it was because she wanted to become a courtesan. This view was promoted by the Catholic Church and reinforced by a colonial tax of fifty francs annually levied on any unmarried *femme libre* (free woman) living within the city.

By the mid-1930s, however, the colonial administration was becoming concerned by Léopoldville's "camplike" atmosphere and uneven sex ratios. Under the official desire to eradicate prostitution and stabilize the lives of workers, women were tacitly urged to move to the city to work as *ménagères*, "housekeepers" for Belgians (with the implicit agreement that these jobs might include a sexual component), or to establish families of their own. Because of the demographic imbalance, women could often choose from many suitors. Some greatly improved their financial and social position by marrying Europeans.

The Belgians trained Congolese men to be doctors, lawyers, administrative workers, and bureaucrats, which created a new middle class—called *évolués*—and meant Congo had an educated wage-labor force twice the size of any other African colony. But the educational opportunities for women, even upper-class women, were rare. They were encouraged to gain proficiency in domestic activities such as sewing, knitting, and cooking. Trapped in the domestic domain and subservient to their husbands, women provided tremendous free labor. This was of such a benefit to the colonial state that a law was passed requiring women to gain permission from their husbands before taking a job outside the home. As a result, women were largely excluded from the rapidly expanding modern economy.

Because employment opportunities were limited, entrepreneurship was one of the only avenues open to them. Even though it was illegal, prostitution was one route, and the most successful women invested their earnings into legitimate bars or property. Others undertook food production and entered into the small-scale and informal trades that men were not willing to do. While village life restricted a woman's mobility by tying her to agricultural fields, in Léopoldville, women could finally find some level of independence.

Throughout the 1940s and 1950s, Léopoldville grew rapidly. As the city expanded, women became increasingly involved in the transport and trade of forest products into urban areas. In their roles as food producers and cooks, they already had an inherent familiarity with bushmeat. While their husbands were stuck at desk jobs and had less time for travel, women would occasionally make the trip back home to their rural villages to visit family. They brought back a surplus of goods to supply their households and sold whatever was left over.

Women were required to have travel permits and frequently needed the permission of their husbands or fathers to undertake such journeys or re-enter the city. Such restrictions gave women the chance to practice the skill of bribery. Many became friends with the colonial officers, trading a share of the profits in exchange for unrestricted movement. Over the years, a matrilineal system of access to the bushmeat trade networks developed, an unwritten knowledge that could be passed down from mother to daughter.

After the vote for independence in 1960, the Belgians quickly exited the country, leaving behind a power vacuum. DRC fell into a brutal five-year civil war, with numerous factions vying for control (Che Guevara even led a group of Cuban guerrillas into the forest to help one group). Kinshasa grew at an unprecedented rate as people left the violent countryside for the relative safety of the capital city.

Independence movements were occurring across Africa by the mid-1960s, and there was a general fear among Western powers that the continent would become a communist stronghold. Mobutu came to power in a U.S.-backed coup in 1965. His party, the Mouvement Populaire de la Révolution, was part political organization, part social organization, and he quickly had a hand in nearly every aspect of cultural life. Because of Mobutu's anti-communist stance, the United States turned a blind eye to his grotesquely violent and increasingly predatory style of governing.

By 1973, Mobutu's power was all-consuming. He reduced the authority of the parliament, suspended provincial assemblies, concentrated governing power in Kinshasa, assumed command of the police, and brazenly executed anyone he suspected of being a rival. He nationalized all foreign-owned industries and invested heavily in urban and mining areas while raising taxes on cash crops. These policies increased the wealth disparity between metropolitan and village dwellers, and further drove a rural exodus.

Mobutu was a charismatic leader and a stylish figure in tortoiseshell glasses, pinstriped suit, and leopard-skin fez. DRC's immense natural resources meant that he was, for a time, the richest man in the world. He took vacations to Europe to visit Western presidents and prime ministers. In 1974, he organized the Rumble in the Jungle, a fight between Muhammad Ali and George Foreman in Kinshasa, calling it the Triumph of Mobutism. The fight was kicked off with a three-day music festival called Zaire 74, which featured performances by James Brown, B.B. King, and Bill Withers.

Despite his Western backers, Mobutu wanted to rid the country of any colonial influences and went about creating the official state ideology of *Authenticité*. He renamed the country Zaire, outlawed wigs, and told the *évolués* to dress, speak, and eat in an "authentic" Congolese manner. Culinary traditions were rediscovered and remade. Newly salaried urbanites were willing to pay good money for traditional meats, and demand for wild game shot upward. Elephant was killed more for its meat than its ivory, as a prestige item for high-ranking officials who thought eating it bestowed a potent virility. Powerful military men were often at the center of this trade. They relied on poorly paid foot soldiers and national park guards to extort game from villagers. Many officers employed their own wives as meat traffickers. In Kinshasa, piles of elephant meat could be found for sale in the markets, out in the open among the flies.

Although life was still under the control of a dictator, there was a sense of freedom that hadn't been felt for generations. Congo became a beacon of cultural progress across the continent, and Kinshasa was at the center of an incredible renaissance. It had one of the best-educated populations in all of Africa. Ambitious public buildings were commissioned in an experimental style that combined art deco, Soviet-style brutalism, futurism, and the geometric designs of village huts to express this new identity of a modern African country.

Music, art, fashion, and literature exploded and started finding international recognition. Soukous, a multi-instrumental genre of dance music that first evolved in Belgian Congo in the 1940s as a variation on Cuban rumbas, became popular again. Musicians started experimenting with synthesizers and performed in clubs in London and Paris. There was acid jazz and psychedelic funk playing from the record shops. On Saturday nights, the upscale bar at the Hotel Venus, right next to the French Club, was the place to be seen.

By the mid-1980s, Mobutu's grip on the country was weakening. DRC was facing widespread inflation and increasing instability. With the end of the Cold War, the United States no longer needed Mobutu's alliance, and international support for his government waned. Civil war broke out in 1996 and lasted until 2003, embroiling numerous other African countries, which supplied troops and support. Almost 5.4 million people died. Another 4 million were displaced from their homes.

The widespread circulation of weapons in the forest became the norm. Rape became a particularly potent and calculated terror tactic. Women were shunned for their trauma. The cities swelled further as people again escaped the conflict in rural areas. Anyone who could left for Europe.

Women in DRC continue to be affected by the legacies of patriarchy, colonialism, and a dictatorship that all actively

166

legislated against their success. The country has one of the lowest rates of female property and livestock ownership in Central Africa. Women continue to have less access to machinery, credit, and advanced education, and still need their husband's permission to start a business or open a bank account. Partially as a reaction to the deep gender disparities, women have begun taking collective action, and DRC has one of the highest numbers of women's organizations in Africa.

Women remain at the center of the wild meat economy, and the most entrepreneurial among them continue to practice the delicate art of bribery, barter, and negotiation with the armed men who now control the trade.

Like the threaded waterways of the Congo River, the trade in wild meat is meandering. And like a river eventually dumps into the sea, most of the meat ends up in Kinshasa.

At the Marché Central, a sprawling open-air market in the center of the city, a man with a bullhorn is selling popsicles. Boys of ten and twelve scavenge for discarded plastic bags they can resell. Men with deformed limbs and other physical signs of a life of great pain wander among the customers. A man sells makeup by wearing the makeup too. Blue streaks on his lids. Pink-purple cheeks. The women line up to bask in his lively spirit. A pile of turtles struggle to right themselves, the dusty market so different from the jungle floor where they were born and raised and ultimately captured. Full fat round grubs wriggle together in a tub. A commemorative dress hangs from a stall, celebrating *le 30 juin*, the overthrow of colonial overlords, celebrating independence in a world where so many remain oppressed.

I meet with the market administrator, a large woman in a floral yellow dress and silk shawl, with a braid that wraps around her head like a crown. She reclines regally underneath a window, half-watching a show about doctors on a small TV propped on her desk amid piles of official paperwork. The room is dark and divided by a curtain patterned with pale-green coconuts. A man in oversized sunglasses dozes in a chair by the door. I hand her my *Permis de Recherche*, signed and stamped by the Madame Secretary General of Scientific Research and Technology. She fingers the creased paper suspiciously. Then she turns to the man. Her eyes are bright and now she is full of laughter. As we leave the office, a small boy with a cloudy right eye follows us out the door and around the market for the rest of the afternoon.

I write down the names of the animals we see. The prices. I write in my little black notebook what my translator, Jack, paraphrases for me. He often wears a black sports jacket and a red shirt with a wide disco collar, buttoned up to the top of his neck. He has a thin mustache, and when he puts on his reading glasses, he perches them midway down his nose, as if they are more of a style accessory than a required object. Jack is eager and anxious and kind and obscuring. His translations generally add another layer of confusion, an explanation of reality filtered through his confident perceptions.

My research assistant, Patrice, a Congolese student studying environmental science, looks less certain about his comfort in these markets. He's never without a packet of tissues to wipe the sweat from his face. On some days, he seems nearly overcome with the intensity, the smell and dirt and smoke. Patrice is an orphan, with four brothers and a sister, deeply religious, and speaks with a slight stutter. He grew up in the countryside, and although he doesn't talk about it, his childhood must have been consumed by war.

One morning, on our way to the University of Kinshasa to interview a professor, we become snarled in a particularly bad *embouteillage.* The heavily trafficked road resembles a roiling river, full of debris, slipping and sliding in halting movement toward its predetermined destination. Motorbikes move like eels between taxi vans, overstocked with people.

169

"In the country, I feel calm. Clean air. Beautiful scenery," Patrice says from the backseat in his staccato French as he gazes out the window. "The city is stressful."

We pass a passenger taxi van with a man standing where the side door is meant to be, his back to the road. It is unclear if he is there to help pull people in, or to make sure nobody slips out.

"There are some good things about the city," Patrice continues. "The Chinese investment has brought new beautiful roads, schools, hospitals, stadiums. It is good for the country. It is development."

He sighs and continues looking out the window. "Although, in the past, only a few markets sold game meat. Now, you can find it everywhere. There is more demand."

A few children, holding more children, begin to approach our car through the stalled traffic.

"Lock your doors, don't talk to anyone, best not to smile," Patrice says with a sudden urgency. I am sitting in the front passenger seat and Lucian, seeing my hesitation, urges me to lock my door with a critical look.

"Lots of theft?" I ask in my simple French.

Patrice pipes up again. "Normally, they will leave the outsiders alone. Only rob the Congolese."

"Why?" I ask.

"They respect the foreigners."

One afternoon, Patrice takes me to his house. His sisters have a makeshift hair salon out front in the yard, and sell other things as well: salt fish and packets of tissues like the ones Patrice is always carrying around. I interview his eldest sister, who cooks daily meals for twelve people. They like to eat monkey and antelope. Or pangolin from the Marché Central, which has better quality and variety, although the prices are higher there. They eat game for marriages, as is the custom. "It's natural," his sister says with radiant eyes. "It's important to know the origin of your food, to know the source. I'd eat it every day if I could afford to. We ate more as children, when we lived in the countryside." The recipe is simple: Soak in water. Remove softened meat. Repeat. Add spices and stock. Cook a long time.

The wholesale port markets that lie on the outskirts of the city are particularly gritty. At Marché Inflammable, the cargo boat captains coming from upriver must navigate past the rusting carcasses of marooned metal barges and pull to shore through floats of trash and rot. The boats crowd in against each other. The decks are thronged with products. Men and women unload the goods, balancing on wooden planks above the waterline. They walk quickly back and forth. A pig roots through putrid refuse on the shoreline.

At the top of a steep rise above the river, women sit on the ground sorting through meager piles of charred wood. Their hands and clothes and faces are covered in charcoal dust. More women are hunched over great big heaps of threshed corn, carefully sifting stones from the kernels.

This market, like much of Kinshasa, smells of smoke. There are many kinds of fire in this city: flames smoking, sparks smoldering, food roasting on open coals, garden plots and empty fields ablaze. The smell of burning earth hangs in the air. It enters your nostrils and stays there all day. This market smells like burning plastic. The atmosphere is acrid with particulate matter.

I interview three women who sit under a broken beach umbrella with a mound of bushmeat. A large crowd of men gathers around us to discuss what I am doing. Jack hands me a smoked monkey and insists I pose for a photo with the women. I crouch in front of them. The women do not smile. I hold up the dead animal. As soon as the camera goes away, the women become kind and jovial, and we make jokes without speaking.

I'm introduced to two sisters who run a bar at the market that also serves as a headquarters for illegal smuggling. The bar is made from recycled lumber, with low ceilings and dirt floors. Light streams in from a few openings cut out of the wall. Plastic trash swirls around the plastic tables and plastic chairs in the soot-filled air. Patrice is dressed, as usual, like a banker: light blue shirt, pinstriped pants, pointy dress shoes. He stands beside me holding a tissue to his nose, like a swooning Southern belle overwhelmed by the state of this place.

"Our father was a trader," the Older Sister tells me. She has short hair, heavy cat-eye eyeliner, and black lipstick. She's wearing a red T-shirt with a striped grey vest and a colorful chunky necklace, with matching earrings and bracelet. "He had a big boat and he sold a lot of things. We took over his business."

"We go upriver twice a year, smuggling bullets to trade for meat," Younger Sister says. She wears a headband with a pink bow and a pink blouse. A necklace with a gold letter *A* rests just above her ample breasts. "We travel to each village, here and there, to find people to trade with. Our mother is still in the village, so we will go stay with her."

The women don't smile but they continue to answer my questions with generosity and surprising candidness.

"You used to be able to get lion meat but not anymore," Older Sister says. "Sometimes we get other illegal meats, like chimp or elephant. These are wrapped in legal meats, or hidden in maize or *fufu*...”

“Sometimes ivory is hidden the same way,” Younger Sister interrupts.

“Are you afraid of being caught?” I ask.

Older Sister answers solemnly, “There is a good understanding between us and the military. Sometimes we give them bribes.”

Younger Sister agrees. “The soldiers cooperate with us, but we don’t trust them. They are not our friends.”

Mothers and Sisters. The markets are full of mothers and sisters, grandmothers and daughters, aunts and nieces. Most of these women are illiterate. Many have been raped. These women deserve an entire book written just about them. Not only because they are long-suffering, poor, marginalized, or illiterate, not only because they are oppressed, raped, and forgotten, but because these women know how to hustle.

As I walk through the market stalls interviewing them, they don’t tell me their names. They are all different, with varied life histories, and yet they are united by their common work in the wild meat trade.

Their hands are quick and talented, wielding machetes like necessary appendages.

“I’ve been selling since 2000. Sometimes I sell on credit. Sometimes I can pay cash outright to the wholesaler,” she says, at the Marché Central. “I don’t personally eat much, although I prefer it to the domesticated meat coming from here. But I don’t have time. It’s too expensive. It’s a special meal. The people who eat it in Kinshasa are the chiefs.”

Nearby is a bag full of animal heads.

A well-dressed customer walks up. "I like different species— buffalo, monkey, antelope," she says, examining the meat on offer. "I like game because it is natural. What we feed our domestic animals is not natural. But these forest animals, they drink pure water. They are closer to God."

These hands are old. They slowly, carefully arrange and rearrange the piles of meat. These hands pinch for freshness. They fuss. These hands offer a taste to a customer, which is refused, so she eats it instead.

"I've been doing this forty-four years," she says. "I know it well. Business is difficult these days. There is a lot more competition. But I don't want to sell something else. This is sufficient."

At the Marché Gambela, she organizes her meat into three piles, each a different kind and price. She is wearing a purple nightgown that is tied in little knots at the shoulders because it is too big. Her red bra straps match her red painted nails. Her eyebrows have been drawn on in thin, quick leaps, and they give her face a celebratory look.

"My sister sells a few stalls down. My mother was selling before us. Every two to three months, I go to Mbandaka and buy a big basket of meat, which I bring back here by plane. I buy elephant secretly, but I'm not afraid to sell it here. They don't care. The hotels and restaurants buy elephant."

As she speaks, she flicks a long, thin knife around in the air, like a pirate. Patrice stands next to her, taking cramped and meticulous notes. He looks unsettled by the closeness of her glinting saber.

"I haven't been directly involved with the military, but we are obligated to pay an illegal tax to hunters who have to pay the local chiefs who have to pay the military."

A pregnant woman admires a large pile of buffalo that costs about twenty U.S. dollars.

"I don't have enough money," the customer says.

"I will give you a special price. Because you are pregnant. The baby needs it."

There is something joyous and playful in these transactions, as if the true nature of the relationship of trade—of mutual benefit—has not yet been forgotten here.

A government employee walks up. She measures the price and weight of game for sale. Her statistics will go to the commercial ministry. She does her work efficiently and walks on to the next vendor.

At this market, you have to stoop down. The stalls are low and the passageways are narrow.

She needs a big supply, so once a week, on Saturday, she receives four baskets of wild boar and six baskets of monkeys. Her parents send it by plane. "A lot of the meat comes from the equatorial forest. The connections were better ten years ago. Boats came more often."

Her hands beckon at regular customers to see the special animals for sale that day.

She hides chimpanzee meat by calling it yellow-backed duiker. She sells it to *premiers citoyens*.

She engages in a friendly, five-minute negotiation with a customer whose favorite dish is buffalo stew. She doesn't like to give her children game all the time because overconsumption causes gout.

An older woman, wrapped in a fleece football blanket, has set aside a freshly smoked monkey for her best client, a Catholic priest.

She has much nicer-quality meat than I've seen elsewhere. "My customers are loyal. People come to me to buy, and then they bring the meat to Europe. But there are less customers now, so I provide options for what people can afford. The price doubled recently, though. There are not enough hunters, and they must do it secretly. It's the dry season and it is illegal to hunt. The wet season is easier."

She displays a mound of turtles that tumble over each other.

She sells smoked serpents, snaked around sticks, with scales
of charcoal shimmer.

She drags a live crocodile by the thick twine tied around its mouth. It does not fight back.

She was trained by her stepmother. But she doesn't travel any longer because her husband won't allow her.

She does not want to answer any more of my questions.

This customer says, "If they forbid it, we don't eat it. We obey the laws."

This customer would eat more game if she were richer. She buys less now than when Mobutu was here. "There is less money in our hands. People are suffering because everything has become more expensive. It's unbelievable, the price increases! Game meat especially. We can't survive."

She is a secretary. She buys game once a month, always on the weekend. "It is not difficult to find, if you know where to go. I eat game because it is fresh, but mostly, because it is *delicious*."

At the Marché Cinquantenaire, there is a mural with large cursive words, *La Révolution de La Modernité*. The open-aired aisles are bursting with an array of vendors. It is very loud and people bump into each other.

She has eaten game since she was young. "My father was a hunter." When she goes home to visit her relatives in the countryside, she takes fresh meat back to Kinshasa on the plane, and then she smokes it herself. If she buys antelope, she takes the entire animal.

She says, "When I eat it, I think about my ancestors. About how they lived. I want to show my children what their ancestors did. That's why I smoke it myself. To show them how it is done."

She stands in front of a yellow wall and thinks hard about her answers.

She has been selling for two years. Her friend got her into the business. She plans to expand and eventually open a drug store because before she did this, she was studying to become a pharmacist.

She is wearing a golden dress.

I try to give her 1,000 Congolese francs (about sixty cents), as I have been giving all these women for taking the time to talk to me. She refuses.

She says, "Why should you pay me? We are the same." She grabs her hair from her head wrap and points to my own dark hair.

She carries a kind of quiet strength, like a spring bud waiting to emerge. She is a conduit for the violence of seasons past, still wary of the frost. Is it truly over? Is it time to bloom?

She is a queen, sitting behind her wild animals, brown and wrinkled like tree stumps, surveying the organoleptic spoils of her latest conquest.

As I leave the market, a refrigerated truck pulls in to deliver domesticated meat.

The Hunter grew up without the security of being surrounded by inanimate objects. The landscape was his home and it was alive. I understood him immediately for this quality. Although our childhoods were vastly different, across continent-sized distances, we both roamed the wilds and explored barefoot. The hills and dry arroyos of New Mexico were my friends, and they were always changing. And so I set within myself a permanent reverence for all such rowdy things.

As I fall in love with the Hunter, I fall in love with the country that has made him. Time becomes a succession of organic experiences, not so much linear but rhizomatic and synchronous, like a growing plant. I start finding mystic signs everywhere. A wasp cleaning itself delicately on the windowsill. The sound of footsteps down an empty hall. The fog on the river in the early morning.

During the day, I visit markets and conduct interviews. The dust-filled air gives the urban buzz a smoky film of sentimentality. I feel love in brief moments of eye contact with the vendors, forgotten before they could be remembered. I feel love even in the tremendous sorrow I experience as I catalog dead wild animals, the sadness momentarily interrupted by thoughts of the Hunter.

At night, we eat pizza and watch movies in bed. We have dinner at the posh French Club and watch the World Cup projected onto outdoor screens. We go out for Chinese food at a restaurant where the menu offers such appealing dishes as "At the End of the Parsley," "Gently Beans," "Salty Food," and "Hot and Sour Little Sheep."

One evening, we go to a play at an outdoor stage. The sky turns orange behind the actors. The play is about a man on a crowded van. He is dressed in a suit and carries a briefcase. He is always traveling, bumping this way and that through his monologues. Then a ghostly woman appears in a spotlight standing on a ladder, dressed in a sheet with a white-painted face. She is still and her voice ripples out toward the crowd. I hold my breath. The Hunter takes my hand.

On the weekends, we escape the city. At a lakeside restaurant with a tragic past, we eat *poulet à la moambé*—chicken in a rich orange sauce made from the fruit of the oil palm and peanut butter. It was here that Mobutu executed a father and daughter charged with treason. Now the lake is an attraction run by a

Catholic mission, and the chicken is delicious. In front of the peaceful water, a music video is being filmed. A dozen women in pale-purple dresses flutter and dance sweetly.

178 We go camping at a tourist resort. In the morning, we hike to a polyphonic waterfall and bathe beneath the rush of prismatic water, then follow the tributary stream down to a wide sandy beach along the Congo River. Pale sandstone rocks, like abandoned ships, moor on the shoreline. The river is the color of sepia. We swim in the strong current and lie on the cool wet sand in the shadow of a boulder.

I realize that life is very simple. It is colors and shapes, shadows and movement of sun-dapple through tree leaves. It is silence punctuated by noise. The roar of humans going about their lives suddenly sounds serene.

The dry-season haze no longer bothers me. I look forward to the nights. To the brief pause between the light fading away and returning again. When we make love, I inhabit myself. I feel like I am home.

One evening, as we lie entangled, the Hunter tells me the name of the remote elephant *baï* in the forest clearing where I should take his body when he dies. It feels like he is sharing the biggest secret of his heart.

Our love becomes unbounded. We are no longer crawling along the solid and somber earth. We are its fecund freedom, embedded and alive. I understand him as I understand myself. Both of us lovely and tormented beasts, which no longer seem quite so ordinary.

It's Friday night and the city is feeling good. At a packed outdoor grillade restaurant called Ngama Cheetah 2, located across the street from a place simply called "Dance Club," a billboard-sized sign edged in flashing lights displays pictures of the available food options.

We sit below the sign, sipping beer and people watching—the Hunter; Lucian, my driver; Jasper, my amiable colleague from the conservation organization; and Raphael, the man who runs errands for the office. We've been waiting nearly an hour for our food. Men selling things walk off the street and up to our table. Shoes, handbags, DVDs. They stand and stare and wait for acknowledgment. Phone chargers and adapters, books, maps. Everything is carried on the body, every part put to use, whether head or shoulder or hand. Carved ebony sculptures, excellent pencil-sketched portraits, fake passports, tools, a single belt. Cardboard pyramids display a hundred other things. The men cycle past us, a carousel of capitalism.

A man with a digital camera around his neck and a backpack full of gadgets has steady business. He takes an overexposed photo of the group next to us, then prints it out on a portable inkjet printer. Proof of their existence, and his, too.

"Here there is a more vibrant sense of time," Jasper says, gesturing toward the busy street. "People walk slowly here. They do everything slowly. To the Western mind, it might seem dysfunctional, but to us, we are not so stressed as all that. Life takes as long as it takes." Jasper takes an extended drink of his beer, as if to underline his point. "We have a saying here," he continues, pausing to take in a breath. *"God gave the white man a watch, but he gave the Congolese TIMMMMEEEEE."*

Adjacent to the diners is a wood-fired grill and a massive butcher's block. Two men stand at the table hacking meat into pieces with the rhythm of drummers. Another cuts open a goat carcass hanging from its back legs. The head chef is dressed in simple leather sandals, a white paper cap, and a white doctor's lab coat. He looks like a surgeon as he expertly flings the bloody meat across the open fire. Then he pauses, stands at idle, and watches the crowd with a satisfied grin. It turns out the wait is just a lack of hurry.

Eventually, our heap of goat meat arrives, served on a paper-lined red plastic tray. The morsels are juicy, caramelized and crispy from the fire, and chewy, filled with gristle and bone. The edge of the tray is lined with slices of unwrapped *kwanga*—fermented manioc (cassava) root that has been pounded, formed into loaves, wrapped in leaves, tied up in string, and steamed—a toothpick stuck in the center of each bite-sized square. The sweet-sour flavor pairs beautifully with the succulent, smoky goat and the tart beer, three simple tastes blending so well, heightened by the light-show ambiance, the vivacious energy of the multitude gathered around us, and my long-overdue hunger, all in the company of such cheerful companions.

After we've eaten, Lucian drives our dinner party to a club. It is located in a basement and the air-conditioning has been turned up full blast. Compared to the languid night, the room is arctic. Glossy-neon lights over the dance floor cast a rippling sapphire and chartreuse haze across the walls. It feels like we are submerged in the slow bend of an eddy. The room vibrates with Congolese rhumbas and satiny soukous from the 1970s.

I dance with Lucian. Papa Wemba's voice is soaring against a backdrop of starry beats. The song is a mix of joy and pity, like a celebratory lament. Papa Wemba was always dressed in his finest, and his followers were called *sapeurs*—men devoted to the cult of dapper style. Lucian spins me around the dance floor, dressed in his finery, an elegant *sapeur* suavely gliding us between other couples. His large hand around my small hand steadies me, and I feel a small piece of happiness. Each note sounds like an immortal and untouchable object.

The Hunter is slumped against the back wall, talking with the other men. When I see him there, I feel that he is doing all this for me. His tranquil indifference to my dancing is a gift. Liberated from the searching intensity of his desire, I exist for myself in the security of his company.

After a few songs, I thank Lucian for the dances and join the Hunter. He does not smile at my approach but lifts his crystal eyes. They have become little satisfied rosettes. I am next to him again.

———

I've been told that people are selling live bonobos at a wholesale market about an hour north of the city, where boats go that don't want to pay the port fees in Kinshasa. The animals are supposedly coming from the tributary rivers around Mbandaka, which means they were very likely captured in the national park.

Some tribes have cultural taboos against eating or touching bonobos because they are thought to embody ancestral spirits. In the forests where the Iyaelima people live, for example, the bonobo populations are actually more abundant near their settlements. But demand for their meat continues elsewhere. It is rumored that they taste like human flesh, very sweet. I heard stories that their bones were highly valued as a cure for sexual impotence, and that people washed their children with the bones to provide spiritual protection.

Bonobos share 98.7 percent of our genetic code and are sensitive and gentle creatures. They were the only animals to die of fright in Berlin's zoo when the Allied forces bombed the city. Baby bonobos that are orphaned by the bushmeat trade are frequently sold into the exotic pet trade. They are tiny balls of rich black fur that must be touched nearly constantly or they will die from lack of love.

On Saturday, the Hunter joins me at the wholesale market to help translate. It is a collection of open-air wood stalls situated along the banks of the Congo River. We walk along a dirt road toward the section that sells bushmeat, passing a table crammed with bottles of home-brewed tinctures, roots, betel nuts, and medicinal herbs. In a shed nearby, children sit beneath a stacked tower of flickering TVs, playing video games and watching cartoons.

We begin talking to an energetic young man smoking a cigarette. He has long, pointy nails and a blue rosary around his wrist. As we speak, the two women sitting at the stall behind us start to yell at us. The Hunter turns to speak with them in Lingala. "They say you will make their business hard for them. Because you work for the conservation people. The enemy," the Hunter translates as the women shout their rough words. "They do not want you to take their picture."

I've been warned that ubiquitous photographing is dangerous. Since there is very little tourism in the country, all foreigners are advised against taking too many pictures, particularly of military buildings, airports, and other government buildings, to avoid being suspected as a spy. This paranoia of outsiders certainly has a long history. To be watched has led to being controlled and colonized.

Now the women begin addressing the man I have just been interviewing. "Don't give her your information. She will use it for her own profit and to our detriment!" The man starts arguing back. The Hunter interjects, speaking Lingala with a tone of irritation, but his face is calm, almost amused. Everyone addresses each other with the customary formality of *Mama* and *Papa* (like we might use ma'am or sir), and for a moment it feels like a big family misunderstanding. But the irate energy is escalating, and tension ruffles through the market.

I can understand the women's anger. I am merely another white person, in a long string of them, here to plunder something that is theirs, even if it is only information. So much of history and the creation of scientific knowledge has been described by outsiders, filtered through their own prejudices. How easy for such an observer to misinterpret or entirely miss the point. The Congolese in this market are merely enacting their power to withhold the knowledge that belongs to them.

It is my own anger and confusion that I am most surprised by, for I suddenly feel quite alone. Up until this instance, the Hunter has acted as my protector, providing me a kind of freedom in a country where I've been warned not to go anywhere alone. Today, it seems, he has disrupted my experience. I've never had such ire directed at me during my previous market visits, and it seems the difference is that when I am with two Congolese guides, I am not seen as posing as much of a threat.

The argument continues for some time, and I walk away. Eventually, the Hunter follows me. The women look tired and strong and persistent and disappointed. My mind is wandering the space between languages and privileges. I want something that I do not know how to have. That I cannot articulate. I want an understanding of the objective reality of DRC outside my perception of it.

On the drive home, we pass Chinese men laboring in trenches and Congolese men crushing purple-grey towers of volcanic rock into gravel, their faces set in tired resignation. We pass an outdoor evangelist church on a hillside—plastic chairs in a field and a well-dressed minister on stage. We drive past a blue-tiled mosque with palm trees; past a dusty graveyard with lines of people (in a city of 11 million, how many die in a day?); past a concrete staircase to nowhere with a sign that reads *Welcome to the Exodus Center*; past beautiful women looking out from old VW buses painted in pastels like metallic Easter eggs. We drive past a half-finished two-story cinder block house with mildewed edges and water stains. The only color is a red scrap of laundry hung to dry and the ochre wrap skirt of a woman out front. She sits and watches traffic. A boy walks to the end of the unfinished steps and stares. We come to a central intersection. Two giant tin-can robots with red eyes and illuminated hands swing around methodically directing cars. As we crush through the teeming roundabout, a child leads a blind man through the traffic on foot. A million little worlds carried inside each of them.

184

The following Thursday, I drive around town with Lucian and Ted, a middle-aged American with a mild southern accent, soft golden hair, and round glasses. There's a restless intellectualism to him, like a boy playing dress-up as a professor. "Oh yes, that place is very nice," he says, pointing to a white-walled restaurant called Limoncello.

Ted's wife works for the British embassy, and he seems both elated and bored to be spending a few years posted up in Kinshasa. He has come along today to ostensibly test out his language skills and be my translator while I survey local restaurants and interview chefs.

"The Lingala word *mosuni* means both 'meat' and 'flesh,' like human flesh," Ted says, handing me a sheet with relevant vocabulary. He has recently completed an English-to-Lingala dictionary for the local expat community. Lingala is sparse and economical. When the Hunter speaks it, I find the melodic clicks and rush of syllables to be a form of music. But when Ted speaks it, the words crunch into my ears.

A pickup truck drives by fast. In the back are a dozen armed men in blue uniforms sitting on benches. I've never been anywhere so openly militarized, and the ubiquitous presence of soldiers does not make me feel any safer.

Ted is like a dog with the windows rolled down, wind in hair, arm stretched out, fingers stretched out further, feeling the anemic breeze as Lucian inches us through Kinshasa traffic.

"We aren't allowed to roll down the windows in embassy vehicles," he beams, "because you know, when things fall apart here—they fall apart quickly."

The traffic is leaden. I watch a taxicab with a smoking tailpipe struggle to tow a broken-down truck carrying a load of immense logs.

As we get closer to the center of town, the promise of a better future is everywhere: billboards advertise evangelical ministers who vow to lift you out of poverty and hardship. Others advertise whitening cream. In an ad for Kerrygold Irish butter, a giant golden wedge towers above happy cows in a lush green countryside. At the central intersection, two digital screens blare music videos and advertisements. They run 24/7, and are a powerful image in a place where electricity is rare and rolling blackouts are commonplace.

A white woman in a white jacket and heels walks along the sidewalk. "A target. She is a target, *n'est-ce pas*?" Ted asks Lucian, first in Lingala, then French, and finally in English, as he points to the woman. "Not a *bonne idée* for her to be walking around alone like that?"

Lucian laughs his full-bellied laugh, a mix of apathy and resignation, and Ted looks satisfied. A man wheels a truck tire through the traffic. Another crosses the road holding a dirty rag. He is only wearing one flip-flop.

"See that hospital over there," Ted says, pointing to a massive institutional building. "The Chinese built it—*l'Hôpital du Cinquantenaire*. It sat empty almost two years, waiting for supplies and staff. Just like when the Belgians were here, it still takes three stamps and four signatures to do just about anything! It's the same with the roads. It used to... Do you see those?" he says, interrupting himself to point to a VW taxi bus with rusted siding. A man hangs off the back, rodeo-style, calling for passengers. "People call those buses *sangui mort*—death wish."

Ted chuckles, but quickly recovers from his distracted state and continues to spew his information. "Anyway, so yes, it's the same with the roads. They are built, then just left to get pocked up all over again. There's no maintenance. And all these Boxer motorbikes you see around, that's new, within the last five years. Cheap and from China and now everywhere. They've totally changed traffic patterns. Of course, some things are better. It used to take nearly all day to get downtown from the airport on the old four-lane colonial boulevard. But in the mid-2000s, Chinese investments replaced it with an eight-lane highway that crosses the city. Now the trip can be done in just over an hour. The traffic lights are a system of arrows and numbers, like they use in Asia."

Ted tells me about DRC with eager giddiness, as if proving to himself that despite being hidden within the walls of the embassy these past years, he has still truly experienced the *real* Africa.

We begin our restaurant interviews at Kinshasa's Grand Hotel, where the tables are covered in white linen and most of the diners are posh Congolese. Antelope shares the leather-bound menus with *Filet de Capitaine* and *Porc Chops au Jus*. Today's special: Porcupine from Bas Congo, US$35, with rice or *fufu* and vegetables.

Game is served at the restaurant Mama Ekila Inzia, where it has been served for forty-five years. Under the Kuba cloth ceilings, steaming plates of boa, crocodile, and turtle are set down before local *Kinois* and, occasionally, foreign expats.

It is eaten buffet-style at Super Aubaine by professionals on their lunch breaks, to the tinkling sound of an indoor water fea- ture. The walls are dressed in colorful paintings, the chairs are dressed in gaudy pink, the waiters are dressed in formal blacks and whites, and the food is dressed in unctuous sauce.

And it is eaten at Chez Fideline, a cramped second-floor room located above a bar. Here the patrons squeeze around four tables while the proprietress has her nails done by the entrance. The clanging and steam from the adjacent kitchen overpower the sounds of the bursting street below. A whole monkey stews in the pot.

With each bite, diners remember childhoods in remote villages, straw huts with mud walls, and forests alive with noise. The songs of frogs at night were so loud they sounded electric. The air was cool and fresh then. The children ran around in rags with broad grins. They laughed so easily it was almost sacrilegious. It was almost a sin. But nostalgia is a tricky beast and the act of remembering is an act of reimagining.

The road back to the British embassy skirts a placid section of the Congo River. The residences of other ambassadors, grand whitewashed art deco buildings, all have neat rows of dazzling flowers and majestic trees behind ubiquitous walls with elaborate entrance gates, each a slight variation on the next. The neighborhood is clean, ordered, and calm. Humanity has disappeared.

As we drop Ted off, he invites me to a movie night happening there in a few days. "It's the newest thing to do in Kinshasa. Somebody bought a projector, and they play movies outside by the tennis courts. Just 3,000 Congolese francs to get in. You just need an ID. And they serve hot dogs and popcorn. Around twenty-five people came last time. Very nice. And such interesting people. Like from the UN. They tell you all kinds of things. Like what drones can and cannot do."

As we pull away, I am thinking about a picture I saw at the University of Kinshasa. It was an optical illusion, a vividly colored hologram. From one angle, the image was of a traditional village hut. From another, it transformed into a pink modern house. Kinshasa, like this picture, is a hologram that changes with the angle at which it is viewed. At one glance, it is like every other modern city—screens, traffic lights, advertisements, patisseries, hotels and restaurants, manicured lawns, and rich parts of town. At another glance, it is none of these things.

Sunday afternoon is hot and stifling. The Hunter and I go to the supermarket. We buy gin, ginger ale, butter cookies, French cheese, strawberries. We buy fresh limes, flown in from some distant place, seamed in yellow, two for ten dollars, and walk over to his friend Ben's house.

It's a gated property surrounded by a high fence with a long brick drive. The guard at the entrance is reluctant to let us in, since Ben is neither home nor expecting us. He's gone upriver in search of *mbenga* (goliath tigerfish), a large freshwater fish with shark-like teeth, and hasn't come back yet. The Hunter's fluent Lingala helps our case, and eventually the guard opens the gate.

Ben works for the United States Agency for International Development and has spent many years in Kinshasa. He pays around US$8,000 a month to live in a house built during the colonial period, a result of the skewed expat economy. The house is heavy with ornate molding and decorative wood accents. The kitchen looks like it was last remodeled in the 1970s, when the house was occupied by a Mobutu government minister, and the cream-white cupboards hang uneasily on their hinges.

There is a sort of decadent decay to the property, like a banquet table strewn with decomposing leftovers, wilted flowers, and melted candles. We make ourselves at home, pouring drinks into crystal tumblers with ice, laying out the cheese and fruit on a wooden cutting board, and sit outside on cushioned wicker patio chairs around a low glass-topped coffee table with a view to the pool, half in shadow beneath large trees. Leaves float on the glassy surface. The yard has been planted with exotic flowers and decorated with stone sculptures, which peer out from the heavy foliage like timid wildlife.

Ben returns shortly after we have settled in, sunburned and scattered. He unloads a large plastic cooler and fishing gear in a pile near the sliding glass patio door. "Nope, didn't catch anything." He smiles, his eyes disappearing into folds. "But the day on the water has done me good. And how nice you have decided to visit!"

Ben's wife left him some years ago, and his daily companion is an enormous aging border collie with an oral fixation. She sits at his feet and promptly falls into a geriatric sleep, only occasionally stirring when her desire to examine some morsel of food or mouthful of conversation is strong enough to overcome her immense lethargy.

Ben is round and red-faced, with a jolly demeanor. But there is a deep furrow in his mannerisms, as if years of pushing money through government organizations has paled his mood.

"Did you hear about the UN official that was recently robbed?" the Hunter asks. "He was walking to dinner, and these men in police uniforms drove up alongside him. As he approached the car, they held him at gunpoint until he turned over his wallet and passport. He was fully terrified."

"I bet, although I'm not all that surprised to hear this. Armed robbers impersonating the police. Sounds pretty standard these days. Not like in Mobutu times. It was so safe, you could walk around with your wallet out in the open." Ben smiles. "Of course, they enforced it by cutting off fingers here and there. Perhaps not the most ethical tactic, but at least it was generally a more secure place to live."

"But of course the instability used to be much worse," the Hunter says. "At the end of Mobutu's reign there were gangs of armed street children roaming the city."

"Yes, that is until President Kabila had them all rounded up and shot!"

"Ah, sure," the Hunter says, reaching forward to cut a piece of cheese, "but truly Congo's reputation doesn't fit its reality. It is not so bad as all that. Compared to Lagos or Nairobi, Kinshasa is so much less dangerous. Yes, okay, a group of armed men took over the airport, TV and radio stations in a protest against the government last December. Some people were killed. But horrible violence happens in America and Europe, too. It's just that we don't talk about it in the same way."

The border collie stirs, moves from hand to hand, licking her way into a frenzy, then collapses back into sleep.

"And this NGO- and UN-ification of the economy has made it all so much worse," the Hunter continues. "All this international money drives up prices. All these high-powered people driven around in armored cars. Coming here, ready to save a country they care about only as long as it takes them to write up a report and pass an audit. And then it turns out those are the same guys smuggling ivory out of the country! UN officials were recently caught trafficking live African grey parrots, too. Or like that conservationist who was recently accused of sexually assaulting local women."

"Ah yes, it sounds like his organization discreetly got him out of the country?" Ben asks.

"Yes, that's what happens. There isn't justice here, only power," the Hunter replies.

I decide to take a swim. How odd to hear these men discuss the sector that employs them with such disparagement. As if their pessimism is a necessary tool to do the work they do, so that they are never disappointed, and in fact, hold out the possibility that one day they might even be impressed. What do you call a crisis that is ongoing and persistent? When does it stop being urgent and become the norm? What if that crisis is simply called "development"?

I swim up to the edge of the pool.

"And how about bushmeat," Ben says, looking at me teasingly. "That's something that seems to be an impossible, perpetual problem. I'm near sick of hearing about it! People have been measuring and discussing it for thirty years. What are we actually going to do about it?!"

He turns to the Hunter and smiles. "I'd say it's time for another drink!"

He shoots up and wobbles into the dimly lit living room, returning with a decanter.

I wrap myself in a towel and we drink amber-colored scotch while the night darkens around us. The dank, polluted air of Kinshasa catches in the climbing vines that course up the sides of the stone outbuildings and slowly eats away at the structures underneath.

———

At the Ministry of Environment, the forest director, a Congolese man with a bushy white beard, in a black-and-white houndstooth tie, is watching the Tour de France. A small old

TV sits on a stand pulled up next to his desk. He answers all my questions with an eye to the bicycles.

"Of course I eat game!" he says, making his point by briefly looking at me instead of the tiny men pedaling uphill. "Red meat makes men strong and intelligent." His voice is deep and confident. "Domestic meat—white meat—we don't consider this meat at all. We must regulate bushmeat, but it has to be based on cultural possibilities. White meat isn't in the culture."

This preference for game is both biologically determined and a result of the accidents of history. There is more protein and less fat in wild meat. The diversity of species, and thus flavors, is more interesting to eat than the standard domestic animals, which have been so overbred they've lost their taste. The desire for smoky meat is a relic of necessity—it was once the only way to preserve animals killed in the forest. Today *boucané* has become symbolic of power. If poaching is hunting by the poor, how do we name the elite demand that is driving it? How do we classify the corrupt ministers and mafia bosses who eat chimpanzee, gorilla, and elephant? The distinction between illegal and legal is really just a matter of who is controlling the resources. As with the great lords of ye olden days, who protected the forests so that they could continue feasting on their precious venison, wild flesh is a status marker, while the peasants have no meat.

The forest director calls to his assistant and tells him to print out the latest version of a sustainable use plan his office has been working on, then turns back to his TV. I am handed a thick stack of paper in a blue folder. The document is a draft, and comments line the sides of the pages, like directions for the future.

The plan lays out the incredible diversity of the region's *Faune Sauvage:*

The Congo Basin forests contain 460 species of reptiles, 1,000 species of birds, 552 known species of mammals consisting of 56 primates, 48 ungulates, and 41 carnivores; 700 species of fish and 2,400 species of ants and butterflies. Plus 8,000 species of vascular plants.

Suggestions for alternative income sources for those living near national parks besides wildlife harvest include small-scale crafts, agriculture, beekeeping, poultry farming, and ecotourism. Ecotourism has "enormous potentials" to generate revenue, but it's failed to take off because of "insecurity resulting from the armed conflicts" as well as "the dilapidation of basic infrastructure." In the margins the comment says: *Raise the problem here of the lack of political will for the development of the ecotourism in the economic sector (Priorities: logging, mines, petroleum).*

As I flip through the document, it becomes clear that part of the concern with the bushmeat trade is that the government isn't profiting from this wildlife resource. The plan to promote ecotourism relies on the hope that wildlife will become more valuable alive than as dead meat, making it possible for local populations to improve their living conditions while also bringing economic benefit to the state. If this works, it would further support the argument for conservation.

There is also a lot of interest in creating taxable "legal" game through stricter regulations, certifications, and farming of certain species, such as muskrat, bush pig, and blue duiker. However, in a country with recurrent governance challenges, this seems like a deeply difficult problem to solve. The economics are also hard to justify as the cost to a poacher—for whom wildlife is free—is less than for a farmer, who must spend months waiting for animals to mature. Moreover, unlike domestic animals, which have been bred to put on fat and convert feed to flesh, game animals are not as efficient at protein conversion.

"Our forests must be protected," the forest director is saying. "Of course, I am against poaching!"

But I am distracted. I am watching the Tour de France.

Later that day, I am just beginning a meeting with Jack and Patrice when my cell rings. It is the Hunter. "Where are you?" he says urgently. "I'm at the office," I reply.

I've never before heard fear in the Hunter's voice. This is a man who rode his bicycle across the country during the civil war and only reluctantly evacuated with the last medical aid workers. But even his particularities have their exceptions. He sounds terrified.

I stare at the faded conservation posters on the wall. Elephants on a pastel map of the country. Chimpanzees superimposed over a labyrinth of rivers. There is static on the line and it is hard to hear him.

"There was a shooting... *chhchehehe*... on the hill... *aahndh shehhh* stay there... *shhehhsh.*" And then the phone cuts off.

I go out into the hall. The news is traveling fast but nobody knows exactly what is happening. Ted's words from the previous week cross my mind: *When things fall apart, they fall apart quickly.*

Emmanuel, the operations manager, is standing outside his office. "Come. I will debrief you."

Emmanuel is normally the most ebullient person in the office, but as I sit in front of his desk, he is serious and grim.

"There has been a shooting. At the military camp near the presidential palace. Some people have been killed. It is a fight between colleagues. Two sides of the presidential guard arguing over whether or not they are paid enough. Whether their conditions are satisfactory. I know this because my nephew is a guard at the camp and his cousin is a doctor, and they tell him what is happening, and he tells me, so I can tell you."

He gives me a small smile. "These stories are still vague but at least they are more accurate than the many other rumors circulating."

I do not feel reassured. Shortly afterward, the Hunter arrives at the office and takes me back to the Bel Vue. The streets seem normal. No one else appears alarmed.

That evening, we fight over nothing, spit ugly words at each other.

"Was this really such an emergency that you had to come get me? I was in the middle of a meeting," I say as we cut up vegetables for dinner.

"Why did you tell me to pick you up, then?" he replies, his back to me as he slices carrots.

"I didn't. I could barely hear you, and then you just showed up to get me."

The Hunter turns to face me.

"Well, I don't think you should be so ungrateful."

"And I can take care of myself!" I say back as I leave the room.

Later, we go to bed with the intensity of two people frustrated and scared and relieved all at once. It's as if death lingers in the corners of the room, watching.

As the Hunter drifts off to sleep, I am wide awake, feeling unconvinced, by this life, by this person. I look at his sleeping face. He looks old. The stubble whiter. The lines on his face steeper and more buried.

The Hunter is usually so calm. So present. He's spent more of his life in the natural world than most people—been privy to its intimate violence. Perhaps that proximity to death has forced this quality of serene living—a bold existence with a stillness at the center. How upsetting it is to see him in a state of agitation.

My mind is in a torrent. *What was that fight? We were both mad with fear. Raw and childish and real. A fear that we might lose each other… A blood fury rife with misgiving, miscommunication, and disconnection… Imagining the black hole of death… A feeling so common to life but one we try to control and distance ourselves from… perhaps if I am diligent and awake, to myself, to my own mortality, to this feeling, I might become more open to love too.*

And as these thoughts whirlpool, I feel like I am floating, nothing touching my skin. My senses are so dulled, I feel everything all at once. All colors become white light… *and if the world ends tomorrow, at least we had tonight.*

The dawn brings remembrances of love and misused time. Kinshasa glows like leftover coals. All day, the sky is grey and low and on the verge of rain. The sun hides. The air remains frigid. I don't text with the Hunter all day. By 5 PM, the light has matured. On my way home, there is heavy traffic, which matches the heavy air. A presidential guard motorcycle with flashing lights turns onto the road in front of us, followed by a black Mercedes SUV. Inside is President Kabila, all alone, driving hurriedly through the city because he can.

Dusk is but a gentler word for nightfall. The evening turns black with alarming speed.

Back at the Bel Vue, the lights twinkle on in loud clusters. I feel a great need to wash off the dust and rancor of the past days. To calm the turbulence of small misunderstandings between the Hunter and me. I go to the compound's pool. The entrapment of water makes me feel dislocated, as if I am anywhere. A man asks me if it is cold in unsteady French. I reply in my own unsteady French, and wonder who he is and why he is here. But his identity is as irrelevant as mine. We are both just here to swim laps.

Adjacent to the pool, the Bel Vue's restaurant, Le Palais, is getting busy. The tinkle of silverware and bursts of laughter float down from the second story. I take a dive off the board, and after some time I go to the sauna and let the hot droplets of water fall onto my skin. Is humanity's greatest gift and talent our ability to forget? We accept that the depleted wild nature we have today is how it has always been. We blind ourselves to the terrors of the past and resign ourselves to what we have left. We shift the baseline, forget the tragedies, and start all over again.

197

Back at the condo, I take a shower. The Hunter joins me. He soaps me tenderly and attentively. He washes my body. We do not speak. His face now looks youthful and glowing, the mountain-shaped lips in a tender smile. His dimples like bright innocent sparks. In that moment, I can see the allure of a world falling to pieces.

Another day sinks beyond the crush of time.

———

Sharon is a family friend from Paris who works in Kinshasa as a professor of international criminal justice and as a lawyer for the Ministry of Justice and Human Rights. A slight woman in her late thirties, with a bob of densely curled chestnut hair and pale freckled skin, she is not, at first glance, what you might imagine an expert on mass atrocities and torture to look like.

Sharon lives in one of the first and oldest Congolese neighborhoods in the city, which just five years ago remained at the edge of town. Today, it lies in the middle of an ever-expanding ring of human settlement. Live wires run along open sewer pits and graffiti for the *Autopsy Gang* adorns crumbling structures. The houses are built close together, enclosed by walls topped with broken shards of glass.

Here, the neighbors speak to each other on the street. They take each other's children out to play, crack jokes, and respond with boisterous laughter. They sell things out in the open and sit in entryways to have faces shaved, heads buffed, and hair twisted into beautiful braids. Here, there is no such disease as loneliness.

Sharon's modest home is hidden behind a high wall. The Hunter and I enter a courtyard through a low door. A porch runs along two sides of the house and French doors open to a sunken living room flooded with books. Sharon has adopted a Congolese orphan, a small boy of about five. He is fresh-eyed and shy at first, but quickly forgets his fear and looks over my face with curiosity.

We take her son and his friend on a short walk to the Académie des Beaux-Arts, a sprawling complex of modernist concrete buildings, with banks of small windows and geometric trim painted in turquoise and red. Founded in 1943 by a Belgian missionary, the school has produced numerous internationally acclaimed Congolese artists.

The place is eerily deserted, a noticeable contrast to the bustling neighborhood we've just come from. We walk past a room of silent printing presses and a sculpture studio with half-made creations awaiting completion. In one corner, a bricoleur's dream of cogs, wheels, cranks, and pulleys, in many tints of metal and pattern, await organization. A small group plays a pick-up soccer game in the dirt expanse next to the buildings. We continue up the hill, past a set of bleachers where a few teenagers flirt, and head toward a wide grassy quadrangle edged in flower beds and an array of sculptures. Murals embellish the surrounding walls.

The Hunter kicks a soccer ball around with the kids. Watching him in this empty space, within the midst of the throbbing city, I wonder about our future, which seems like a ghost whose presence is only known after it's departed.

As the sun begins to set, we go in search of dinner. The narrow streets are a parade of people. Side stalls sell *pondu* (cassava leaves) and rolls of *kwanga*. Displays of fresh fruit are illuminated by candlelight. At one stall, under a glowing beach umbrella, a dozen waffle machines are plugged into one meager outlet. Each appliance is covered in smoky burns from previous electrical fires. We pass a man pushing a cart carrying a popcorn maker, the cord hanging loosely as he goes in search of a free outlet. Bonfires line the unlit side roads, like sacraments to survival.

We sit outside under a string of lights. The restaurant is busy, and we order beer, chicken, and fresh river fish. We call over a boy precariously balancing nearly a hundred hardboiled eggs on his head. He looks relieved to set down the stack of cartons on our table. After placing a plastic bag over his hand, the boy removes an egg, cracks evenly all around it with a slim-bladed knife, then quickly and rhythmically uses the knife to peel off the shell. When his careful work is finished, he deftly slices the egg in half and scoops dried *pili pili* into the middle. The whole performance takes less than a minute, and then he is back to wandering among the tables under the strain of his precious cargo.

"The street food isn't what it used to be," Sharon says, delicately eating peanuts, one at a time, as if her hands were little birds. "In the past, you could get turtle, crocodile. Now you have to go to a fancy restaurant to find that."

"The street food will give you the shits," the Hunter says, smiling at me. "But not because it is dirty or unclean. It is merely full of local bacteria that your body is not yet used to. If it were so bad, it would make everyone sick. They call it travelers' diarrhea for a reason: it only afflicts those who are passing through." His eyes are playful in a way I have come to find so comforting, like he knows the role he is playing for me by heart.

The river fish arrives in a neat leaf packet that has been cooked on simmering coals, perfectly poached in a clear broth with onions, tomatoes, and hot peppers. The bones are so tender you can eat them whole. For dessert, we eat fresh beignets with amber forest honey that tastes like nectar.

A few nights later, we take Sharon out to dinner without her son. She is wearing a grey dress with a brilliant-red shawl, a cascade of pearls around her neck, and a shock of fuchsia lipstick and looks much too elegant for us—the Hunter in Chaco sandals and khakis, and me in a wrinkled linen skirt. I admire her expansive energy, the self-determination she radiates, her solitude: a single mother, with a house full of books, putting away the grief of a day spent with mass atrocities to play with her son.

We go to a restaurant famous for its wild game. The restaurant is made to look like you are in a forest village. We sit at a table on an elevated platform with a false ceiling of palm leaves. TVs in the corners play flashy beat-heavy music videos full of fast cars, bling, and bikini-clad women. The restaurant is full of laughter, and I feel warm among so many eating happily.

We order purple-black caterpillars that catch in my throat and crocodile, the flesh white and fishy but firm like meat. We order duiker, although it's impossible to know if it was hunted legally or not. It has been slowly cooked in tomatoes and spices. It is tender and smoky. It tastes neither wild nor domesticated. It tastes like the hard labor of many hands, of chaotic streets, and polluted Kinshasa air. It tastes like the sadness of many millions killed in war, like the pulsating beats of Congolese music and the vivacious colors of their fabrics. It tastes like the cool wet quietude of a threatened forest. It tastes embedded.

With each bite, I am not just tasting meat. I am tasting soil and sunlight, bacteria and metabolites. I am tasting everything the animal once tasted, a web of relations we cannot replicate. I eat a landscape of magic. I eat the past.

⊹ 7 ⊰

SMOKED GAME
AND FAKE CAVIAR

To Let the World Disappear—Thoughts and Details—
Deemed Delicious—Unidentified Meat—Richest, Poorest—
Something of Free Will—Wild Filaments

I DO NOT REMEMBER leaving the Hunter. It is as if in an instant, I am in Paris, and he is no longer by my side. "Remember, no news is good news," he told me before I left. His time is measured by the hunting seasons, and sometimes he might be gone for weeks in the forest. "If you do not hear anything about me, it means I am okay."

How will I get used to him being so far away and out of touch?

I lie in bed and look at our old text messages.

I wish to be in the forest with you today, to let the world disappear.

Yes. It is important to disappear now and then... puss.

═══════════════

At the headquarters for the environmental and pharmaceutical crime department of the National Gendarmerie, the conversation with Lieutenant Colonel Deforest, the deputy head, is long and sprawling. It must be a slow day for illegal wildlife trafficking, or perhaps no one else had ever taken such an interest in his work. He has blue eyes, short bangs, and a goatee-mustache combo grown just past the stubble phase. There are two swords hanging on the wall behind him and a lamp of twisted wood on the filing cabinet.

Massive trade networks transport food products from Africa to the growing diaspora in Europe. Semi-legal container shipments arrive at European ports regularly, packed with vegetables, fish, and fruit. But wild game is brought to Europe in a much different manner. Each week, flights from Kinshasa and other African cities carry immense quantities of smoked meat, crammed into passenger luggage, smuggled by hand. Paris has become a hub of the illegal trade.

"We spend a lot of time going to grocery stores looking for fraud," Deforest says. "Most manufactured products—80 percent or so—are legal. But the rest, there are issues with stickers and logos. Like French products with labels written in Polish. Not serious fraud, but something we are tasked with enforcing. The vegetables and fruits, those are often imported without sanitary declarations—so they might have pests or banned pesticide residue on the peel."

He sits back and smiles, pausing only for a moment before continuing on. Behind him is a plaque declaring him a knight of the brotherhood of Gastronomes of the Sea and Wine Companions, an organization that requires its members to say an oath of loyalty to Muscadet, a type of dry and fruity wine that pairs particularly well with seafood.

"Only some stores sell bushmeat, not all, and at 99 percent of those that do, it is hidden in the back office or underground storage. Most of the time, it's on demand—you have to order it ahead of time. The meat comes mainly through commercial airlines, mostly Air France in hand luggage, so we've conducted systematic raids targeting certain flights from Africa. It's a mix between people bringing meat on opportunity and more formal trafficking. But nobody cares about bushmeat in France, not in terms of the concern for wildlife. And if they do it's because of fears about pathogenic agents—like Ebola."

I had heard about this concern over Ebola from other Westerners as well, but it seemed more rooted in fear than reality. The highest risk comes from hunting the animals, as the hunters are exposed to blood and other bodily fluids. However, there is a slight risk that if the meat trafficked into Paris is raw or not entirely cooked, it could carry the disease. So far no one has gotten sick this way, though.

"In theory you get one year in jail or a €15,000 fine—that's the CITES code for illegal trafficking of endangered species," Deforest says, continuing his explanation of the law. "Although if you are part of an organized crime conspiracy, then it's up to seven years in jail and a €750,000 fine. But wildlife crime really isn't a priority of customs. They are more concerned with narcotics, contraband cigarettes, and counterfeit items."

He turns his computer monitor toward me. "Here, I will show you some videos. For Africans, bushmeat has very symbolic value. It is tradition, yes, but almost religious, like spiritual."

We watch shaky footage of recent airport luggage raids. One woman is visibly distressed—"It's my medicine," she cries as the masked scientists in lab coats and plastic gloves carefully unwrap hunks of meat, which have been packaged in black plastic, white paper, and tinfoil. "I am sick!" she says, over and over. A man in a police uniform tries to calm the woman down.

"Some of the meat we find, like fresh lizard meat, is red and nearly raw and you can see worms," Deforest tells me. "In November 2012, the control at Roissy-Charles de Gaulle Airport found a whole fresh fish, without the eyes, just superficially smoked. It measured four feet by two feet and weighed fifteen to twenty kilograms. Once they found the head of an antelope. Another time, an elephant tail."

I watch the screen as another uniformed man, with a gun in his holster, photographs a jumbled collection of brown smoked pangolin and muskrats that had been confiscated from a different passenger.

"Besides the airports, we also did a raid in December in the Château Rouge neighborhood," Deforest continues. "There were a lot of public order problems with that one. When we arrived, twenty or twenty-five women were lined up on the sidewalk waiting to buy bats. It is a meat that is quite appreciated during Christmas and Easter. So it is understandable, all the women shouting and crying, trying to prevent the confiscation of several dozen kilos of bushmeat. Imagine if all the turkeys in New York were taken away two days before Thanksgiving. There would be riots!"

"What do you do with the meat that you confiscate?" I ask.

"After we are done with it, food control takes it. At first, we were just throwing it away, destroying it by pouring detergent or washing powder on it, and putting trash bags of the denatured meat in front of the stores that were selling it. But then we started hearing stories of people taking the meat inside and washing it—that would produce loads of foam! So now food control has to take it. They burn it."

And then the conversation meanders and Deforest is telling me about all the wildlife trafficking he has encountered in his job. He explains the underground market in France for the ortolan, the tiny songbird that is drowned and cooked in Armagnac, eaten whole, bones and all, while the diner wears a napkin placed over his head, so that, according to tradition, he doesn't offend God with his luxury. He tells me about New Caledonia and French Polynesia and the turtle meat consumed by locals and French citizens. About the endangered glass eel, which is trafficked by highly organized, industrial-scale poachers, who send the live eels by cargo plane to China or Korea, although indirectly, with a detour first to Morocco, where the eels are fattened up before being sent back through Charles de Gaulle, but because they are in transit, customs can't touch them. He tells me about black-market caviar, and Chinese caviar farms, and raids on caviar shops, and "caviar" made of agar-agar, and how the internet is full of fake caviar. He tells me that the iconic escargot snails have been so overharvested in France, they are no longer found in the wild, so they must be sourced from Poland or Hungary. He tells me about the farms for red deer and pheasant and roe deer and ostrich. About zebra farms in Eastern Europe and eating kangaroo, and how the American crayfish was accidentally introduced in France, wiping out the native river crayfish, and that because of heavy pollution and the drying of swamps, their edible frogs have almost disappeared, and now 99 percent must be imported from Turkey or Hungary, Romania or the Czech Republic; he tells me about the savage hunters in Japan and the Faroe Islands killing whales and dolphins, about crocodile farms and donkey sausage, and eventually we arrive at edible bird's nest soup from Borneo, where the most traditional tribes still primarily eat nuts, fruits, and forest vegetables.

"I'm a crazy traveler," he says. "They eat this jungle fern! It has become an urban delicacy. I tried it in Kuching. Very good!"

I can hear my stomach grumbling. It is time for lunch.

In times of war and famine, almost anything will get eaten. Sometimes, those foods become so ingrained within cultures that the prejudices against them not only disappear, but the food is actively desired for generations into the future.

People have rarely eaten carnivorous animals, as they seem to hold a certain unworthiness as human food, but in the winter of 1870, the Franco-Prussian War was in full force and the stomachs of Paris's elite were desperate. They had been under siege for ninety-nine days when the city's gourmands decided to expand the sphere of edible things. The zoo animals of the Jardin d'Acclimatation—originally founded to promote the domestication of exotic species—were bought by an English butcher who made quite a profit selling them at a rate of twenty-five francs per pound. At least two elephants were killed, Castor and Pollux. Their trunks were sold as a gourmet treat for forty-five francs a pound, while the cheaper meat was made into soup.

For the midnight Christmas dinner held by Alexandre Étienne Choron at Voisin, a much-celebrated restaurant located on the rue Saint-Honoré, the menu included *Cat Flanked by Rats*, *Terrine of Antelope*, *Elephant Consommé*, *Roast Camel with Fruit*, *Stuffed Donkey Head*, and *Kangaroo Stew*. The meal was finished with a nice Gruyère cheese and a bottle of 1827 Grand Porto.

Over the course of the war, hunger led Parisians to consume at least seventy thousand horses. After the war, the taste was so desired that horse meat became a staple in butcher shops for the next one hundred years and can still be found in many grocery stores.

In the afternoon, I visit the Forensic Entomology Laboratory, which houses the scientists who analyze the trafficked wild meat after it has been confiscated by law enforcement. I am hoping to gather more information about the kinds of animals they have found.

The entry hallway is hung with pictures of blood and spatter and lined with glass cases full of bones. Voclain Baudin conducts genetic studies for the wildlife crime investigations. Post-it Notes line the sides of his computer.

Baudin is lanky and friendly, with a long neck and specks of grey in his hair. He is much less animated than Deforest and speaks in a roundabout way, diverting this way and that, like an insect. As he talks, he sprinkles in the Latin names of species.

"It's really only in the last three years that there has been such a focus on non-human DNA in criminal investigations. The Barcode of Life project has allowed us to do this work," he says. "We have been working with the National Museum of Natural History. We take meat samples as close to the bones as possible, the bloodiest parts, because otherwise the DNA is likely damaged from the smoking process, or the meat is too dry to obtain good results. About a third of the samples we take are unidentifiable. In some cases, it's because they don't match any of the species in the database. In other cases, it's the stage of decomposition. The DNA is too degraded."

He goes on: "In one targeted search of passenger luggage we found ten species and the trunk of an elephant. In another raid—this one was over the course of ten days, one plane per day from DRC, Congo Republic, and Cameroon—we found three tons of vegetables and fish, and many kilograms of bushmeat! You could smell it in the luggage. But really, it's a huge quantity and diversity. Twenty species! Big rats. Five species of monkey. Snakes—those were very smoked. A mole. We found fresh bats—fruit bats—in decay. *Anthrenus africanus* beetles are frequently found infesting the meat. Crocodiles. A fresh lizard.

Pangolin. Eight of the species were on the CITES list of endangered animals. We confiscated one bat that, at the time, was an unidentified species, now called *Eidolon helium*. Another, earlier operation, they found a six-and-a-half-foot crocodile!"

Baudin pulls out a binder with sample results and images.

"There was *Manis tricuspis*, that one was fresh, well, rather, frozen. And *Thryonomys swinderianus*—also very common coming from Cameroon. Plastic bags with leaves. Ants! Python!"

He turns to an image of a brown lump.

"That one was unidentifiable just from looking at it. So much of the smoked meat is. Some moldy or full of maggots. Of course, the main problem is with disease, you know, Ebola, and the unsanitary condition of the food. But we've confiscated more than thirty kilograms headed for shops in Paris and London. A pangolin is worth a hundred euros. I remember one young woman, very kind. The meat she was transporting was laid out on a whole table in clear plastic bags. She had a very expensive haul there!"

He shows me lots of photos of small dead animals, sagittal cuts of boar, brochettes of unidentified meat, followed by crime scene images of the airport setup: a little room for taking samples and another of a big fridge. The scientists wear turquoise gloves and put the DNA samples in plastic tubes.

He is quiet a moment. Vivaldi plays softly from his computer speakers. "Do you like cryptozoology? There is a very interesting scientific study on the potential genetics of Bigfoot..."

His voice trails off as he begins searching his computer for the article. The room is lined in black, grey, and red metal filing cabinets, each with numerous thin drawers. He catches me looking at them.

"My hobby is collecting butterflies," he says, pointing to the cabinets. "About a hundred cases of specimens, there. I go to South America quite often. I've discovered twenty-five to thirty new species. *Arctiidae*—it has orange and cream genitalia. Beautiful..."

———————

The next day, I wander around the food market at Château Rouge, a neighborhood on the outskirts of Paris with a large community of African expats. *Congo is the richest, poorest country on earth.* Something about that phrase keeps rumbling through my brain. In the streets outside the shops, the market feels nearly as alive as the markets I visited in Kinshasa. There are women pushing shopping carts of maize, with metal grills filled with charcoal for roasting the corn on the spot. Women line the sidewalks, crouching or sitting on small stools. They are from many different countries—Senegal, Guinea, Cameroon, DRC. They are chatting in the shared trade language of Lingala, attempting to outcompete each other with better prices on the same products. Brochettes of small blackened fish—ten euros. Bag of caterpillars—five euros. Purple fruits—five for one euro, twelve for two euros. Kwanga—1.50 euros. Kwanga—four for five euros. Kwanga—one euro.

The women lay their wares on squares of burlap cloth, the corners easily pulled up into a makeshift sack when the market police come around, because selling on the street like this is illegal. False alarms surge through the market. I walk into a shop with a busy meat counter. A newspaper clipping of an image of Mfumu Kimbangu, a Congolese spiritual prophet known for fighting injustice, is pasted to a wall. When it is my turn, the pretty smiling woman behind the counter says no, she does not have bushmeat, and as she talks, her eyes have already moved to the next customer, hands in the air, passing parcels of chicken meat and sausages.

After finding it difficult to interview Congolese women at the market—most refused to talk to me—I am put in touch with Frédéric through a contact. I meet him at the cramped, two-room headquarters for his nonprofit organization, which works to stop the spread of HIV. He agrees to tell me about the experience of eating wild meat as an expat.

When I arrive, Frédéric is sitting at a conference table that takes up nearly the entire room. Some suitcases rest against the wall. He is a thin, balding man with an elegant face. He came to Paris from DRC in the 1970s, just barely in his twenties and an idealist even then. He tells me that bushmeat's wholesomeness is maintained by the smoking method of preservation, and that it is important to know where the meat comes from, although he acknowledges that what he buys in Paris could just as likely come from DRC or another country in the Congo Basin.

Frédéric's wife cooks game when there is a reason to celebrate. How to even imagine a richer life, in which it would be eaten more often? It would be like weekday dinners of caviar and lobster. His family won't take the risk to bring it here because control is increasing. Frédéric believes that wild meat coming from Africa is feared in part because the trade is difficult to regulate, but primarily because of its association with the unknown.

There is an acute dissonance between the white and Congolese perceptions of bushmeat. The white people tell me it's unsanitary. Ebola is seen as a terrorism from the forest, a virus hitching a ride on networks of trade and migration. The Congolese tell me bushmeat is more sanitary, a *source* of health. That the presence of maggots shows the meat has not been adulterated by chemicals. Whose knowledge is true?

It's important to deconstruct our own reality every once in a while. To see something novel you didn't know existed in the familiar. The difficulty then becomes how to reconstruct the world again, with this startling new knowledge, to remake reality with a coexistence of intelligence rather than a succession of beliefs.

Humans have been hunters forever. But we all live so much closer together now, next to fragmented ecosystems experiencing devastating deforestation. The sick and stressed animals at the interface of people and forests has allowed for new diseases to emerge. We pass diseases to the animals, which morph and return to us in the form of new zoonoses.

This of course happens in domesticated and industrialized ranching, too. Swine flu and bird flu are two of the most prominent examples. In the United States, there's concern over chronic wasting disease in deer, which can affect livestock. So why do we consider bushmeat more risky? Perhaps it simply comes down to racism.

———————

That evening, I lie in bed. I write in my notebook, in thick, well-spaced words: *I knew the moment I met him that I had already lost him.*

I put the notebook down and text the Hunter.

Goodnight lover, I write.

Will I ever see him again? Meeting the Hunter didn't feel like destiny but something more like the flow of a river. There is an inevitability to a river. Its general course is known—from high elevation to sea, from small to large, from past to present. Yet it remains unpredictable, subject to internal pressures and oscillations, such that it might abruptly jump its banks, flow over its borders, and find release in a new direction with unexpected ease. Suddenly passive to fate, we glimpse something of free will.

My phone beeps.

Puss and good night. Hold your face and kiss you, he replies.

And I drift off to sleep, knowing we will be together again.

————————

As game disappears—from diets, from the forest—important cultural possibilities are lost with it. We lose an ancient and deep relationship between people and the non-human world. The intimate knowledge of the forest that hunters carry. The culinary inventions of a wild game chef. The increasing standardization and regulation of every aspect of our lives will deny us a future of significant differences. It will be a bland existence.

Is it possible for me to ever fully understand the pleasure and cascade of memories that a bite of buffalo or smoked wild antelope brings?

When families visit relatives in the country, taking with them the products of the city, and return home bearing gifts of game wrapped in brown paper and tied up in string, a very deep ecological history is transported. The market women, the restaurants, the poachers, the hunters, the conservationists and park rangers, the scientists and military are all wound together by wild filaments.

Imagine each piece of meat moving along this chain of trade, visualized not as meat at all but as a living animal. Imagine each step of the way, and all at once: the animals would stream from the forest like a torrent at high tide! Each time the animal changes hands, a new vortex emerges, a momentary configuration, a brief perturbation in transience, and with each step we become enfolded in a cycle of nutrients. We are dispersers of the ancient soil and infinite sunlight, now in the form of dead animal flesh, now transmuting across time and space to be recomposed within the prisms of our own bodies.

PART 3

SEASONS OF FEAST AND FAMINE

⋆ 8 ⋆

MOOSE WITH CHANTERELLES IN CREAM SAUCE

The Rumored Bear—Daybreak at the Black Lake Blind—
Working Country—The Extent of His Experience—The Dust
of Nostalgia—Taking Apart the Body—Virtues and Vices—
Moose Burgers—Notes from Butchering—Ephemera—Unbounded

T IS ON my third day in the forests of northern Sweden that I see the black bear. She is ruddy and heavy skinned, tearing down the mountain toward the safety of the brook below. I can hear her hairs bristling as she runs past me.

I am alone in a hunting blind perched on a moss-covered granite boulder. The Hunter has left me here alone while he goes in search of an injured moose.

The wide view before me is thrown with cut and broken trees, scattered among shiny stumps. Young aspens grow through the slash, and tiny fat birds hop around in the disorder picking at

215

the lowbush blueberry. Behind me the stubble of a wheat field is golden with autumnal decline.

My lookout tower is crudely fashioned from unhewn branches. A pale blue plastic tarp that once made for a rough ceiling has degraded into noisy streamers, and the sun and rain blow through with the fast-moving clouds. It is a good place to watch for moose, as they run from the hills to my left into the valley below.

When the bear startles out of the woods at the top of the rise, the sun is low in the sky, and I am reading Borges, struggling to stay awake through his constant metaphors of mirrors. The body reacts much faster than the mind to sudden animal encounters, and the prospect of death by this wild beast turns me hot. I sit perfectly still and try to slow my breathing. I am a two-minute walk from a field. I can almost see houses across the river. I hear the passing cars. I feel afraid.

A survey of my lunch: thick slabs of pork, burnt hot dogs, the digits of cold pink sausages. I will throw it all at the bear if she returns.

In the late afternoon, I go back to the barn. The old men take a break from their butchering work to gather around and discuss my luck. They are dressed in hunting attire—orange hats, camouflage jackets, thick rubber boots—fashionable and new, but not so fancy as to be prideful nor so clean as to be unsullied by work. Some drink black coffee, sweetened by a sugar cube on the tongue, and like the coffee, their jokes are both strongly bitter and strongly sweet. They look at me with minced grins. They press in toward me.

A short, fat man with a white beard and orange suspenders smokes a little cigar. He has a buck-toothed smile, and when he speaks, his words protrude out of his mouth like he is spitting seeds. "Yes, we heard there was a large bear roaming the hills.

But so far no one has seen it. To see this *Björn*, this is very good fortune." He interrogates me with the sense of authority that comes from standing on one's own land, and his ridiculous little cigar holds a certain weightiness as he teases it through the air. "Should we bring you a new set of pants? You must have shit the ones you are wearing?" he says. "But where was the Hunter? He left you all alone? Out there with a *Björn*?"

The men continue to toss out their jokes, and we all smile through them.

To be a hunter is to chase the light. We hike in at dawn, down an old logging road slowly filling in with new trees. This day promises a break from the steady rain of the day before, which had made sitting watching for moose quite unpleasant. It is still dark out and the mist hanging in the tall Scots pine trees is suspended in a state between ice crystals and dew. The Hunter walks in front of me. His bootlaces are untied, a forgotten detail in the rush to beat the sunrise. We do not speak.

It has been months since I have seen him. He goes home to Sweden for hunting season almost every year, and I was pleased when he invited me to come along. It would be a chance to see him again. To understand him better, in this new environment, immersed in a tradition that weaves throughout his life. To understand myself better, through the act of killing a wild animal for food.

In late fall, these boreal forests take on the beauty of a season in decay. Small-leaved cranberries blush against a slate of reindeer lichen. Paper birch trees shed pulls of silver bark. Lingonberry shrubs proudly display clusters of sour fruit, best harvested after the first night of frost, when they are lustrous with benzoic acid and the last of their summer sugar.

The spruce sap the green from their needles and store it in their roots for the long cold ahead. Their branches wait for winter adorned with tassels of sage-colored beard moss.

218   The tire ruts we have been following disappear into a spongy swamp, a forest of heathered seaweeds. The low hills weep water, pooling at every slight depression. We walk over auburn feather-moss carpets, dimpled with emerald rosettes of new growth and the petite grey stalks of depleted spore capsules.

We are not remembered for long. Our boots sink into the mass. The ground springs back and erases us.

We come to a lake blackened by shadows. Canada geese sound across the cerulean surface, and a couple of grouse respond to the message in scratchy hoots. Woodpeckers hammer the pines. Mist seeps down the forested slope of the opposite shore.

A dilapidated hunting blind is nestled in the shrubs along the shore. It reminds me of the forts I built as a child with flotsam gathered from the side yard. The open-aired hut is constructed of scrap wood and lichened logs, with worn netting draped over the sides. A rustic wooden bench has been placed at the back of the blind, and an old metal canister-drum stove with a jagged pipe and a rust-twisted door sits at an angle near the entrance. The trees overhead release their dewdrops, rattling the green tarp roof in a staccato hymn to the warming morning.

We stoop forward in the low shack and go about our preparations with slow, careful movements. Even this early in the day, before the long hours of silent sitting, we dampen any frantic tendency we may have accidentally carried into the woods with our supplies.

The Hunter unpacks his waxed-canvas backpack with the meticulous consideration of a religious rite. His bag is well used and frayed at the edges. He unstraps his gun and gently sets it on the bench. The stock is made of a dark wood and carved in an intricate geometric pattern. Next, a thermos of hot blueberry tea. Another of coffee. Radio and GPS receiver. Extra warm clothes. Each item is handled as reverently as his gun. He takes out a box of large-caliber rifle cartridges, designed to keep their mass and expand outward upon impact, and places them next to our lunch.

219

I remove my hulking camouflage coat and hunting pants to layer on more clothes over my long underwear—a crimson wool shirt, two wool sweaters, and a heavy, velvety jacket. Another pair of thick wool leggings. A wool balaclava, an orange fleece-lined hat, a thin scarf, and a big checkered scarf. Knitted red-and-blue wrist warmers, then yellow mittens that come to a delicate point at the end—both handmade gifts from the Hunter's mother—and over these, thick leather-palmed mittens. My limbs are stiff and hindered. The tops of the trees turn orange with the rising sun.

Armed for action, situated in a hidden place, we begin the long, slow wait of infinite vigilance. The day's first rays dapple us with light. A shiver passes through my body.

———

Compared to the industrial feedlots where most of our meat comes from, this land is distinctly unspoiled. But it is hardly wild. It is *working country*, made by human hands, a landscape not for observation but for labor. The land is managed for timber forests and farmland, and so, in a way, it is also managed for moose.

To me, a moose is a bizarre animal, an outlandish and abnormal natural invention. The prolonged nose; the tiny tail; the white, gangly legs and splayed feet that kick with tremendous force but were designed for delicately stepping through swamps; the downy, oversized rabbit ears; the prominent eyes; the dewlap of loose flesh hanging below the chin and the massive tongue used to slurp up tender catkins and the leaves of water lilies. The largest adults are nearly ten feet tall. The male's curved antlers look like hardwood, can grow six feet wide, and are shed each winter after mating season. But to the men and women who have hunted since childhood and now teach their own children this way of life, every animal should look like a moose.

Moose rut in early fall and carry their babies until late May—a gestation period a week longer than humans. The babies are born reddish and fuzzy, weighing thirty pounds, and stay under their mother's protection until the following May. Although they will nurse for upward of six months, the calves begin testing different plants within a few weeks of being born—a nip of willow or aspen, a tuft of grass, a leaf of rowan. By late July, they eat a massive amount of vegetation, particularly the buds and shoots of baby spruce and pine. By the approach of their first winter, a healthy calf will weigh three hundred pounds.

Wolves are the natural predators of moose and tend to prune away the weakest individuals. A wolf family can kill 120 moose a year. But in Sweden, wolves have been targeted for extermination since the fourteenth century, when kings Magnus Eriksson and Christopher of Bavaria declared it a civic duty to kill them, as they were seen as a threat to both people and livestock. Under the penalty of a fine, everyone but parish priests and landless women were required to take part in the wolf hunts. Over the next few centuries, the wolf population was decimated.

In the nineteenth century, Swedish forests were maintained as common spaces for grazing livestock and collecting firewood. Locals gathered wild plants to make beer and liquor, and spruce resin was chewed as a refreshing gum. In periods of food scarcity, the inner rind of pine trees was dried and pulverized, then kneaded with rye or oat flour to make a coarse bread.

After World War I, there was a rise in demand for export timber, charcoal, and pulp. As Europe's leading suppliers of trees, Sweden and Finland created a joint export cartel to regulate prices and quantities, as well as defend their positions against the threat of cheap wood coming out of the Soviet Union's vast forests.

By the early 1940s, concern arose over the low volume of remaining timber in the two countries. To remedy the shortage, Sweden adopted the methods of scientific forestry. Over the next five decades, the country's forests were clearcut, drained, burned, sprayed with herbicide, scarified to expose the mineral soil below the leaf litter, dusted with nitrogen fertilizer, and planted with new, even-aged stands of Scots pine and Norway spruce.

With wolf numbers greatly reduced, and each newly planted timber stand providing an ample source of shoots and buds for baby moose to eat, the moose population increased dramatically. The animals' appetites caused significant damage to the tree crops, killing many seedlings and stunting survivors. By the 1980s, there was such a glut of moose, the Swedish Forest Agency enlisted the help of hunters to control this pest. With few laws to regulate the hunt, some individuals shot eight hundred to two thousand moose a year.

Today, hunting in Sweden is highly controlled. Each county sets its bag limits, with input from both the appropriate forestry districts and the local hunters. In order to participate, each hunter must own a certain amount of private forestland property, although some people pay forest owners a bit of "rent" to join a communal hunting party. A lottery determines where each individual is allowed to hunt during the collective chase.

There is a rule that you can't shoot more than one moose at a time, in case you don't kill the first animal and it runs away to suffer. Across Sweden, eighty to a hundred thousand moose— roughly a third of their total population—are killed every year to keep their numbers in the desirable balance.

222

The Hunter has the lithe body of a stripling, and in Congo, he exuded an ageless quality. When I think back to how he looked in our first days together, at the edge of the rainforest, he appears different in each recollection, as if his face changes shape depending on the memory and the mood in which I captured it in my mind.

But this morning, months later and a continent away, his face shows the extent of his experience. I am startled by his greying stubble and deeply lined forehead, uncertain how they can belong to this same man who forgets to tie his shoelaces.

In our time apart, he sent me lots of sweet missives. *Good night my love. I hope I dream of you so I can sleep. Miss you next to me.* But then they would stop, and he would disappear for a while. I have been trying to get used to this inconsistency, to the ambivalence it brings up in me.

I huddle into his warmth as a respite from the cold-bones and monotony. I am not sure the feeling of comfort is reciprocal. He has hunted here many times before without my companionship. We do not speak, even in whispers, for many hours. But I do not mind. It is enough to be next to him again.

The Hunter's childhood in the Democratic Republic of Congo was marked by one requirement—he must master unfamiliar territory. When he was a boy of six or seven, he walked with a friend along an unlit rainforest path that ran between their two villages. They walked alone for an hour amid the gloomy sounds of invisible nocturnal animals. Having conquered this shadowy journey, he never felt afraid of the dark again.

He learned to speak the language of the locals, to hunt with bow and arrow, to eat *fufu* with his hands, and to ride motorcycles barefoot and shirtless. But even as he grew fluent in the forests, he remained as white as his companions were black.

On holiday trips back to Sweden, he tried to unlearn all these things, to replace them with the lessons of subway trams and grocery stores, and he wondered at the novelty of sharing the color of his skin and the blue of his eyes with those around him. He learned to live with the instability of these half-inhabited worlds, and over time the persistent quality of not belonging set itself within him, too. It was in the unknown that he felt most comfortable.

When the Hunter moved to Stockholm for university many years ago, he made a pledge to himself: he would never run to catch a train. To live a life enslaved by someone else's schedule didn't make sense to him—instead, he wanted to embrace all the extravagant possibilities of spontaneity. He refused to submerge his freedom under the institutions of time, and an enduring resistance was fashioned out of those small moments of protest. He did not live with a sense of hurry.

I, too, have tried to live life this way. Maybe it is why I feel so very seen and accepted by him. It is an experience of being present that I have never found with anyone else. A trust in the timing of all things. A celebration of our independence, such that returning to each other is a comfort held in gratitude rather than a lazy acquiescence to the familiar.

Here, in the forest, we live by the clock of nature.

When the sun crests the trees, we eat rye sandwiches piled with cold cuts and butter, and sip hot blueberry tea from a paper cup. It is a welcomed break from the cycle of my thoughts.

I stare into the forest. The hazy vegetal shapes morph into moving animals with each gust of wind, like a rush of phantoms careening through the trees.

The bright-loud crack of the rifle rings out, like someone diving into deep water amplified ten thousand times. The moose has been hit, but he does not fall then. He twitches forward and flees away into the obscuring forest. We wait in the blind, senses alert to the creak of a stick, the snap of a twig. The trees to our left shiver.

The light is cold and stark.

The moose returns some minutes later. Blood pours from his nose and mouth. He walks like a man in chains to his execution—the struggle gone, with only the final death before him. In generous resignation, the moose presents himself to us as an unwilling gift.

The Hunter shoots again, striking below the ear and into the head. The moose drops instantly and is still. Moments later, the back legs kick, the torso rocks a bit, reeling with fatal melancholy, the animal dead but the body intent on releasing obsolete nerve signals sent seconds before the last breath.

As I watch the moose die, my emotions swing between excitement and horror. I've never been hunting before, nor have I seen such a large wild animal die. Still, there is something deeply familiar about it, a feeling just beyond the reach of my memory, not fully formed, like the dust of nostalgia for an experience buried in the heritage of my DNA. I want to kiss the Hunter, now, in this moment, to acknowledge that we are here together, to somehow slow time and float in the stark immensity of existence, but I am as unmoving as he is.

Within mere minutes of death, an animal becomes a carcass.

This is not just a matter of semantics. There is a perceptible shift in the body. It crosses some threshold and living beast becomes insentient flesh, skin, hair, muscle, tissue, blood.

But there is no time to think about the dead animal directly, to consider the weight of mortality. Any elation, sadness, or grief must be ignored. The mind turns to practical matters.

We need to gut the moose quickly before its body heat spoils the meat.

The Hunter is looking tense.

"You don't want to do it?" I ask innocently.

"Yes, but it is a lot of effort," he replies, and I realize that although this is a moment of adventure for me, his experience of nature—his intimate knowledge of it—is one enmeshed in toil. There is no regret, nor any triumph. There is only work to be done.

Our moose is three to four years old, a powerful male with fifteen points on its rack—seven on the left, eight on the right. He looks like the forest in which he has lived. The antlers are a deep golden, spotted with greenish imperfections, like hints of lichen in late fall. His neck is thick, with strong, striated muscle fibers to hold up such large antlers. He is covered in cankerous growths, mushrooming between thick patches of black-brown hair glazed in tiny droplets of water. His eyes bulge out. The blood around his mouth has congealed and darkened.

The Hunter takes his handmade, bone-and-brass-handled hunting knife to the thick, elastic hide of the abdomen. He is careful not to prick the innards, which could spill their noxious gastric juices and make the animal inedible. He deftly cuts upward, with the blade toward the sky.

I pull back on the skin and push against one front leg to further open the belly. The Hunter reaches into the cavity and, with some struggle, carefully severs the tissue at the rear wall of the body. He pulls out the bulbous stomach, then the dusky liver and blooming intestines. He throws the innards steaming into the cold air, onto the soft forest floor. Over many seasons, they will mingle with the detritus of other deaths and replenish the ecosystem where this moose has lived and died.

As we disembowel the moose, there is a brief gurgle, a slight belching, a *pfft* of air, releases more mechanical than biological, signs of the great buildup of pressure inside the animal upon death. The more we work, the stronger the smell becomes. It is a bit like domestic cattle and soil, but mostly it is of earthy bog, as if the perfume of the forest was pulled into the moose's muscles with every breath, held as a kind of life force, and now with these final exhales, these moribund sighs, the odor returns to its source.

The Hunter has blood up to his elbows. He stands over the empty chamber. It is large enough that I could crawl inside it and disappear. I am struck by the sheer volume of blood, glittery red and frothy. The first shot hit the moose just below the shoulder, then passed straight through the lungs. This meant the blood drained away from his skull and into his lungs, where it was oxygenated one final time.

We are nearly finished gutting the animal when we hear a distant shot and chatter on the radio. A young bull is close, pursued by other hunters nearby. We return to the blind and make a charcoal fire in a bucket. We roast hot dogs, which split lengthwise. The ends curl up and the skin shrinks and the innards burst out. They are deliciously hot and crispy and greasy. We drink coffee and more blueberry tea. I eat a candy bar. The Hunter eats grilled sausage cut into rounds, browned at the edges.

Within an hour, the ravens discover us. They perch in the high trees and gossip. Sometimes the excitement of fresh carrion is overwhelming, and they take flight and circle above. The circling is some kind of signal. More birds arrive. They sing the death rites to the sonorous lake.

We build up the fire and sit in silence again. Small gnats buzz the carcass. The moose's front hoof is behind his antler, set stiffly above his head with rigor mortis, and he resembles a playful dog on his back. The distended stomach and intestines lying next to him have become swollen and hard.

After some time, a man arrives with an ATV and a plastic sledge to pull the moose out of the forest. Before we leave, I make an altar to the dead moose, like my parents taught me to do as a child whenever we came across dead wild creatures in the dry arroyos of New Mexico. I place a collection of flowers and bent twigs, curled leaves and smooth stones in a gentle balance against a decaying stump near the red-stained moss where the moose died.

We tear up this mute place attempting to pull out the eight-hundred-pound quarry, great churns of black earth stewed into a brown soup, the sedge grasses, pink and yellow-gold, laid flat. The earth will bear the mark of our actions. It will face the winter with scars on its back.

━━━━━━━━

Back at the barn, the late sun is fading behind a forested hill. The silhouetted spaces between branches are more substantive than the trees, a tangle of deep purple-green shadows. To the east, a vermilion farmhouse with white trim gleams in the setting light. It is some distance away, and partially obscured by the muted rainbows of an unkempt meadow.

A group of men break from their work taking apart the body of a female moose in the barn and congregate in the yard. Some drive hydraulic Range Rovers or big trucks. The less fortunate drive tin-can cars from the Czech Republic. The most insecure among them has nothing good to say. He is always trying to put the others down. "Ah, that's not such a big moose," he says, or "Ah, your shot wasn't so great."

They chew tobacco and pass around a spent bullet retrieved from the body of one of the dead moose. It looks queer and deformed, like a burnished mushroom twisting through the earth. To retain this warped metal, especially if it is placed next to the discarded head of the moose, is meant to bring prosperity to the killer.

Meanwhile another moose arrives. Just as our moose had arrived. The mouth hangs open. The tongue hangs down. The body is in the rigor mortis pose of an elegant ballerina en pointe, as if it had died in the midst of a pirouette. The Hunter's best friend, Tobias, has shot this young buck. He has small, furry bumps, the early sign of horns, and could not have been much older than six months. When the buck fell, he became wedged between two rocks.

Tobias names his hunting dogs after Swedish soccer players, and this was Zlatan's first successful kill after more than a year of rigorous training. Cynegetics—hunting with dogs—is an old art form, and different regions of the world have their own hunting styles and preferences for breed. When a well-bred canine finds a scent, she flattens like a tabletop—sleek tail stiffened, head aimed forward—and then runs toward the quarry in pursuit. The dogs flush the moose out of the woods and toward the hunters waiting in their blinds. If the dog comes across a moose, she barks wildly, keeping the animal in a state of frozen fear until a hunter can catch up and kill it. By listening to a dog's barks, the hunter can tell subtle details of the prey he will find: whether it is alone or in a group, injured or on the run. These dogs wear GPS collars so they are easier to track, which has also cut down on the long-standing tradition of arguing over whose dog brought down the moose.

It takes three men to carry the small calf from the flatbed of the truck to the V-shaped metal dressing cradle. The front legs are skinned. The back feet are removed with an electric saw. Hooks are pushed into the hocks, and the animal is hoisted upward by a rash of chains. His nose touches the floor, as if he were suspended halfway through a front flip. The head is sawed off. The esophagus looks obscene protruding from the neck. There is the smell of bone dust in the air.

The hide is peeled away by an electric winch. It makes a faint sizzle as it disconnects from the luminescent layer of fat. The half-removed skin hangs down like a cape. When the tug of the rope stops, there is the reverberation of dripping blood. The hide will be scraped, salted, and laid on a tarp at the edge of a field. In a few weeks, it will be sold to a leather company.

The flesh beneath the skin is blood red and marbled in alabaster foam. As it cures over the next few days, the mono-chromatic tones will differentiate into pale rose, purple-blue, pink, cerise, and ruby wine. A young calf, much bluer to begin with, will age to a lighter color.

The men saw down the length of the moose, opening up the initial field dressing further. Blood pours out. Any innards not removed immediately after the killing are pulled out. The heart, penis, and testicles are cut out. They spill into a small black bucket. Fur and dirt stick to the raw flesh.

Someone gets a hose and sprays the inside of the carcass. Another person with a rubber squeegee brooms the red-tinted water and the thick ribbons of blackened blood toward a drain in the concrete floor.

One front leg is cut off and tossed out the open barn door, followed by the other. They make the hollow sound of chopped wood as they land in the gravel. The hunting dogs roaming the yard are quick to retrieve these *curée* treats and retire to the grass to chew on them sinisterly.

———————————

Humans have been hunters much longer than they've been herders and farmers, so when we are confronted with the feral violence required to kill a liberated animal, there is an innate reckoning. The Latin verb "to hunt," *venor*, is a deponent verb— passive in form but active in meaning—suggesting that hunting is not only a direct action but also a transitory state of being. Hunting is an ephemeral act that means something different each time it is performed. It ties the body to the forest in ways both physical and metaphysical. It's as if the hunter not only chases the game but hunts himself as well.

A large portion of the hunt is devoted to understanding the peculiarities of the prey animal: what food it eats, when and how it moves, the time of day and year it is most active. If the habits of the prey animal change over the course of its life, the hunter will know this too. To be a hunter is to be aware of the virtues and vices of an entire landscape.

Hunting has always been an ecological act. Just the fear of a predator can make prey act timid, the effects of which ripple through the entire ecosystem, eventually affecting even the vegetation and carbon cycle by shifting the location of grazing animals. In these ecologies of fear, it is the weak and odd animals—sick, deformed, discolored, very young and very old—that are most often killed. Hunting—like all predation— is a force that pushes forward evolution, making prey animals stronger, faster, or more evasive.

Hunting may seem like a relic activity, an archaic and brutal form of acquiring food that has become more symbolic than essential in today's world. But hunters have always used the most modern technology available to them, and the moose hunt is no exception. It relies on so many of the trappings of civilization that it begins to resemble the simulations of war. With each invention, the killing becomes more efficient.

Yet hunting remains rooted in the peculiarities of its traditions, and hunters are perhaps the most agile naturalists left among us. As it borrows from this heritage, hunting is set apart as an activity that is outside the progressive thrust of history. In its ability to be both modern and archaic, sport and necessity, hunting is its own moral impossibility.

———————

That evening, after we have killed and dressed our moose, we take good hot showers and sit with cold beers around the large metal island in the kitchen. We are staying with Tobias, his wife Sasha, and their three little girls in a rambling farmhouse overlooking a wide river valley. The train tracks run nearby, and the rumble can be heard faintly at regular intervals throughout the day.

The kitchen is the only room to have been recently renovated, and the garnet walls and black-and-white checkerboard floor are quite different from the rest of the house, with its stray rusty nails, doors that don't shut properly, and carpeting mounding upward from unseen moisture—each room hoarded to the ceiling with stuff, some useful, some garbage, all seemingly unorganized. It is difficult to tell if the residence is well lived in or just neglected.

A Russian submarine has been discovered a few miles off the coast of Stockholm, violating Swedish sovereignty agreements, but we are more interested in discussing our hunting success than the new Cold War. As we talk, Sasha cooks moose burgers and crispy baked potatoes, a meal less elaborate than some of her others during my visit, but made with equal precision and skill. She has a new, six-burner stove and a Sub-Zero refrigerator. The kitchen is stocked with fancy Japanese knives and equipment to purée, sous vide, confit, and cure. A shelf above our heads spans two walls of the room, neatly displaying cookbooks detailing the elaborate techniques of molecular gastronomy.

Sasha was adopted as a child from Sri Lanka, and when she learned to hunt, she made herself a part of Sweden. Sometimes, her little girls go hunting too, but on this and many other occasions, they are glued to the screens of their iPads. Sasha is in a good mood, as cooking game is one of her favorite things to do, and the room buzzes with the accomplishments of the day.

"My grandfather started our hunting club," Sasha says as she cuts up potatoes and sprinkles them with salt and olive oil. "My father never learned anything because his dad did it all, but my brother and I, we watched. We learned a bit. And one day Tobias said to me, 'Okay, Sasha, it's your turn to take over.'"

Tobias is tall and wiry and has a hard time sitting still without something to occupy his hands. As we sit around the kitchen island, he is taking apart and cleaning his gun.

"Our hunting group is very friendly with the one next to us. But they have a problem with a neighboring group who tries to steal their moose," Tobias says, finishing his beer and opening another. "Although hunting moose here is more like culling moose. We are practically feeding them with all the trees we plant."

"Yes, up here in the north, we are sick of moose meat," the Hunter says. "But down in the south, it is not so common, and people love it."

"We could make a fortune from our meat!" Tobias responds.

After dinner, as Sasha puts the girls to bed, Balvenie whiskey is poured and talk turns to a topic not often discussed—tracking and killing injured quarry that has gotten away.

"We have laws about not letting the animal suffer," Tobias says, "but there are so many miraculous stories of animal survival. How are we to determine when to stop that fight, that struggle? Instead, you do this to feel better about yourself, because otherwise you couldn't live with yourself—knowing you are causing this suffering. Even though in many ways, it is the wrong thing to do. To chase down this injured animal and make sure it meets death."

"Do you remember that story of the bear in northern Sweden?" the Hunter says. "The one who was shot in the eye and tagged and given antibiotics? Well a few years later, he was the biggest and the best. He became the pack leader."

On the far wall of the kitchen, a magazine article has been pinned up. It is a story about the Hunter. About him taking down the most notorious criminals involved in the illegal wildlife trade in the Democratic Republic of Congo. There are photos of men with automatic weapons and bonobo mothers, with hanging teats, high up in the canopy trees. In another picture, the Hunter grins through his crooked teeth, like a boy with a secret. But his sweet-pea blue eyes are sad and his brow is wrinkled. I am absorbed in the image, trying to square this flat depiction of his work with a reality that is so much more complicated.

The Hunter's soft lilt brings me back from the past and into the kitchen again.

The men are still discussing the act of killing. To me, the death of the moose was sudden, but for skilled hunters like them, who've spent more of their lives in the natural world than most people, the killing takes place in their minds some time before, days earlier, long before the prey is even seen.

"You see, killing is the easy part," Tobias says as he pours more whiskey into my glass. "It is the decision to do so that is difficult."

"Yes, it is true, my dear," the Hunter says, gazing at me adoringly. "Even so, sometimes you might shoot a moose straight in the heart, and it will keep on running."

234

On butchering day—the last day of the hunt—everyone from the hunting association convenes at the barn. It is early, and the peeling black-and-scarlet metal doors are hinged open to the smoky blue light of daybreak. A girl sits on a parked ATV with her younger brother and watches the activity inside.

The girl has dark hair and murky eyes. Her skin is sallow, and a front of greasy bangs sweeps across her forehead above feral eyebrows. She is twelve or thirteen, and by the way she holds herself, it is evident she does not yet feel steady within a body that insists on aging. The girl watches the men in the barn do their butchering work with a look of longing absent in her childish brother. On the grass next to her is a moose head. Curious flies examine the bark of its antlers and the dried blood around its throat.

The boy is blond and distracted, but the day before, when he drove the ATV into the yard pulling a moose on a plastic sledge, he was talkative and looked much older than his seven years. Now he stares quietly at the naked moose carcasses, which hang in a macabre line from the barn ceiling like a still-life painting.

A pair of geese honk by. Small black-and-yellow birds ply the fields. A flock of blue jays rise from the line of trees. They fly west briefly, then arc east. Moose legs, chewed down to the bone, litter the yard.

Behind the barn, three men build a wood fire in the lower part of a rusted metal barrel stove with a tall, thin chimney. Inside the top half, water slowly comes to a boil. The steam and smoke of the fire mingle with the steam of their breath and the smoke of their cigarettes, and this sundry cloud leisurely drifts toward the sunrise. It gathers in the trees next to the adjacent field like a rising fog. The men fill black buckets with the boiling water.

235

Another group is stooped over teal plastic bins, numbered one through forty-six, although at least ten numbers are missing. The bins are laid out in front of the garage in three rows—two long and the other short. The garage door is open, and the inside is crammed with bikes, old furniture, discarded items, piles. Six bins are removed, seemingly at random, and brought to the fire. The men pour in an inch of hot water and add a squeeze of green liquid soap. Each bin is scrubbed, then rinsed with the garden hose.

The first time I saw an animal killed and butchered was in New Mexico. I was twenty-five and my friend decided to have a pig roast for his birthday. We bought a live one from a man named Elvis, who lived on San Felipe Pueblo. After we unloaded the sow from the truck, we gave her cheap white wine and let her drunkenly wander the dusty yard. My friend Katherine Lee shot the sow in the head with a .44 Magnum revolver. Did it require two shots? I can't remember.

This was a new tradition for us, and we didn't entirely know what we were doing. It wasn't an unthoughtful act or done purely for indulgence. It was an attempt to remake an ancient pattern in the fabric of our disconnected lives. To kill what we ate. Hung by her haunches, dipped in an oil drum of boiling water, and seared with a blowtorch. The art of killing hadn't been passed down by fathers and mothers. We found it in the pages of forgotten books.

In the half-light of this morning, though, eleven men, ages fourteen to seventy, and two women, both mothers, work steadily in the barn. They do not speak often, but the occasional glint of their knives silently signals the progress of their work. The unmaking of the moose is highly ritualized: like medieval aristocracy after a chivalrous deer hunt, everyone knows their rank and role. The order in which the carcass would be dismembered was never discussed but known from many years of practice. They have done this a long time and know where to place the knife.

The cavernous room is laid out with a row of makeshift tables, wood planks resting on sawhorses covered in thick white plastic sheeting. Where the plastic is not long enough, black garbage bags have been sliced down the sides and laid flat. The carcasses hang in a giant, ugly row against a white wall. They are massive and overbearing. In this oversized butcher shop, we have all shrunk.

One man wears a Bluetooth receiver in his ear and a full white Tyvek suit. His black belt is threaded through a clear plastic double-sized sheath that holds two blue-handled knives, side by side. Two white towels are looped through the belt, one at his belly and the other at his mid back. A moose-butchering ninja. He drives a Hummer, and as he works, he complains about how much gas it uses. Wires and cords dangle from his pockets.

Everyone else wears plastic aprons. Most wear clear-white surgical gloves, vinyl, powder-free. A few wear thicker rubber ones. Next to the box of surgical gloves rests a carton of Aqua Resist bandages and a roll of paper towels splattered in blood. I hear the sound of a knife sharpener, but do not know which one—there are at least three kinds.

There is something tender about butchering. The fingertips lightly pulling the meat. Swift little cuts like quick kisses. The meat glistens with a layer of fat. Breaking down the animal is gruesome but carefully attended to, conducted with restraint and notable joy.

Archaeologists study the fossilized bones of hunted animals for the marks of butchery. The striations of the cuts and blemishes from sawing and chopping tell as much about the culture that consumed the beast, and the methods of its distribution, as do other artifacts.

I watch the butchers do their fluid work, and the old man with the little cigar watches too.

The front legs are sawed off. A man on a wooden stepladder cuts away the meat and fat of the belly in large pieces and tosses them down onto the tables. The large pieces are cut into smaller pieces by a line of workers below. The chest cavity widens with each slice. The man pokes the meat between the ribs with the tip of the knife. It sounds tight going in.

He saws through the rib cage along either side of the spine, all the way to the back haunches. The ribs are cut off and thrown onto the table with a loud smack. The carcass looks like a grotesque, long-necked bird hanging upside down.

The spine is sliced off at the midpoint.

Finally, the hips and hind thighs are cleaved in half from the bottom up. When they come apart, the separated legs clap together as if they are applauding.

At the tables, the men and women go about their work with calm, committed movements. They carve meat away from bones and ball joints: where the back encounters the shoulder; the inner thigh; above the butt; from the cage of the ribs in long, narrow pieces. They trim the thin white fat away from the solid red flesh.

Sasha wears a brown baseball cap, and her dark hair is tied back. Her pants and boots and shirt sleeves are splattered with blood and blobs of meat goop, but she does not notice.

During short breaks, the butchers eat pastries with bloodied gloves, popped into mouths quickly, and gulp at polystyrene cups of stale coffee. They pass thin slices of salted, peppered, and sugar-cured meat from last year's hunt.

238   The oldest men no longer trim the primals—their eyesight is not so good anymore—but that does not remove them from the work. They carry red-stained black buckets and rinse and scour them with white kitchen scrubbers. The little boy tosses the scrap bones into the back of a small trailer attached to the ATV. There is blood on his face, lightly rubbed over his nose. Each time he emerges to toss out an unwanted chunk, he is illuminated by slanted sunlight. At the end of the day, this pile of waste will be returned to the woods.

When the sun fully crests the eastern hills, and the last of the night's rain clouds blow away, the harsh rays stream in, making the butchering look beautiful but the work more difficult. So the hinged doors are closed, leaving just a small gap for the boy to transport the bones and the old men to bring out the finished cuts. The barn is dim. The uneven light casts ornate shadows.

Another table is brought out from the wall into the center of the room.

Within an hour, one moose is gone and another halfway. In two hours, there are four bins full of meat to grind, about a hundred pounds in each, and a long table outside of prime cuts, arranged by kind. Loin, medallion, rasher, rack, escalope. Later, these will be placed in the teal bins and divided up as evenly as possible, not only by weight but by quality. Everyone will draw numbers to decide which bin they will take home.

At midday, there is pea soup and open-faced sandwiches and the flies have gathered to inspect the effort. There are three full moose left, small calves, and one more at the long-necked bird stage. Ten people work at the butchering tables. The wild is ordered, labeled, numbered. The moose is reduced into meat.

Before hunting became a privilege—the rewards reserved for

a few—it was a communal liturgy. Producing food was both a challenge and a confession of loyalty and love. It was magic and spirit tied to the material. It existed in a community so that each member came to know that she was constituted not only by her own thoughts and actions but by the thoughts and actions of others. Together they made a map for how to live. This is how such work derives its power. Through careful repetition, we make relations with the land. Today, the daily work is usually concealed and done by others. Most of us can hardly imagine acquiring food with such attentive reverence.

As the evening sets in, the Hunter and I drive dirt roads past farms and forests, and talk about what it might be like to live here among the wet-fragrant woods, built by generations of snowfalls and decay. We stop to admire a cute red cottage overlooking the river valley. "I've built a home like this before," the Hunter says solemnly. I wonder who he built it for, where she is now, but quickly turn my thoughts to our own future together.

"Someday I will take you to New Mexico," I say. "I have friends who hunt elk there. Like moose. We could go with them."

"Someday, I would very much like that," he replies with a smile.

━━━━━━

The Hunter has given the head of our moose to another hunter, who admired it for being the largest, with the most antler points, of this year's hunt. But he has held onto the slug. To him, the lethal bullet is the more important trophy. It keeps the death with him. And yet, he cannot keep track of it. One night, I find it in the pocket of a pair of his pants while looking for something else in a pile of dirty clothes. I stick the metal flower behind the elastic band of my underwear for him to find. "Lie back on the bed," I tell him. "I have a surprise for you." He misplaces it again the following morning, but discovers it and puts it in his toiletry bag. A few days later, he mislays it once more, and after I locate it, lost among life's rubble, he agrees to leave it at his parents' house in Stockholm for good keeping.

The beauty of the hunt lies not in its particularities and details but in the battle of instincts. The prey animal is perfectly matched to the predator. The hunter pursues with sharp weaponry and reason. The hunted flaunts speed and graceful evasion, making itself seem to be merely an illusion of the predator. By taking a life, the predator pays homage to the prey's strength, and defines its own strength in the same act.

How foolish, then, to catalog the contours of our moose's body and pore over the details of his corpse. I'd hoped these visible attributes of his death might reveal something of his hidden life. But the wild can never contain some pure, knowable essence, for in becoming absolute and static, each minute internal oscillation would cease to exist at all. Enthroned in his casket of lush moss, the moose was a momentary temple to nature's ceaseless striving.

To the moose, these boreal forests were a terrain of war. But to me, this land holds its own legend, and to labor upon it was to worship it, was a kind of ceremony.

When we go to bed that evening, the acoustic splash of the bullet echoes in my mind. I close my eyes, and the Hunter speaks softly, as if to himself. "My heart is stuck," he says. I fall asleep to these ringing words, uncertain of exactly what they mean.

———————

We travel south to the Hunter's cabin to have some time alone. I feel unbounded. During the day, he goes hunting, and I lie on the couch idly reading about the spread of HIV out of Congo's forests on highways of trade and prostitution. I stoke the cast-iron stove with split wood, doze, and stare at the fading light.

When the Hunter returns, he prepares moose flank in cream sauce with gathered forest chanterelles. He sets the cast-iron pan on the wooden table, and I light a candle. The meat is delicious and tender. The mushrooms are supple and faintly sweet. I could get used to eating like this.

After dinner, we drink red wine and dance, half-dressed, to French punk music in the darkened living room. The wood stove glows from the kitchen. Outside, the forest is cold and quiet. In this moment, there is nothing new to be learned. I am home. The Hunter's smell mingles in the fabric of my skin and the folds of my hair, and I carry it with me as long as I can.

A few days later, I board a bus to the Stockholm airport. The rain slaps the windows, and the Hunter fades into a blur of water. The frozen, vacuum-sealed moose in my suitcase begins to thaw.

⋆ 9 ⋆

NESTS AND
BLOOMS

*Packing Again—Finding the Boat—Anatomy of an Emperor—Two-Way
Domestication—Pure Money from Heaven—Caves and Crevices—A Rat
Ecosystem—In Search of Something—Writing by Candlelight—Forest Phero-
mones—A Tale of Two Futures—Memories of the Hunter—Ancient Soup*

MY DAD HAS been slowly preparing me for the apocalypse. It is subtle. Each birthday or Christmas, a new tool to add to the mix. A Mylar blanket. A PocketMonkey. A Survival Frog whistle. I keep them in a drawer with my knife collection. I don't think these gifts come from a place of paranoia, but from a desire for me to be self-reliant. A few years ago, he taught himself to hunt. And now he sends me gifts of elk jerky and dried cherries.

I am thinking of this one night in December as I pack for another trip, this time to the island of Borneo in Southeast Asia. I pull open the drawer with his mess of presents, wondering if

I will need any of them. Will a heavy-duty flashlight come in handy?

I'm slightly drunk, so when I arrive at my destination, unpacking my suitcase will be a surprise. Sundress. Leech socks. Chaco sandals.

For someone like me, it is staying home that is hard. I have always been like this. I like the excitement of seeing far-off places, of exploring, putting myself in just the smallest bit of danger, surrounded by new smells. I like the experience of watching myself searching.

Is this why I want to fly around the world looking for wild things to eat? To remember that feeling from childhood of indulging in a curious appetite? First aid kit. Audio recorder. Rain jacket. Camera.

The Hunter has been increasingly distant since I visited him in Sweden. Our weekly Skype calls have stopped. No more sweet messages—*Sleep well love, think of me holding you, keeping you warm.* No more veiled poetry—*Yes my love, so empty in the bed and you've now slept next to me in all my beds so all are empty.* In fact, I haven't heard from him for nearly a month. *No news is good news,* I remember him saying.

Maybe I'm to blame. I'm not the most tamable woman. Binoculars. Waterproof notebook. Field pants. Should I pack a knife?

———————

I'm on the back of a motorcycle driven by a geriatric misogynist. He is dressed in military fatigues and driving fast down a wide dirt road lined in towering electric poles under construction. I'm on my way to a little village in the highland mountains of Borneo that is only accessible by boat. We are trying to find the boat.

Johnny, "Joh-nay Be Good" as he calls himself, works part-time at the airport greeting people and chain-smoking. He wears a gold cross charm necklace, and with each bump, it flies up into the wind. I hold on tightly as we pass over a worn-out wooden bridge, bike wheels precariously stuck in the ruts. We hit a deep pothole and my butt leaves the seat. "Ah, now we are horse-riding!" Joh-nay Be Good shouts. "I am an Indian chief and I've kidnapped you from your father. Am I a dirty bad man? No, I am a *romantic.*"

The ride is exquisitely uncomfortable and seems to be taking forever. If I mince the minutes or fence about the passing of time, it becomes unbearable. Perhaps I should give up an explanation for this moment in order to experience it?

When we finally find the boat, it is just about to leave, and I am unexpected weight. I squeeze in with five other women, fierce-eyed all of them, who laugh in giggly ripples as the water nearly tops over the sides of the tipsy, overloaded wooden boat. The motor is not quite powerful enough, so we make our way upstream slowly.

Driftwood logs and eddies of bamboo float downstream, obstacles to be avoided, and occasionally the overhanging tree branches are so low, they caress our ducked heads. The air is wet and damp. The water is cool. The sun beats down, and it is hotter than possible.

Water skaters collect themselves in groups on branches poking out of the river, then shoot out like Roman candles as the boat passes. A white butterfly fringed in black dips down to drink. Maroon dragonflies flirt along the edges of our wake. A green kingfisher hoops over us. All I can hear is the drone of the engine and the rush of wind. Around a bend, on a sandy beach, we see a peacock-like bird. The women point their fingers like a gun and say *boom*.

After we disembark, the hour walk to the village is up and down mountains of rare rhododendrons and exotic orchids, punctuated by bouts of shin-deep mud.

246　　This adventure began simply enough. I wanted to study the trade in edible bird's nests, which are made from the spit of a cave-dwelling bird called a swiftlet and have become one of the most expensive wild food products in the world. Often prepared as a soup, these spit nests are deeply ingrained in Chinese mythology and tradition. There is a long history of nest collection from the limestone caves that pocket Borneo's tropical forests. Some swiftlet species use echolocation—like bats—to navigate the underground caverns. Some of these caves were once occupied by millions of birds at a time.

———

The first time I see the edible nests for sale is on my way to Borneo, at the Shan Medical Hall in Singapore. Behind a long glass counter, there is a bank of wooden drawers with decorative brass pulls and rows of mirrored shelves lined with jars. Beneath the lighted countertop, flat borosilicate glass pans display more mounds of products. Amber-colored powders, fans of desiccated worms, shaves of bark, twisted dried fruit, flakes of ivory wood, lumps of peat, sea slugs like old pickles, sea fans the color of cream, tropical seedpods, roots like gnarled fingers, mushrooms of all sorts, and piles of bones. A wild pharmacopeia.

The shop was established in 1955 and looks as though it has hardly changed since. The customer seated on a marble stool in front of the counter is much the same. His skin is very fine and unwrinkled, and it is difficult to tell if his mass of ebony hair is dyed or naturally still dark. He's dressed casually, in a long, tan T-shirt and ill-fitting jeans, but carries himself as if he has the anatomy of an emperor. "How old do you think I am?" the customer asks me in a soft, musical voice that makes his vanity seem friendly. "You will not believe it if I told you."

Some origin stories are lost to time. This is certainly true for the trade in edible bird's nest. Chinese porcelain dating to the Ming dynasty (1368 to 1644 CE) has been found in Southeast Asian caves where bird's nest would have been harvested, and archaeologists believe this is strong evidence that these items were exchanged during this period. Chinese merchant ships followed the cycles of the monsoon, traveling south in summer and making the reverse trip in the winter when the winds shifted north. They traded porcelain, textiles, and glass beads for tropical products including fragrant woods, pepper, and wild animals. These fortune seekers knew that whomever could bring back foods with the most precious taste would gain favor with the Beijing elites.

In one story, the famous explorer Zheng He presented a chest of sixty bird's nests to the Yongle Emperor. He was duly intrigued, but it was such a small quantity, and he had hundreds of noble consorts and imperial concubines. How would he decide who would share the pleasure of experiencing this new flavor? He certainly didn't want these neurasthenic women fighting among themselves. So he ordered the cook to prepare a soup that everyone could share at a feast in the opulently carved Hall of Splendid Canopy. They loved it so much, the emperor declared it a royal delicacy.

By the early seventeenth century, bird's nest soup was fully entrenched as an important food for wealthy Chinese. It was served at the Manchu Han Imperial Feast in 1636—a banquet that lasted three days, with over three hundred dishes—as one of the "Thirty-Two Delicacies," along with shark's fin, dried sea cucumbers, bear paws, fish maw, live monkey's brains, deer tendons, ape's lips, quail, peacock, swan, and rhinoceros tails.

Not only an elite food, bird's nest was increasingly viewed as a medicine. In *Dream of the Red Chamber*, written by Cao Xueqin in 1791 and considered to be one of the oldest and longest novels in the world, bird's nest is suggested as a necessary, although expensive, remedy for the respiratory ailment that afflicts the main character, Black Jade.

In the distance between source and consumption, myths filled in the gaps of knowledge about the birds that made these nests. They were said to take their water from the clouds and build their nests of whale sperm, seaweed, ocean spray, or wind. The birds were supposedly too weak to stand, so their feet never touched the ground. The result was a bird of magnificent purity.

This sentiment has endured through the centuries. "How do I look so young?" the eager shopper I have been chatting to continues. "Well, I take ginseng and Cordyceps—one every other day—and crocodile oil. This will cost me $3,500." He gestures to the pharmacist weighing out concoctions on an old pan balance hanging from a notched stick.

"But primarily it is the bird's nest that keeps me young." He points to some jars on the shelf behind the pharmacist. Inside are quarter-moon-shaped cups woven from translucent strands of hardened spit, like delicate baskets of layered lace. They are organized by color, from bleached white to honey to lemon yellow.

"It is very good for women, too," he says, smiling, his eyes gleaming with a mix of mystery and forcefulness, as if he has just shared the secret of immortal life. "The wild nests are double or triple the price of the farmed nests, but they are worth the cost." Another smile, but this one is turned inward as his gaze settles back on the pharmacist, so I leave him to his obsession with the past and worry over the future.

That evening I text with the Hunter.

Me: *You've been so quiet. Are you mad at me for something? I miss feeling your love. I feel like I've lost you.*

Him: *No not at all, just quiet.*

Me: *Why quiet?*

Him: *Don't know... Not much to say I guess. My existence goes quiet sometimes, just reflecting on all this craziness around.*

Me: *Well I look forward to when you emerge from your quiet again and want to be in my life. Enjoy the cold forest. Kiss.*

Him: *Oh, didn't realize I wasn't. Kiss.*

Jet-lagged fever dreams. The Hunter is covered in ashes. I hold him tightly, hold onto his frenetic energy, like he's a scared child, and then we both sink into a calm silence.

———

"Historically it was an imperial dish. But we all eat imperial foods these days, don't we?" Lord Cranbrook says, cocking his head to one side, his long, distinguished nose offset by a head of fluffy white hair. He speaks each word in a mannered British accent, as if it took years of practice to master just the right tenor and emphasis. "It's not really a gourmet food for the rich; it's a therapy. Traditionally, bird's nest was steamed in a porcelain vessel, on a double boiler, for a long time, with just a touch of ginger in it. Then at the end of the day, you sit down, calm down, and you reflect on things. You have a quiet conversation and you sit with these little glasses of fluid. It is quite solemn."

He shifts toward me and widens his pale eyes. "And now in Hong Kong they've reduced it to a pill!"

He pauses to chuckle to himself. "I was once at a dinner party and all the men around the table started telling me, 'Look, you've let yourself go, and if you start eating bird's nest every day, you might smooth your skin out.' Well, I used to joke, 'He's a rich man, he probably does take bird's nest every day, but he can also afford a good dentist and a good doctor!'"

Dr. Gathorne Gathorne-Hardy, the Fifth Earl of Cranbrook, is in his eighties and a legend among zooarchaeologists and conservationists. He has spent nearly his entire career in Borneo, and it is rumored that his torso is covered in traditional Iban headhunting tattoos. He's been returning to the hotel in Kuala Lumpur where we meet for so many years that the staff keeps a bag of his belongings in storage between visits.

As one of the first people to study the biology of the edible-nest swiftlet, Lord Cranbrook has an encyclopedic knowledge of the birds. Swiftlets have a natural habitat range throughout the tropical archipelagos of Southeast Asia. Of the twenty-four species, only a few produce edible nests. The two most commercially exploited are the prized white-nest swiftlet, with nests consisting of 95 percent pure saliva, and the black-nest swiftlet, with nests containing around 50 percent feathers.

During the past three decades, overharvesting in caves has led to a crash in the wild population, and nearly 95 percent of Borneo's edible-nest swiftlets are gone. People have begun raising the birds in specially built houses, and Lord Cranbrook's current project is trying to understand the genetics of these semi-domesticated house birds, which appear to be a new hybrid white-nest subspecies.

"Domestication has been a two-way process. It's the birds who started it! It's the birds who came into houses first!" he tells me excitedly.

From what Cranbrook can deduce, the Javan white-nest subspecies in Indonesia began nesting in people's homes on their own volition sometime around 1880. In the 1930s, an economic slump led to an excess of abandoned shop houses, providing more habitat for the birds. After World War II, people began to darken the houses to encourage the birds, making them more like caves, and adding horizontal struts to the ceilings to create corner spaces where the birds like to nest. By the 1970s, people in Java had discovered that you could transfer eggs from the desirable white-nest bird into the nests of the more common non-productive swiftlet varieties, and they would incubate and hatch. As adults, the white-nest birds would breed in this new location. People started transferring the white-nest eggs all over the Southeast Asian archipelago, thus establishing new white-nest colonies. Eventually, entrepreneurs started building cave-like concrete birdhouses specifically to rear the birds, a process called swiftlet ranching.

With the expansion of China's economy in the 1990s, the demand for bird's nests grew tremendously. Caves were over-harvested with little regard for the life cycle of the birds, and the trade became increasingly disorganized, illicit, and violent. The population of wild birds crashed dramatically all across Malaysia. A meeting was held in 1994 to consider placing the edible-nest swiftlet on the Endangered Species List, but as the proceedings continued, more and more swiftlet ranchers came forward to testify about their birdhouses, determined to convince the panel that the birds were not in fact a threatened species. For the first time, the true extent of the industry was known.

"Astonishing change over the last years," Cranbrook tells me. "A lot of optimistic building—eight thousand birdhouses in the state of Johor alone."

There are specialized architects and consultants swilling advice, and legions of Facebook groups dedicated to hashing out the finer merits of the bird business. To prevent infestations of dust mites, bacteria, cockroaches, and bird bugs, the houses are routinely sprayed with insect repellants. Control rooms regulate humidity and temperature. The houses are generally made of concrete, some of which was likely quarried from empty limestone caves that once housed wild swiftlets.

At the same time, there have been protests and ongoing struggles to remove nest houses from cities. The smell wafting from these buildings can be unbearable, as can the noise. The screeching melodies of recorded swiftlets—up to 180 different sounds, including one song titled "Duress"—are played on both internal and external speakers, twenty-four hours a day, to attract and soothe the birds.

"Part of the process of domestication is that these birds are now looking for houses to build their nests in, which you can explain in simple ornithological terms," Cranbrook says. "The bird knows where it should build its nest from its natal experience. It's a natural behavior to return. But that's what I find one of the most interesting things—these birds have no inclination to return to the wild."

Nest houses are harvested each month, with at least 30 percent of the nests left behind to protect the breeding stock. Each breeding pair is harvested up to four times a year. Wild cave nests, though, must follow the seasons and are usually harvested just three times a year. Because of the rarity of wild nests, they cost nearly four times as much as the house nests. One wholesaler told me he had sold two kilograms of wild cave nests for US$43,000.

"People say the house nests are soft, pulpy, disintegrate in water too quickly, and that only the wild nest has got real value, but it's up to opinions," Cranbrook says. "What is very distressing is that the tremendous rise in house farms has not prevented the continued looting of the wild caves." As he explains, large caves often have many entrances, making them highly accessible to thieves. Only if you have a comparably small cave—and money to pay for guards—is it possible to manage the caves properly, allowing for at least one reproduction cycle to occur each year.

"The high price has stimulated constant theft and misman-agement by ignorant people who don't know what the breeding cycle is," Cranbrook says, leaning forward. "Some of them look like complete gangsters, with gold, gold all over themselves. Even the houses must absolutely have guards, burglar alarms, intruder alarms, CCTV monitors. People will get a bulldozer and knock the house down."

The wildlife laws in Malaysia state that swiftlets (genus *Aero-dramus*) are a protected species. It is illegal to have, hold, or handle them. At the same time, the agricultural department has a special section for the promotion of swiftlet house-farming.

Cranbrook lifts his eyebrows. "The law is very peculiar. They haven't worked out whether this is or is not a domesticated bird. So that's a bit of a dilemma. And as it so often goes in the world, you've got a law that is being totally disregarded by the lawmakers. I don't think an X-ray machine can see the nests if your suitcase is full of them. They haven't got sniffer dogs trained to detect them yet, so I suspect there's a great deal of informal trade."

Although Cranbrook has the objective quality of a scientist, he clearly hates to see the loss of wild birds—not for sentimen-tal reasons but because it makes what he studies less interesting. As he speaks about his recent research expedition, there is no mistaking the curiosity that fuels him.

"We took a fishing boat two hours out to this island with the most beautiful cave. I spent an enormous amount of money and only caught one bird. And it was the wrong species! Most expensive bird..." His eyes flare and he lets out a hearty laugh. "But it was such a good adventure, I don't mind a bit.

"Luckily, I've got a friend with a micro-pathology labora-tory in England, so this poor bird had his mouth thoroughly swabbed for my genetic studies, and I pulled out two feathers. You know, it's quite difficult to go into a house and say, 'Excuse me, may I kill a few of your birds.' But if you say, 'May I take mouth swabs...'"

"So you don't have a suitcase full of dead birds?"

"No, just a tiny package of mouth swabs. Ah, it was such a good adventure." His cheeks flush with the memory. "I'm not sure I shall be back. I'll see..."

His gaze returns to me, wistful and nostalgic.

––––––––––––

Once a home-based cottage industry dependent on wild cave birds, the edible bird's nest market is now worth over US$5 billion. The therapeutic claims are generous: bird's nest will make the skin supple and pure; provide relief from cough, phlegm, and sore throats; cure insomnia, joint pain, arthritis, and cancer; make the body strong and the libido powerful; prevent aging; and tweak your psychology. Whatever problem you have, bird's nests will solve it.

With the proliferation of swiftlet ranching, the price for house nests declined, spawning the creation of new products aimed at an upwardly mobile younger generation uninterested in traditional nest preparation. Instant coffee and face creams; premade bottled drinks and daily gummy-bear snacks; stem-cell-repairing-wrinkle-fighting-anti-cancer cookies in a variety of flavors (black currant, oats, chocolate chip, cashew nuts, or mint chocolate with mint filling); NUSGx active glycoprotein drink premix with honey (fifteen sachets for $180, now on sale for $160); and tiramisu almond milk-chocolate bars (sugar-free with stevia)—to name just a few.

The first legal swiftlet-ranching investment scheme in Malaysia, the Swiftlet Eco Park Group, has its headquarters on the third floor of the Brem Mall, in a suburb of Kuala Lumpur, Malaysia's capital city. Opposite the reception desk is a display of products in a backlit case. A bowl and spoon sit next to an open black box with a bright-red velvet interior. In the center is a white bird's nest. On the shelf above, a collection of crystals sparkles on white satin fabric. Next to the showcase, occupying nearly the entire wall, is a glowing image of two golden eggs with the words *Build Your Retirement Nest on Edible Bird's Nest.* Another poster depicts two long, white buildings, surrounded by palm-oil fields. A highway runs through the top corner and an enormous swiftlet flies toward the viewer.

Miss Hanis, a senior executive at the company, places a small blue cup and saucer with a gold logo portraying two swiftlets in mid-flight down in front of me.

"Here you are. A sample of our four-in-one Royal Bird Nest White Coffee, which comes in instant individual serving packets," she says. "Actually, in Malaysia, it is not easy to use the word 'Royal.' But we have received permission from the mother of the emperor. She is our chairman."

Swiftlet Eco Park Group is ten years old and has fifteen subsidiary companies across all sectors of the industry. They have investors from Malaysia, Japan, Brunei, China, and Dubai and more than five thousand people involved in a multi-level marketing scheme to sell their products.

Miss Hanis picks up a small nest from a plastic tub on the table. It is three inches across and very white. "Just like we like entertainment—jazz, ballad, country music—we have different sounds to attract the birds to come into the house," she says, referencing the bird melodies played around the clock in the nest houses. "When in the cave, the environment is not controlled. But in the house we can control the results. It is *pure.* We follow the GMP—good manufacture practice, and the

GAHP—good animal husbandry practice. The Veterinarian Services Department suggested the prospectus. During export, we use an RFID [radio-frequency identification] tag to trace the nests and a special coating that identifies the country and company that the nests come from. And, the local university is looking into robotic nest cleaning for us.

"With this nest extract, we produce a lot of products." She says, holding up a jar of fine white powder the consistency of sand. "It's all product innovation. That is why we are working with all the biolabs to test the best things to transform it into other products."

Through a collaboration with the International Medical University, Swiftlet Eco Park Group claims to have isolated eighteen types of amino acids from swiftlet saliva, as well as discovered an epidermal growth factor similar to human skin growth proteins that purportedly has stem-cell-rejuvenating properties. Another compound, SGB, supposedly binds to cancer cells and causes them to self-destruct. The company is trying to get Food and Drug Administration approval to sell bird's nest as a medicine, instead of just a food. If they do, the value of bird's nest extract will increase by a factor of ten.

"Our goal is to have house nest units in all of Malaysia's states. Next year, we will expand our marketing to Indonesia. We trust and we believe in the future market of bird's nest," she says proudly. Her conviction mirrors a similar sentiment I heard from another house-nest entrepreneur, who told me, a bit more flashily, "It's like money from heaven."

At the bottom of my empty coffee cup, there are chewy sugar-like granules. My tongue is slightly numb.

Later that week, I visit a pharmaceutical-grade nest processing facility. Traditionally, cave nest cleaning was done by the women in a family, sitting around a table straining their eyes to pick out impurities, the nest passed from grandmother to daughter to granddaughter, who finished the job with her youthful sight. But with the increase in house nests, cleaning has become a highly regulated part of the industry.

I watch the processing through a large one-way window, the workers beyond like projections. A dozen women, and one man, dressed in teal surgical masks, blue latex gloves, and hairnets, sit hunched over their work at metal tables lit by harsh fluorescent lights. Their tools are spread around them: plastic containers with unprocessed nests; metal bowls filled with water and nests soaking; towels and ceramic plates for laying out the softened nests; toothbrushes, tweezers, and scissors to pick out the impurities.

The processing room has green floors. The workers do not talk. A man checks their progress with magnifying glasses strapped around his head like a mad scientist. There is the sound of running water and the rhythmic clink of tweezers hitting metal. The nest cleaners work robotically. The discarded feathers float like grey shadows in white ceramic bowls.

A woman and man in the far corner lay out the strands of clean nests onto baking sheets in equally sized rectangles. If a nest is mostly intact after it has been cleaned of feathers, it is drained in a small mesh strainer, then arranged into a crescent-shaped plastic mold, held in place with metal clips, and placed in an air dryer for up to a day.

This facility processes about 825 nests a month. Each worker cleans five to ten nests a day. It's hard to find people who want to do this work. Some months, the facility has a 50 percent turnover rate.

The owner hands me a small jar of premade nest drink. It is warm, foaming, and has almost no taste. How disquieting to watch the women work while I swallow the drink made from their labor, as if I am consuming them, too.

A cave is built by coincidences. The location of stalagmites and cascades of limestone are determined as much by the accidental flows of water as they are by the opposing forces eating away the walls. To be in a limestone cave is to experience geologic time as a tangible form. The slow passage of water constructs a city of solid relics, monuments to past movements, while at the same time, the ripe air, thick with wet, stinging with acidic bat guano and bird droppings, lashes away the progress. In some caves, the waste of these flying creatures was so powerful that over thousands of years, the caverns doubled in size. A cave is a total entity in a constant state of flux. The biotic and abiotic are lost notes without each other.

There are many legends about Borneo's caves. In one myth, a woman was turned into a stalagmite by a crawfish. In another, a curse transformed a group of cruel villagers into stone columns. It is said that the presence of Dewi Walet—the goddess of swiftlets—can be felt by a gentle gust of hot air, carrying on it a particular musky scent. As spiritual places, and historically the sites of burials, a few caves still hold the remnants of centuries-old, intricately carved coffins made from rot-resistant ironwood, the bones wrapped in beautifully woven cloths and snuggled in with gongs and machetes.

In Niah Cave, an anatomically human skeleton was found dating from the late Pleistocene period, some forty thousand years ago. Did the smoke from the fires of these prehistoric humans cause evolution in the swiftlets or bats? Like most bird nest caves in Borneo, Niah was traditionally owned and managed by local families, usually of high status, and shares were passed down to the next generation. By 1978, Niah had over a thousand owners and was no longer being harvested sustainably. Thieving was rampant. An enormous iron gate with spikes and a heavy padlock still blocks the main entrance, but given the extent of the cave complex, there are nearly fifty other routes in. At one time, Niah was home to nearly 4 million swiftlets. Today, there is an eerie silence.

Lady Brassey visited Borneo in 1887 as part of her round-trip yacht expedition from England to Australia. She was "very anxious" to visit the Gomantong Caves, but was "assured by everybody that the difficulties would be found insurmountable."[1] I find the going much easier, and drive to the cave like every other tourist, although there are monitor lizards and mongoose to confront as they delicately cross the road.

With fourteen separate caves, Gomantong is one of the most famous black-nest sites still harvested. Depending on the weather and season, each harvest produces eighteen thousand to twenty-five thousand pounds of nests. There are usually three harvests a year. In the 1990s, the complex was guarded by men with Kalashnikovs, but since then, the government has stepped in and developed a system to bid out access—itself a process rife with corruption.

The cave is hot and humid, with a persistent odor—not so much a smell but a feeling, like vinegar in the nose. A shallow river runs through the center of the gaping space. Crabs sidestep in the water. Bats swirl in sepulchral crevices. And everywhere, swiftlets. Swiftlets whiz out of the cave entrance through overhanging vegetation in a chaotic flight pattern, calling in a high-pitched one-two-three trill, the tone of an emergency whistle. A ruckus of sheer numbers. They ring the clouds looking for flying insects. Inside the cave, they hasten the air, releasing cascading clicks as they echolocate through the dark canyons.

Nests were traditionally collected using long bamboo poles, complicated riggings of rattan ropes, and wooden ladders strung together hundreds of feet tall. While more modern techniques are increasingly being employed—such as headlamps instead of oil lamps—it remains an incredibly dangerous job, and the workers have very little protection.

I watch men rapidly and gracefully pull the nests off the high ceilings by hand. A man dangling from a tall rope ladder with wooden rungs holds a bamboo-handled orange net. He swings into action, pulled from one section to the next by guidelines. Four men secure the squeaking ropes below. There is the reverb of water dripping. Urgent yells echo across the walls. The foreman sits and points with a laser. Anyone not busy watches, transfixed.

Some men sit on the railings of the wooden walkway. Others sit perched on logs or in the muck of the cave floor, which shivers with a mass of insects. But the men are unconcerned with what's beneath them. They crane their necks upward, an impatient audience, amused, resigned, hypnotized by the acrobatics above. They've heard many stories of men who fell to their deaths. An old man flicks his cigarette butt into the black abyss. A rock falls from above. A shout of warning falls after it. A young worker with sad, beautiful eyes stares and stares at me as he waits his turn to ascend into the vaulted gloom.

When I emerge from the cave, I am covered in green and black specks of bird shit. A man in a stained white tank top with a pink rag on his head lies in a hammock and yammers into a walkie-talkie. A woman in a wooden tower, like a captive princess, counts the ledgers. December: one ton of black nests. In the eaves under her stilted house, a chicken sleeps in a cage. On the elevated walkway to the cave entrance, an orangutan mother and her baby watch the toiling men inside.

Borneo has one of the highest deforestation rates in the world and a long history of boom-and-bust resource exploitation. First it was spices, then timber and plantation agriculture—rubber, breadfruit, and sisal—followed by rattans, acacia, and cocoa. Still, up until just a few decades ago, the island remained nearly 75 percent forested. But that changed with the now ubiquitous palm oil.

In a palm-oil boomtown, the bank is the busiest place in town. Followed by the machine shops and insurance agencies. Trucks carry gasoline, tires, laborers, fertilizer, palm fruit—"the golden crop." Motorcycles and fancy cars carry men and women thinking about money as they rumble past signs for a new condo development called Palm Heights. The air is heavy. The breeze is sticky and acrid.

On every horizon is a menacing sea of identical trees. The monolithic palms creep to the edges of every roadway. Each tree is a clone, all the same height and evenly spaced and heavily fertilized. The trees have such a short productive life span that they are replaced with new trees every ten to fifteen years. The understory is dark and ghostly. A smattering of coconut trees sway above the uniform rows, like the masts of invisible boats, their hulls lost in rough waves of palm frond. In the distance, bald hills crisscrossed with roads wait to be planted. The gothic structure of a palm-processing facility rises above the eerily ordered forest, spewing smoke into a perfect blue sky.

The extensive logging and palm plantations across Borneo are likely partially to blame for the crash in wild swiftlet populations. A single swiftlet eats up to a thousand flying insects per day, and the modified landscape appears to have a lower carrying capacity for their food source. New wild populations will not reach the abundant numbers of the past, and there is very little room for further domesticated expansion.

One evening, I go to a small gathering at Dr. Stephen Sutton's office. Considered a pioneer of upper canopy research, Dr. Sutton has spent much of his fifty-year career studying the unseen inhabitants of tropical forests. He was the first scientist to use a mercury-vapor lamp in Central Africa to collect insects, during a source-to-sea expedition of the Congo River with a group of army personnel and members of the Scientific Exploration Society.

"There's very little point in drowning if you are trying to publish later," Dr. Sutton recalls with a laugh. "But I tell you, the entomologists were the only dedicated lot on the trip. Not like the parachute regiment. If the way was blocked, they'd just blow apart pristine swamps."

Dr. Sutton initially came to Borneo to catalog pyralid moths. Now, one of his primary projects is to increase access to this entomological information. As in other places around the world during the colonial period, Borneo had a vibrant trade in taxonomic specimens, especially insects. Every time a new species was named, it had to be accompanied by a type specimen—an individual sample of the species. These were housed in major museums in the United States and Europe, and used by subsequent researchers as comparisons for their own taxonomic work.

But for Malay scientists, studying the type specimens from their own country requires an expensive trip overseas. Returning the specimens home would cost even more in museum construction and staff. Dr. Sutton is passionate about reparations for this history. Along with three other researchers, he is helping to return Borneo's natural heritage through the creation of an online database containing 3-D digital type specimens, DNA analysis, images of wing patterns and genitalia, and facsimiles of the original descriptions for nearly twenty-five hundred species of moths.

The room in which we sit is crammed with so many books, you can almost hear them breathing, like living entities, far outnumbering the human guests. Leeds University was selling sixty thousand library books for scrap, and Dr. Sutton was tasked with compiling a collection of eleven hundred books for a research center here in Borneo that studies forest fragmentation.

"The old story is that Borneo's forests were once so extensive, a gibbon could swing from tree to tree all the way across the island," Dr. Sutton says. "But now palm plantations have fragmented what little forest remains."

"A lot of species don't live in palm plantations but do feed on the palm fruits," replies a balding ecologist who studies ants. "The Tabin Wildlife Reserve is one of the best places to see wildlife at the moment. Quite lively traffic of animals commuting between the primary forest in the reserve and the palm-oil plantations next to it."

The place where two different kinds of habitat meet—in this case a forest and a palm plantation—is called an ecotone. These edge spaces have various impacts on biodiversity. Orangutans have been known to nest in the palm plantation trees. Pangolins love palm fruits, too. And rats eat the leftover fruits that fall off during harvest. Then all these rats are a favorite food of snakes, like the king cobra.

"But these plantations cause a lot of local extinctions," Dr. Sutton responds. "And orangutans nesting in palm trees are often targeted for extermination by plantation workers. Overall, palm ecosystems have reduced diversity and complexity compared to a primary forest. It's a Rat Ecosystem!"

As the sun sets, we follow Dr. Sutton to his office, which overlooks the ocean and two small islands, to verify his claim that the view is "the third-best sunset in the world." Large schooners are anchored in the bay, and as the sky floats toward twilight, speedboat wakes flash like white lightning against the consuming darkness. A stately desk is piled with papers and old research journals. Classical music plays and a cuckoo clock ticks out a metronome accompaniment. I imagine Dr. Sutton here late at night, listening to one of Beethoven's concertos, examining his moths, ruminating over their endangerment and the best methods to archive those that still exist, making do with the shadow of former glories.

I feel exhausted. Another day, another empty white-nest cave. Someone had burned a tire in the cave complex during a family conflict over who controlled access. The bats stayed, but nearly all the swiftlets left.

I'm beginning to think my idea of finding a remote location where virgin caves hold glistening white nests worth more than gold is purely fantasy. This bird nest research has proven more exasperating than I could have ever imagined. It's a secretive world full of double-back stories, fuzzy numbers, and obscured details. The truth is so difficult to pin down. There is an infinite amount of information lost in translation.

Many of the people I interviewed gave me dire warnings— *You have to be careful. You can't just go around asking questions. You will get in trouble. There is a lot of corruption in the wildlife and forest departments. This is a dangerous subject to be pursuing.* I suppose there has always been a certain suspicion of curiosity. Especially in women.

Borneo is a place where men have come for generations in search of something—headhunters, horsemen, wild women, and pirates—or simply to chronicle a vanishing way of life, as the cultures that existed in the extensive rainforests disappeared along with the trees. I had come to Borneo for much the same reason. To find something primeval and elusive—the last vestiges of pristine nature.

But it seems there are no wild frontiers left anymore and I am merely pursuing feral domesticates. The forest ecosystems that the nineteenth-century explorers wrote about are no longer in existence. The wisdom of these places has disappeared forever, like the burnt manuscripts in the Library of Alexandria. We continue to demolish what little remains before we've even had a chance to glimpse the mysteries there to unravel. Borneo is losing forests at twice the rate of the rest of the world's tropical regions. Unknown species are going extinct before we can even discover them and add their deaths to our grim statistics.

I am tired of looking for wild birds. If there is a deeper mystery or meaning, it has eluded me. I am tired of searching in general. This quest has become much like what the nests represent: a fountain of youth, a utopian dream, a paradox without solution, a romantic mirage just beyond the grasp of my persistence.

I spend the night in an elevated cabin at a nature reserve. After dark, a wildlife guide takes me out into the swamp forest, an archaic and disquieting menagerie—there are floating spiders, fire ants, striped wasps, a black scorpion the size of a banana, and a translucent frog bursting with eggs. Tiny phosphorescent mushrooms cover the ground. Iridescent birds, balled into fluffy slumber, perch in the trees, while snakes curl asleep in the high branches. The frogs warble in resonant waves, like they are inside my own head. It starts to rain. The animals take shelter in the trees, disappearing into protective verdure, and I return to my cabin.

I feel unsettled. Like a bird asleep in the dark, caught in the sudden bright terror of a searching light. The last round of texting with the Hunter has made me want to retreat.

Distance is sad but nothing has changed. This is how distance turns out, he wrote.

In the landscape where we hunted the moose, beside that lovely lake, beneath tall trees and the calls of ravens, bundled together and silently in the company of our love, we reflected each other, like luster upon the water. Could it really be over so quickly?

You shouldn't chase anybody, he wrote. *I can't play the role you want in your life for now, and I understand if you don't want or feel you can't keep in touch.*

I feel a sense of crisis both inside and outside me. It's as if I can't separate our meandering love story from the consequences of this age of extinction. As if history exists not in time but in space—not a linear narrative but a collection of occurrences. My mind feels like a chaotic reflection of a fragmented ecosystem, broken apart, fractured and split, no longer a cohesive whole. A famine spreads across the landscape of my heart.

I go out onto the back deck. Borneo is a 130-million-year-old island. The unique ecosystems that have evolved over such a long period of isolation are incredibly complex. There is inexhaustible beauty in this tiny remnant of rainforest. It is a place where Nature expresses her divinity through visual metaphor. Where it is possible to experience deep time diversity. What a different perspective a tree must have that has lived five hundred years. These beings mark the tide of the seasons as we mark our days—a swift rise and fall of the sun.

What does it mean to love the Hunter? To be loved by him? What does it mean to truly love the wild? Our need to control and define and bolster ourselves against vulnerability only leads us to heartbreak. To love the wild is an act of uncertainty.

Perhaps I am not capable of love. Perhaps I never loved the Hunter, but only the idea of him. But I do not believe any of these thoughts. As soon as I think them, they are false.

Perhaps this has been an experience of being unmoored, of having to find a home in myself. To love the wild is an act of spiritual liberation.

In the dark, beneath an empire of foliage, I shed my clothes 267 and bathe naked in the rain. A million leaves ring drops of water into fervid white noise. The wet falls on my body. Ants of remarkable size crawl up my legs. The gorgeous world slides by in muted tones as if in suspended animation. The downpour gathers itself up and reaches a new crescendo.

All I can hear is my breathing and the dull roar of the rain.

This minute holds all eternity.

My grief breaks into a million little stars.

The trees eat time above me.

———————————

The bird's nest trail has gone cold. So instead I am here, a day's journey from anyplace, in a roadless village in the Kelabit Highland mountains, where there are no wild caves and tradition is not quite dead but definitely showing signs of aging. I'm staying with Daniel, a rice farmer who runs an ecotourist business out of his home with his wife, Jasmine. Their children are away at boarding school—the school here closed down for lack of students and resources. It is odd to be in a community without young people.

Their lofted open-air house is not insulated from the vagaries of weather, from the smells of the earth, the sounds of the forest, or the occasional bird flying through. When the rain comes on, the wet air rushes in.

I am writing by candlelight because Daniel's generator has broken, and he needs a part from town. Last night we had electricity, though, and we listened to American country music.

Daniel hands me his headlamp because mine is on the fritz. "Take mine." He pushes it toward me like he's pushed cigarettes, fried onion dough, and rice over the course of the past few days. It is an aggressive sort of hospitality, one I'm not quite sure what to do with. Declining feels impolite but so does taking advantage of his kindness. It reminds me of the stories about my grandmothers pushing food on their children. *Eat, eat! You are too skinny.*

The villages around here take their names from the rivers, and it is customary that the inhabitants change their own names at least three times: when married, after the first child, and after the first grandchild.

Rice is such an important part of Kelabit culture that they have different words for each stage: seedlings, mature stalks, unhusked rice grains, husked rice, crushed rice after pounding, rice porridge, rice flour.

The walk to the paddy fields feels like a great adventure. From the back of the house, through light-loving ferns that have grown up after the area was burned, then into a wide-open pasture. The lumpy ground is filled with puddles and the protrusions of tree stumps, everything covered by crabgrass, clipped short by the water buffalo. The only other vegetation is purple ground shrubs they won't eat. At the edge of the pasture, a buffalo jawbone has been wedged into the crook of a dead tree like a signpost.

Then into a forested area, past a two-thousand-year-old stone megalith, cracked on one side. There are numerous stone monuments like this one throughout the forest, each constructed for one purpose or another: to honor the wealth of a chief, to mark boundaries or rites of passage, make prayers, show strength, connect to the spirit world, or bury heirlooms for safekeeping— such as antique Chinese dragon jars brought by traders from the coast. In exchange for the labor required to construct them, the chief would throw a great rice feast for the entire village and usually the neighboring village, too. When he died, land was cleared and another megalith made to mark the funerary rites. Glazed stoneware pottery stored the bones of the dead and the charred fragments of burnt rice accumulated around the base.

The forest path has worn through the thin dark humus topsoil, exposing layers of sand beneath. Scramble up embankments, balance on moss-slick logs, shoes sucked into sticky silt. Then, another pasture opens wide and beautiful, with a view past sloping grass, dotted with water buffalo staring—melancholically, dumbly, calmly—among their white egret sidekicks, and green-grey trees beyond, draped in fog. After a few minutes, there is a gate. Over a stile made from a tree split into two, with notches cut out at regular intervals like stairs, slippery with mud. Then, down a winding path to a bamboo bridge over a small stream. Last week, a flood of nearly eight feet of water topped the banks, almost taking the bridge with it.

Cross the bridge, past a stand of bamboo, and enter a small fenced orchard of sago palms, banana plants, and fruit trees. Beyond are the sparkling rice paddies, emerald and flaxen against the backdrop of a lush forest.

"This is our simple life," Daniel says, gesturing at the wide expanse. "Farming here not like America: big farms, good job, very rich. Here, you are a farmer, you are poor. But I like it anyway. We grow the best rice in the world."

Despite its grandeur, this is not a pristine landscape and likely hasn't been for many generations. In the past, a form of swidden agriculture was practiced here, very similar to the kind found in the forests of the Congo Basin. After a part of the forest was cleared, usually by burning, the thin layer of peat was only fertile enough to support rice crops for a year or two, after which it was planted with cassava, yams, and oil palm, then

269

eventually abandoned altogether. Over the next ten to twenty years, the terrain slowly grew back into forest.

After five years or so, communities would leave their long-houses for a new location, but before doing so, the inhabitants planted fruit trees like durians. When they returned to these sites some time later, the mature trees welcomed them home again. Some areas of primary forest were conserved for hunting. There were also "women's forests," secondary forests maintained for a variety of resources: plant foods and medicine; poison for blowpipes and fishing; leaves for house construction and cooking; rattan palms to make baskets; and dammar resin, which was traded for beads, pots, and iron with people who came from the coasts.

This kind of shifting land management, practiced throughout the world's tropical forests, was particularly good at capturing soil carbon and created a dynamic landscape with a diverse bounty of edible food. Each disturbance and abandonment caused new forest configurations to occur, creating ecological niches for a whole assortment of creatures. This human-nature partnership was a different kind of domestication—a recipro-cal, unpredictable relationship—that did not degrade the land, but in many cases was actually biologically richer than people-less forests. The distinction between nature and culture was nebulous.

The Kelabit switched to wet rice cultivation in the nine-teenth century—the technique likely introduced by Christian missionaries—and the villagers still plant the heirloom vari-ety first planted by their great-grandfathers. The ponds are watered by mountain streams filtered through the rainforest. The paddies are habitat for dragonflies, butterflies, and other pollinating insects, as well as for catfish and tilapia. After the rice is harvested, the water buffalo eat the plant remains, and as they walk through the water, their defecations help to fertilize the next crop. The threshed rice straw is fed to the pigs, made into brooms, or burned, the ash used as fertilizer in vegetable plots or sprinkled back into the paddy fields to return the nutrients. After two to five years, the ponds are left to fill in with sediment, and these areas eventually grow back into forest.

The men are in the paddies with hand-forged machetes. Daniel is a handsome man, small and wiry, with a neat mustache and close-cropped hair. He works quickly, helped by two young men in brightly colored coveralls. They plod through soggy fields, resign their boasts, and forget their pains. The men spread the cut rice stalks on woven mats to dry in the sun.

The women sit in a shaded hut and beat handfuls of the golden grass against a mat-covered floor. With each thump, grains fall from the plant. It gathers in heaps. All around us is birdsong and laughter.

Three hunting dogs, medium-sized and striped like tigers, lounge around amid the activity, happy for a day to do nothing.

Daniel's wife, Jasmine, wears a blue jumpsuit and simple gold hoops. After threshing for a couple of hours, we go fishing in a fallow rice pond. She stands barefoot in the muddy water with a net, prowling for small, silvery minnows and long snake-like fish. Suddenly, she hits something sharp. Her toenail has been ripped up and is bleeding. With hardly a moment of pain, she picks up a hand-forged *parang* machete knife, slices off the hanging piece of nail, and resumes her work.

I am surprised by her piercing bravery and subtle charm. For the past few days she has said little—an apparition off to one side, always just out of measure—a cast of light behind the shadow of her husband. She reminds me of the stoic women who sell bushmeat at Kinshasa's markets—powerful in their quiet existence, determined to find some measure of joy in the hard task of survival.

Jasmine catches a mess of fish and scrapes the still-squirming bodies with the *parang* until the scales float on the water like vibrant jewels. For lunch, she boils them with chili peppers and garlic over a fire by the rice fields. We eat them with mashed rice wrapped in *daun isip* leaf, a staple food that is eaten with nearly every meal. It is an ingenious method of preparation— the rice will stay good for up to two days without refrigeration and the paddle-shaped leaf provides its own plate.

After lunch, I walk home barefoot, the mud squishing between my toes. Green-spotted brook butterflies surround me like phantasms. One lands on my nose. The sky darkens with late-afternoon monsoons. A flock of birds dash the clouds in anticipation of the impending downpour and veer toward the eaves of a house. An older woman is fixing her fence. A man sits at an open window reading the newspaper. The gong from the church in the center of the village rings out, like a sigh after a long day, and is met with a chorus of dogs, barking their pleasure.

In the evening, we eat more of the rice-paddy fish. Jasmine throws them into hot oil. A fecund roar emanates from the wok and the fried smell lingers in the air like mountain mist.

I hike into the primary forest beyond the rice paddies, pausing frequently to listen to the unfamiliar bird calls and biotic sirens—like screeching tires, rusty faucets, and the electric *ding* of a grandfather clock striking twelve; the *whoopee* mournful cry of the jungle peacock; the *quack* of a silver leaf monkey. I watch a troupe of tailless gibbons swing above me. Trees weep white sap like candle wax and shed their skins. Bizarre poisonous caterpillars covered in long white hairs look like displaced sea creatures. Leeches reach out from leaves and branches looking for a ride to somewhere else. Pitcher plants and orchids burst forth. Edible white mushrooms emerge triumphantly out of the leaf litter, a life that lasts only a few days. The canopy trees refract the splendor of light. A living library of unruly forms. A symphony of biodiversity. An enumeration of what is essentially unlimited. When I stop to take a breath, the forest pulsates, vibrates, an orgy of living and dying.

The rainforest has layers of density and depth. Each step is like entering a new room. The air smells different. Sometimes it is sweet like jasmine. Other times it is putrid and skunky. But everywhere, it smells verdant, with hints of delicate rot. The aroma unfurls around me—the rowdy pheromones of the forest.

Although tropical forests make up just 7 percent of the earth's terrestrial surface, they contain nearly half of the planet's living species. Despite this great variety, there is not necessarily an abundance of any one species. The role of biodiversity is therefore redundancy. The forest doesn't work as a series of competitions. Rather, it is based on a framework of mutualism and interdependence. Having many species that play the same functional role means that if one is wiped out by accident, the many creatures that rely on it can still survive.

At irregular intervals between two and ten years, numerous tree species conduct a synchronized flowering event. The forest becomes gregarious with fruit and nuts. Evolutionarily, such events helped to suppress seed predators—by overwhelming them one year and then starving them in the intervening years, population sizes were kept in check, thus increasing the likelihood of tree-seedling establishment. We do not know what sets these masting events into motion, although it is likely due to chance fluctuations in subtropical monsoons. Similar group masting occurs in forests around the world. Perhaps trees just prefer to unfold their engorged reproductive rituals in the company of others.

In this small section of highland rainforest, there are more than 819 plant species, 668 of which have been named, including 151 species of orchids, 30 ginger species, and 41 species of ferns, plus 8 genera not identified to the species level. A study undertaken in 1922 found that people living here used 148 different plants on a regular basis for over 250 different applications, ranging from medicines, foods, and spices to building materials for houses, boats, handicrafts, household implements, charms, and toys. They used plants to make hunting dogs fierce and treat diseases in buffalo, as fishing bait and as a source of water, and even to stop a child breastfeeding. It seemed the rainforest provided nearly everything they needed.

I come across four men making a dugout canoe from an enormous downed tree. It will take them some weeks to complete the project. As I watch the skilled men wield their chainsaws and hand-forged tools, the crack of gunshot and the squeal of a wild boar sounds from somewhere just over the hill.

There is a heap of empty bottles and beer cans piled beneath the house. "From Christmas," Daniel says. They drank forty liters of scotch whiskey over the holidays. Slaughtered a water buffalo. Had the whole village to dinner. Danced.

Daniel has invited a few people over for dinner tonight and has gone to great lengths to make sure we have electricity. His generator is still broken, and he's been quite worried over the meat in his freezer, which is beginning to smell spoiled. Today, he struck a white electric wire through the trees, along a fence, taped together, propped in the V of long poles he cut from the forest, and across the village to a neighbor's generator.

"Not so strong," he says, pointing at the flickering bulb above us, "the power." American country music plays from a cell phone. The sheeny twangs of "God Must Be a Cowboy" bounce around the room.

We eat dinner at a long handmade wooden table. The open-aired room has a thatched roof and elegant pastoral views of the water buffalo, with their twisting black-tipped horns, grazing in the rosy sunset. The free-ranging chickens scratch under the elevated house, laying eggs where they please, unbothered by the dogs that lie in the dirt among them. The sound of gibbons booms across the valley. Ambrosia and nectar lace the cool breeze coming from the forested mountains.

We eat "the best rice in the world" with fresh-picked cucumber in salt water, bowls of salty broth made from wild boar gristle, and jungle fern, which Jasmine picked on the way home from the paddies. Next come flaxen-colored mushrooms, cooked in a big silver pot with garlic and locally made salt. It is too expensive for the local people to buy, but Daniel's friend borrowed his water buffalo to go to the forest and pull out the firewood used to evaporate the mineral spring water, so he was given a little container of it in exchange. The mushrooms taste mild and buttery, like chanterelles that have taken a bath and lost some of their woodland grime.

"From our jungle supermarket! Very fresh every time," Daniel says, setting down a dish of wild ginger flowers in scrambled eggs. I had helped prepare the dish earlier in the day, pulling the slender, hot-pink petals carefully away from the stems. They taste tender, like ginger root blushed and fell in love, with hints of the same strong, earthy flavor but more subtle and sour, an alchemy of moist air instead of soil.

While domesticated pigs are only eaten for special occasions, wild boar is eaten for daily meals. Tonight, we eat wild boar spareribs, grilled over a fire in an old oil drum, specked with coarse singed hairs, sweet and spicy, perfectly cooked. I heap a spoonful of expansively hot chili paste onto the meat.

276 My appetite keeps expanding. The excess of water in the rainforest makes the food mild and the flavors watered through. But the high altitude and coolness add pungency, an interesting sharpness on the tongue.

The delicate palm hearts required hacking down an entire sago tree, which was ringed in black spikes like a medieval torture device and home to a colony of ants. When I went with Daniel to harvest it, we walked past two disconnected PVC pipes that ran along the muddy path. "No water for the village," he had said with a mix of frustration and resignation. Just the innermost core of the palm is sliced into thin circles and cooked with garlic and shallots. It is nearly translucent and patterned like snakeskin.

In contrast, the tapioca leaves are bitter, toothsome, a buzz of phytonutrients. I feel drunk on chlorophyll. Before being cooked, the leaves are pounded to a pulp in a tapered wooden vessel with a long, heavy pole. It is quite difficult work, but Jasmine made it look effortless. It was the same with the massive stone mortar and pestle she used to crush spices, mash garlic, and make chili paste.

She cooks with a kind of reverence that comes from careful habit, determining the flavors of the evening in an improvisation with the wild foods themselves. In these small moments, when she thinks no one is watching, I catch an adumbration of her divine smile. She is not an invisible object to me.

For dessert there are fried yeasted dough twists and pineapple, harvested from a neighbor's yard earlier in the day, sprinkled with the brownish-grey Kelabit salt. The juicy, sour pineapple and sharp crystals of salt are a revelation of flavors. I devour two more slices. A perfect end to the meal.

I keep thinking about the lunch I had at Noma eight months earlier. Is this what Noma is trying to do? To recreate this sublime sense of the land providing for us, of a relationship of mutual thriving? Foraging here is quite different from the foraging I did in Copenhagen's Assistens Cemetery. Here it is common practice. For me the wild banquet laid before us is an extraordinary feast. For everyone else, it is simply dinner.

I spend much of the evening talking to the man sitting opposite me. "When I first left for school in Kuala Lumpur, I cried," Aguan tells me. "Me and all the country boys did. Cried our eyes out and went fishing in the city gutters to try to stop our sorrow. Everyone made fun of us."

As an adult, he worked all over Borneo trading in tires, rarely returning to the highland village. Aguan seems to have a contradictory relationship to this place. He yearns for the past and its traditions, and yet holds a prejudice against them, rooted in some deep shame about his upbringing. "My mother is the last one in the village with stretched ears and heavy brass ornaments. When we were growing up, we didn't have plates or silverware. We just used jungle leaves for everything. We used to joke, 'The Kelabit are rich in plates!' The old people would cook rice by wrapping it in leaves, stuffing the packets into bamboo, and throwing it into the fire. My kids can't appreciate what life was like here before. The unsanitary food. Living off the forest completely like we were monkeys."

Aguan pauses a moment, a look of contemplation sweeping across his face. "But in other ways, it is worse now. There was once a clinic and a school here and an L-shaped longhouse around the field. Even a landing strip for planes. There used to be two hundred people living in the village. Now it's down to at least half that. Only fifty-seven hundred Kelabit left in total. The local language is dying out. Our culture is nearly dead and the children don't learn how to do anything in the forest."

He takes a bite of mushroom, holds the remainder up on his fork. "Even I didn't know you could eat these mushrooms until recently. They aren't organic mushrooms—they are the original mushrooms from the forest!

"But I am hopeful more young people will return here and preserve our knowledge. The paved road is coming and that will help. Supposed to be finished next year, although they've been saying that for years and so far nothing. But, it will be good. Of course, not everyone agrees with me about the road." He looks around the table to see if any dissenters, like Daniel, speak up.

Places without roads are rare and getting rarer every day. For the first time in human history, more than half the world lives in urban areas. Many push-pull factors are contributing to this shift, and the numbers of both urban dwellers and roads are projected to increase. It's a transition that will have far-reaching and somewhat unknown evolutionary consequences—for both us and the planet.

Here, the road represents possibilities and guarantees big changes. It will bring wealth in some forms but will also bring control imposed from the outside. Reliance on the land will diminish. Whole mindsets will cease to exist. There is concern the road will increase the drug trade. Accessibility will mean more things to buy, more garbage, and more noise.

What does it mean to be from a place? To have an intact culture? What does purity mean anymore? What does it matter? This village is already a hybrid place. Already globalized. It has been for a long time. Daniel is just as likely to reference the Discovery Channel when explaining something in the forest as he is to draw on ancestral wisdom. And somewhere in Berlin, a woman is stretching her ears and hand-forging kitchen knives.

Still, there is something undeniably different about this place, about its remoteness, something important that we should not lose. It is a place where life takes time. It takes as long as it takes because there is immense non-monetary value in a life lived this way. Learning to read the forest requires years of practice, and it is only with knowledge of the forest that conservation is possible—without it, cutting down the trees and forgetting what was once here becomes easier.

Can this village support an influx of tourists, whose presence is often more detrimental to local people and wildlife than it is beneficial? Is ecotourism a solution? I don't know. If modern conservation becomes a purely consumptive experience, there is the risk that nature will fall further under the logic of efficiency and capital, no longer retaining its wildness. Commodification is its own kind of domestication.

But without the wealth of visitors, will these places survive at all? Is it not better to save some wildlife, even if it has been habituated to the lens of a camera? To save some traditional skills, even if they are not for the sake of themselves but as art for purchase? And who are we, as tourists, to say that these places must remain "wild" for our pleasure, to deny the rice farmer the same material benefits and technology we enjoy, even if we've come here to take a break from such trappings?

I wonder about my own motivations for visiting this place. Was my desire for a transcendent escape into the wilderness and an encounter with the locals rooted in a colonial mindset? As I recount the simple pleasures of my excursions, it is easy to forget that these moments rely as much on the materials and wealth of a destructive economic system as they do on the mountains and forests, stoic against time. I have the privilege to forget the capitalist grid upon which my retreat into the wilds depended. Ecotourism allows us to divorce the idea of wild nature from work. It allows us to believe in the pristine even while destruction occurs just over the next hillside.

With dinner over, the men smoke Indonesian tobacco, rolled in papers without glue, holding them just so as they burn so that they won't fall apart and to pieces. The white smoke disappears into black night, pulled away and into nothing by the wet wind. A hint of clove mingles with the stench of the green mosquito coil burning at my feet. Dolly Parton's voice drifts toward us from the radio. Jasmine's middle finger is swollen and red from a bite she got yesterday, and she keeps worrying over it, touching the hot area as if the insect were still there.

Without warning, a dragon-like wasp with a long stinger dive-bombs the table. Daniel's niece squashes it in half, then burns the sharp end in a candle so no one will accidentally get stung. Apparently, this species is dangerous even after it is dead.

The cicadas prattle. My head is full of village politics.

After the guests have left, Daniel and I look at the stars. I point out Orion and the Southern Cross, arbitrary names and patterns for universal spots of light. In so much of the world the stars are gone, driven to obscurity by a million brighter lights. But these stars are luminous, like the stars of my childhood. The sky is clear and the lack of cloud cover means the air is unexpectedly cold. There is occasional lightning on the horizon, a distant storm illuminating the silhouettes of mountains hidden in the dark. They remind me of the mountains in New Mexico, just as the call of gibbons at sunset sounds like coyotes hidden in desert arroyos.

Thoughts of returning homeward loop in my mind, like a Möbius strip. I realize I have been experiencing the grief of placelessness. I miss a wild home that no longer exists.

Is it possible to feel homesick, not for a place, but for the past?

The memory of the Hunter haunts me like a ghost in the room. Fragments of the time we spent together float like dead leaves, residues of past seasons on the glassy surface of the present.

One afternoon, I find Daniel sitting in the kitchen, smoking while he heats water in a black metal teapot. Grotesque wild boar fat hangs from a nail in the lichened tree that forms one wall of the kitchen.

Daniel hands me a sautéed caterpillar. It bursts in my mouth, releasing hot eggy water. The chewy body gets caught in the back of my throat like the caterpillars I ate in Congo.

The bottom of my chest falls out. I'm deluged with thoughts of the Hunter. Making his coffee over a kindling fire as the dawn wakes up. Walking through the forest on his epic one-month quests in search of poachers. I think of something he whispered to me one night as we lay in bed. "You know I have been shot at—on more than one occasion. There is a rumor among the poaching gangs that I am invincible. This is a very bad rumor to have when you are trying to stay alive."

My sadness leaks into my eyes and I must look utterly insane, this lonely tourist girl who asks so many questions, following everyone around with her curiosity, camera in one hand, notebook in the other, always and spontaneously on the verge of tears.

On Borneo, birds were once used as omens, because their own unpredictability perfectly matched the irregularity of the world. They were a reliable way to randomize action. The circles of causation between things were not independent but interlinked.

How do we retreat back to the point at which a decision led us to failure? How far into the past must we go?

I remember the night toward the end of my stay in Kinshasa when the Hunter and I went out for a meal at the Greek club. The contents and setting of this meal are obscured by the feeling I had as we ate. Each bite was to be savored, interlaced with sips of sweet wine and pauses just to smile at each other.

The Hunter was dressed in a white suit jacket, borrowed and too big for him. Three men played basketball in the crumbling concrete courtyard next to the long porch where we sat with our crystal and porcelain. The old Greek waiter had tired hands. He served us little fish in oil and pale-green olives. The evening felt atemporal, existing only as it existed, not tied to the past or prophetic of the future. Each heartbeat held a universe. The night was rugged with time, and yet each moment still felt too brief.

282

* * *

The house shakes as people wake up. The tinkle of teaspoons. Jasmine sings softly. It has been raining all night and I rise to more. Torrents blacken the sky. The yard is a series of ponds and rivers. Daniel left early this morning to take his sister and niece to town, and it is unclear if he will make it back today with so much water and so much mud.

I visit another homestay and meet the older owners, Saleha and her husband, Tuan. Potted orchids line the long wooden walkway to the entrance. Their house is full of artifacts, beautifully decorated porcelain, and items Saleha has beaded. A pantry alcove is stocked with canned goods like a country store. On the walls are faded vintage travel posters: *Hidden Paradise of Borneo, Golden Days in Sarawak, Rainbows End in Sarawak,* all in soft colors. In one, hibiscus flowers crowd the edges around a woman with doll features. She wears a headdress and smiles enigmatically. In another, an orangutan flirts among blue butterflies while a hostile-looking monitor lizard walks along the bottom of the poster.

I drink tea in the dining room as Saleha sits across from me. We look out enormous screened windows at tranquil rice fields edged in pineapple, with green pastures and the articulated mountains beyond.

Saleha recently went to the city and told them she didn't want the road. That she wanted this place to stay as it is. "You are very lucky to have come here before the road. With the road, we will be just like every other connected village. It will happen this year, I think," she says, defeated. Maybe she's been fighting this change a long time.

"Although people might just come for lunch if there was a road," Tuan says, trying to lift her mood.

"Yes, but I want the government to help make river travel more reliable. Take out the flooded debris. Tourists come for the inaccessibility and the tradition. Anthropologists and archaeologists come here to study. Tell us, why are you here?"

And so I explain my failed search for wild bird's nest soup.

"You don't say," Saleha says, looking at me mysteriously. "My sister is married to a man whose grandfather owned a bird nest cave in Middle Baram. One of the most high-quality caves, with both white and black nests."

Saleha suddenly stands up and disappears into the kitchen. She returns with a pink Tupperware container full of bird's nests her sister had given her many years ago.

"These come from a limestone cave on a big piece of land planted with an orchard and oil palm, next to hilly jungle and a river. It's a low cave, only seven or eight feet high, so you can just touch them. The government wants to quarry the cave. My sister registered it as a bird nest cave and protested. But still there is a threat to grab the whole area."

As Saleha talks, I slowly realize this was one of the caves I had tried to visit but had been unable to reach. I look at the nests. Compared to the farmed nests I have seen, which are pure white and uniform, an accurate reflection of their industrial production, these wild cave nests are beautifully complex and aesthetically disordered. They absorb minerals from the wet cave walls and look like stalagmite seashells—striations of oranges, pinks, and yellows, with warped reddish-brown edges and just a few traces of grey, downy feathers.

"I never imagined someone would come here looking for bird nest..." she says, trailing off to stare out the window.

I return later that evening. Saleha has put on a string of rust-colored pearls. The bird's nest soup is served in a porcelain teacup. It is made with salt, eggs, and a mushroom that "arrives between hot and wet weather." The long nest strands float in the broth like a galaxy. There are bits of feather drifting in the soup, which slipped beyond Saleha's old eyesight. I am touched by the work—both human and natural—that went into making this meal.

I take a spoonful. The nest is soft, but discernible, with a chewy, slippery, almost leathery texture. Another spoonful.

"Slowly, slowly. We eat slowly here."

What does time taste like? *Slurp.* This soup is a luxury that passed through sisterly hands and many years and great chance to find me. *Gulp.* It is a luxury best eaten with friendly strangers in a remote valley with glorious views—in an outpost at the end of a violent world that creeps closer every day. *Sip.* This soup is a relic, an artifact, of a vanishing way of life.

"Can you feel it?" Saleha says, smiling.

In the beginning of any search all the possibilities present simultaneously. But to continue the search requires pruning away some potential paths. When we make the discovery of what we are seeking, the first impulse is to focus only on what has occurred, as if this were the most important part of the story. But the missteps and dead ends, the endless list of what we gave up, that is also what allows us to find our way. Our memories are only those experiences we failed to forget.

There is no way to separate out the details of this feast from the experience itself, nor speak of the experience without mentioning its small differences from any other meal. All the components, inorganic and organic alike, seem to sing to each other in the mutual improvising of a hymn.

I take another sip of soup. Perhaps the birds were looking for me the whole time.

⋆ 10 ⋆

WILD GRASS

─────────

Infinite Beginnings—A Future of Survival—A Map of
Ten Thousand Years—Sympatheia

M Y JOURNEY BEGAN with a renunciation. I withdrew toward the wilderness to strip away the superficialities— to regain contact with the essential. To let my mind wander so that I might feel the passage of time unbounded by the clock.

But since beginnings are relative and multiplicitous, and one beginning often contains another, I will begin again.

I am on a train in Poland. It is some months before I first meet the Hunter.

I visit forests filled with memorials to mass murder, generations of grief, too closely related in time and blood. Planting, thinning, logging, the march of soldiers' steps. The trees at right angles mock my moments of anxiety. I eat delicious soups and mystery meats, pickles and cabbage, so much cabbage it moves past a joke and into a kind of culinary purgatory.

I suppose there is something else I've been searching for. A feeling of home. Of nourishment. Something that perhaps lies within myself. I think about the ways my great-grandmother controlled her own wild nature. How strange it must have been to forage from places with such a violent history.

I visit grasslands filled with rare birds. The lapwings and corncrakes glide between the tall stems. These grasslands are not natural. They are the relics of a haymaking culture that no longer exists. For centuries, the fens were grown and cut, sliced down with sickle and scythe. Over time, these archaic fields became their own wildlife habitat, an ecosystem that is home to a unique and threatened mix of species.

The Polish conservation organizations must grow and cut the hay fields every year—not because it is still profitable to do so but to maintain the birds' habitat. Forests are such a tenacious mark of our absence that many of the world's grasslands would not exist without human intervention—as soon as we stop burning the grasses or cutting the fields, the trees and shrubs begin to invade, sprouting up like sentinels on watch.

To save the rare hay birds requires a fight, requires managing lands for what would otherwise not survive. We've come to appreciate this antiquated anthropogenic nature and are willing to spend massive resources to freeze it as such, as though it were self-contained and timeless and permanent. We have essentially domesticated an entire landscape. Is this post-natural or re-wilding?

The idea of Wild Nature has long been a reflection of our appetites and longings just as much as it has been rooted in a real physical place. Our desires remake the world from one of objects into a landscape of subjects, and the meanings we attach to the wild are a distorted reflection of our own domestication.

Wild Nature is no longer such a vivid example of what humankind is not. This changed nature is a complicated totem.

When all our natural landscapes are found to be anthropogenic, we are no longer borrowing an innocent symbol. We have become implicated in it. The worship and devotion that Wild Nature conjures in our hearts, the sublime awe and terror, invariably leads back to us. Once divergent, now combined. Overcoming and being overcome.

Like natural selection, domestication is a small, slow practice that eventually leads to large-scale changes. While hunting occurs throughout the zoological scale—and symbiotic or mutualistic relationships are quite common—domestication between other species is relatively rare. It seems to be a form of resource management particularly suited to colony species. And if domestication was once seen as bending an animal's natural instincts to suit our needs, it is now considered to be one of coevolution. It was not a spontaneous invention but an extension of the common practices already occurring within hunting and gathering culture, combined with the preexisting natural instincts and characteristics of certain animals and plants.

Why our species evolved to enter into such a large number of these symbiotic relationships, and within such a relatively short period of time, remains a mystery. To take the sphere of the wild into our homes required that we underwent our own domestication. By many measures, we are no longer as healthy as our gatherer-hunter ancestors. The benefits to the domesticates can be debated, but at least in terms of numerical success, they far outrank their wild counterparts. Dogs have become the most abundant large carnivores on earth. For every tiger in the wild, there are 100,000 domesticated cats.

But genetic studies have shown that wild/domestic categories are not rigidly fixed—they depend on changes in just a few regulatory genes. Domestication is a spectrum of relationships. The most interesting ones occupy the liminal spaces, full of fragments and unified by their discontinuities.

Wildness and domestication have never been pure categories. There is no border, no solid line between territories and definitions. The captive beast cannot always be tamed, and sometimes, even the most cultivated must return to feral lives.

———

The train is rushing through a land of water gardens. We skirt a river that snakes into the distance to meet the shimmer of a far-off lake, windswept and edged in water grass. A white stork examines the detritus. The clouds have gathered above, and the bird is an omen bringing news.

At the edge of the lake there is a concrete bunker, built into the ground during World War II. The forests that had been hunting areas for kings and czars became hunting preserves for Nazi generals, who burnt down any surrounding hamlets suspected of harboring partisans and blemished the local woodlots with secret tunnels and mass graves.

The metal doors of this bunker are a sallow pink and buckled with age. Thick tree roots tear apart the musty interior. Fulvous mushrooms sprout from the soils of the dead, like natural monuments to wartime slaughter. The forest slowly takes back what had been given to human hubris.

On top of the bunker is a simple wooden altar, the color of honey. At the apex of its steeply pitched roof rests a Christ on the cross, carved of white ash. Two rows of pews, simple benches constructed of hand-hewn wood, are set out in front of it with a view to the lake. It is a church meant for worshipping in all elements. If you were to sit here long enough, under the godly roof of orange-tipped Scots pines, you would witness the trees growing like spinning tops, poking toward the sky in slow spirals. As they layer themselves with lignant fibers, the trees would shed their reddish bark in flakes the size of hands. You could count the whorls of branches to mark the passing years. The wooden crosses, affixed to trees by thick nails, would grow upward and more distant with each passing year, like the grief they represent.

I imagine the worshippers, each prayer a reminder of wars and occupations. Each hymn a testament that given enough time, trees will always grow back.

I think about what can't be recovered. I think about the colonial naturalists who bartered free passage on merchant ships to collect specimens. On many occasions, the sea had its own plans, and the months and years of careful work would be lost in shipwreck, tempest, or pirate attack. Lost to the boiling waters of some unnamed place. The thin-papered drawings and scribbled notes scattered on the waves. The pressed leaves and vessels of insects dipped into obscurity, useless and water-logged history.

I think of enslaved Africans on similar ships, carrying nothing but their mother's knowledge of medicinal and poisonous herbs, and a few seeds of their most treasured foods, like relics of freedom, while the immigrant settlers went to war unsparingly against the abundant wild birds, feasting on the ruins of fowl day and night. I think of the Indigenous Americans erased from their homelands to create wilderness preserves and of the unfathomable abundance of green turtles, dismembered and consumed, that no longer exists and likely never will again. I think of the men and women in the Belgian Congo, losing their hands to the rubber and ivory trades, and their ancestors today, hunting among familiar ghosts.

My maternal history has also been lost, to wars and migrations. I am displaced from my homeland. Most of us are. We have become exiles in the places where we should belong. We all carry the weight of our mothers. The weight of their mothers.

It is in our bodies. The stress of our births. The sacrifices they made to love us. The silences they carried in order to survive.

In losing wild foods from our diets, from the landscape, we lose something unnamable. The silences are so loud, they have become their own sound. We face a spiritual crisis, an existential loneliness greater than any heartbreak. To be without the ecstasy of the wild is to face a bland future.

Of course, we can't all go back to eating wild foods. There are too many of us, and not enough wild places left. We would need many Earths to satisfy our hunger. Yet for many people, wild food remains a necessity. It will never become a luxury. It is scavenged from the roadsides, dropped off still steaming in the back of pickup trucks. It is a gift from the land and the people are grateful for hearty stews on cold nights.

We are at an inflection point. A moment fixed in history, rerouting the flow of the future, while all the rest remains as fluid as time. How do we regain our lost rites and make new mythologies? How do we learn to nourish ourselves so that we might heal the wounds of the past? To be re-enchanted by wild hunger requires severing ourselves not from the grid, but from a grid mentality. Every action is an ecological act. We must become comfortable with the dark and quiet again.

My sister has learned my mother's gift for botanical alchemy. She sings to her plants. They are her babies. Her garden is always messy and abounding. A tangle of beans around the corn stalks, with tomatoes in between the leaves. Her squashes commune with the carrots. There are songbirds among the flowers.

My sister is becoming a seed saver. She trades these seeds with others. She recently received heirloom varieties of amaranth and lemon balm from a seed vault on Tesuque Pueblo, just beyond the land where we grew up. She likes to tell me about a watermelon variety she was given that was cultivated in these

desert valleys generations ago. It has a thick rind to retain moisture and can thrive in places with hot days and cold nights.

Are my sister's botanical rituals a form of protection and
prayers for the earth? Is she taking responsibility for our stew-
ardship of the planet or acknowledging that we are but tiny blips
of light? Is it grieving or celebration? Perhaps it is both.

The idea that humans are a vital part of keeping nature wild
is a very old one that must be remembered. We are capable of
creating the conditions for abundance, for the mutual thriving of the infinitely diverse creatures that share our home, the
Earth. Of loving the wild back into existence. It is up to us to
dream the direction we wish to go, casting these incantations
in whispers to the stars.

These ancient seeds light our way like sacraments to a future
of survival.

A plate of food is an emblem of the intangible, of space and time,
of economies and Nature. It ties us into the web of history. How
lofty the act of eating! But rarely do we find ourselves in awe
of such magic, because eating must be done. Too little and our
stomachs grumble with pain, too much and our intestines bloat
with discomfort. We eat together and we eat alone.

Our appetites—whether as rich tourist or poor refugee—
have driven us around the world. Intentionally or not, we've
molded nature to satisfy our deepest culinary yearnings. The
world still runs on instinct. We want fat and sugar and rarity.
We want loud music and fast cars. Straight trees and rowdy
wildlife preserves. We want stability and wild love. So many
conflicting desires.

In some beginning, we hunted and gathered, and so we
became human. Once we overcame the necessary matter of

survival, we turned our great intellects toward perfection. We innovated and truly believed to have broken with tradition. But then, almost as an aspiration, we tried to conjure the past, with its pure and simple feelings of hunger and satiation, the immediate experiences of the senses, unadulterated by the bitter taste of excess. This contradiction lies at the center of our appetites. We are comforted by the dullness that comes with domestication, but we crave the flavors of the wild.

There is infinite anguish to live in such contradiction. But it is all we have. It is our most beautiful flaw. To be both mortal and godly, element and subject, body and mind.

What were the branch points in this evolution? Did it begin when we learned to tame fire and invented cooking? With the first spark, we began to believe in our independence. Or was it the rise of agriculture? We began to settle in one place, ignore the passing migrations of wild animals, and dampen down our own instincts to move with the seasons. We cast off the knowledge gained from action and invented History, being nothing more than a way to account for the accumulation of inert facts, which seemed to grow more unruly each season, like the weeds in our fields. Maybe it was the expansion of colonialism or the Industrial Revolution? Relationships of mutualism were exchanged for those of power. In the course of so many generations, we came to believe that time was linear and Wild Nature was separate. We became seduced by the idea of scarcity. It drove us forward. It shackled us with the burden of progress.

But even if we make an accounting of the facts, a demarcation of the boundaries between one century and the next, it is difficult to know how this current path began. Perhaps there is no single explanation. Like the branching pattern of a tree or the coursing tributaries of a river, many forces came together, natural and human alike.

The Nature we have today is an artifact of this history, and the Nature we leave to the future is a map of our own. Today we feel not just our own mistakes but the cumulative impacts of a thousand generations. The land tells the truth of what has been done to it. The species that will survive our onslaught are those that can live at the edges, in the transition zones between one type of land use and another, the spaces we have disturbed and left behind. They slot their fragmented lives between systems of management, rebels fighting against the standard state of affairs. Wild Nature is still everywhere, even if it has become too familiar to be exoticized.

Perhaps the frontiers were imaginary the whole time, phantoms we chased to mark the measure of our wanderings. Perhaps, in the end, I know nothing.

We might understand history to be the authentic repository of facts, but it relies solely on the materials that were salvaged, that did not perish by casualty or neglect. It is an act of gathering. Arbitrary and fortuitous. The first archives were records of randomness, built not by methodical catalogs but through the collection of what was saved, and by a willed forgetting of what was lost.

What if the maze we wish to find a way out of is history itself? What if, instead, we could draw a map of ten thousand years? How would it look? It is a contemplation that seeks no answers. Such a map would surely be a mess if we included all the lives that have been excluded. The small things that hardly anyone noticed. The frayed remnants of recollection. The quiet details of an intimate story.

I once saw a photograph of the Hunter as a little boy. Skinny, shirtless, and barefoot on a motorcycle. He looked serious but had a gentle smile, like he already knew the secret of universal tragedy, and that within it, one could always find joy. He has always been a man with a conflicting identity. Of hunter and protector of wildlife. Of scientist and sentimentalist, lover and solitary figure, playful storyteller and somber cynic.

296 Sometimes, when I am at my desk, trying to write, I think of him, walking silently through the deep forests of another place. It is not a small thing that he risks his life for the elephants and bonobos, but I didn't fully grasp his deep sense of commitment and sacrifice until after we had parted ways. As I survey the contours of my own life, spending late nights composing sentences, twisting the words around until they feel right—*altered, alienated, artifice*—perhaps he sees the midnight moon from a makeshift forest camp, surrounded by military men awake to the sounds of poachers in the distance.

Our love story emerged out of the turbulent chaos of the past. The Hunter and I were lovers by circumstance, already fitted together by a vicious and environmentally destructive colonial history. And we were lovers by accident.

We found a fleeting home in one another. It was not a carefully tended garden or a decadent wilderness. It was built by layers of earth and blood, flowers and fruits, the first tender shoots of spring and the heavy beasts of fall. It was a deep recognition of something already inside me. To love the Hunter was an encounter with our luxuriant planet, undomesticated, free, and full of wild grace.

I cannot say that I was anything more than a tourist in these wilds. Ultimately, we are all tourists here. We consume the pleasures of the earth for a brief moment and leave behind only our recollections and refuse. The past survives as memories of the future.

With every hunt—as with every great love—there is the ritual of the story, a telling and retelling of the pursuit and eventual capture. In each subsequent rendition, the details vary slightly, but the overall meaning only solidifies. It is a tale of the existence of two individuals engaged in an ancient game. They both know this mystery of entangled destinies, but neither truly understands it.

With each love lost, our hearts break open even further, allowing us to love again more deeply. The legacy of disappointment and crushing destruction must be carried along, but the heart is expanded with the knowledge we gain about ourselves.

The provisioning of wild food, like the provisioning of love, is always wrapped in narrative context. It is tied to a place, to its inhabitants, to the devoted hours of hushed waiting, to the communal process of butchering it down, to the blood on your hands, a taste of game on your tongue, and the suddenness of an end we always knew was coming.

When I began my journey, I did not know the Hunter, and it is difficult to say if I truly know him now. Still, I have discovered the beauty of his pursuit. To be a hunter is to chase the light. But to gather is to search the shadows.

The train is picking up speed. Forests become small towns, become suburbs of bigger towns. A haggard man peers from the top-story window of a concrete apartment building, grey from rain.

I find myself waking in a panic too often these days. Perhaps it is merely sensory sympatheia for the raped lands I am passing through. I've often felt wary of trusting the future, especially if the past is any measure of its path. But if we don't believe in the future, we must live in the unreliable present.

Foraging, by its very nature, is unpredictable. There's no prognosis, so there's no roadmap. You can't plan. You can't expect. You don't know how long it will take, what you will find, or how much worse it will get. It is this condition of the unknowable more than any other quality or countenance that distinguishes gathering from agriculture.

298   Foraging is an experience of the relativity of space and time. It requires the focus of a quiet mind so that your perceptions can become distorted. Time speeds up and your eyes scan the small details of the forest floor, as if they were designed to spot the exact size and color of a mushroom, berry, or herb. And then in the next moment, everything is slowed down and spacious. You can see the whole forest floor all at once, the undulating mosses, the soft curve of fir seedlings, the play of light through beech and alder trees.

The land is no longer a static catalog of minute internal oscillations but a simultaneity: it is event and representation. Our vision is reoriented away from any one dominant view, toward a de-homogenization, a pluralism. We inhabit ourselves. We are home.

My great-grandmother passed this quality down through her DNA, this affinity for working with hands and bodies, this belief in searching, this compulsion to find the discarded and insignificant, curiosity driven first by necessity and then by desire. We all have this in our bones. It is our heritage as humans.

When I go to the mountains of New Mexico to look for boletes beneath the aspens, I evoke something hidden in the recesses of my memory, an experience I did not have but that was so vital, it was passed down through lines of blood. A sensory adaptation fixed in my body, a forest hysteresis. Perhaps these are corporal memories, made from generations of fear and survival. When might we eat again? *When will we return home again?*

I don't imagine Esther was particularly unhappy, but rather rarely satisfied and always overworked, a woman simultaneously proud and self-critical. Perhaps she found the forest of her childhood to be a comfort, a place to break from the confines of a small village. The woods were a place of deep tranquility and quietude, like a cavernous temple, with a soft needle floor built by generations of the fallen, the pine bristles above undulating in a perpetual embrace with the breeze, and the air filled with the slow odor of moldering wood, like sacramental incense. Perhaps because Esther's whole life was built on a strict adherence to an outside order, to a structure imposed by others, those moments of unscripted everyday life were eerie and unruly medicine.

The invention of new traditions will not be an event but an accumulation. Even as history tries to silence the many little, recurring moments with which it is built, we can hold onto our memories, embedded in the ever-changing landscape and the food it provides. Remembering that this is a beginning, not an end.

What was that wild plant my great-grandmother gathered? Was it hogweed or cow parsnips, wild plants sometimes used to make borscht, substitute ingredients in difficult times when there was no money for beets? Was it sorrel? Something bitter with oxalic acid?

We know the action but not the details, the event but not the time, the landscape but not the plant. Perhaps it shifted, like the borders, with the seasons.

The train keeps moving.

Now the light is fading. The fields and houses and shopping malls look lovely and simple, betraying such a complicated past and uncertain future.

Was it the flavor that Esther loved, or did the taste bring back remembrances, each sip a retrospection, her mouth flooded with nostalgia? Perhaps it was a way to sort through the broken bits and rubble littering her past, to quiet the longing for her childhood spent foraging in the shadows of baroque palaces, an antidote to the poison of misery, a tonic for the grief of place-lessness. To find some stillness amid the noise of a displaced life, in a new city, so bright and mad. To remember that most experiences arrive from far away and of their own volition. Perhaps as she finished the last sip, she vowed not to be afraid, for in her heart, she knew that everything returns.

ACKNOWLEDGMENTS

I T IS A pleasure and a privilege to express my gratitude for the people who have supported me during the creation of this book. First and foremost, I wish to thank my immediate family, to whom this book is dedicated. They held me up during every step of this endeavor.

I am beyond thankful for my aunt and uncle, Madelyn and Steven Wils, who graciously hosted me during the final years of this project—I would not have completed it without their generosity.

Numerous friends provided motivation, fed me dinner, gave me encouragement, and generally kept me sane. They include Megan Anjali, Rebecca Brooke, Meredith VanAker, Angel Hertslet, Cary Simmons, Mi'jan Celie Tho-Biaz, Lydia Sisson, Maclovia Quintana, Ainissa Ramirez, Sameera Savarala, Sophie Young, Jacob Brancasi, Volker Eckles, Thea Gregarious, Alida Borgna, Maggie Hanna, Hannah Kirshner, Margo Harrison, Ashley Fried, Rosa Kozub, my Cambridge family, my Yale tribe, my Santa Fe homies, and my Creamer Street babes.

Nell Tivnan, Kendall Barberry, and Elisa Iturbe were invaluable help in reading early drafts and cheering me on. My aunts Liz Anastasia and Terry Antman kept my belly full and my spirits high on many occasions.

This book would also not exist without the incredible support of my professors Brian McAdoo and Verlyn Klinkenborg, my agent Jenny Stephens at Sterling Lord Literistic, and Jennifer Croll at Greystone Books. I wish to extend a special thanks to my editor, Paula Ayer, whose ample wisdom and time stewarded an unruly draft into a completed manuscript.

I am eternally grateful for the innumerable people I spoke with during my research who entrusted me with their stories. Their candid and heartfelt interviews make this book what it is. I've changed some names, identifying information, or other details to preserve the privacy of the people mentioned. Any mistakes or omissions in the book are my own. Finally, I wish to thank the many other people I'm forgetting but who should be remembered.

To all the lost creatures in the world, this book is for you.

302

NOTES

Chapter I: Herbs and Insects

1. "thirty thousand plant species"; Aaron Reuben, "Conservation Through Cocktails," Yale School of Forestry and Environmental Studies, July 1, 2014, https://environment.yale.edu/news/article/profile-ashley-duval-conservation-through-cocktails/; "What Is Agrobiodiversity," Food and Agriculture Organization of the United Nations (Rome, 2004), http://www.fao.org/3/y5609e/y5609e02.htm#bm2.

2. "luxury, lust, and intemperance": Paul Freedman, ed., *Food: The History of Taste* (Berkeley: University of California Press, 2007), 305.

3. "a perfect digestion": Samuel Hammond, *Wild Northern Scenes; or Sporting Adventures with the Rifle and the Rod* (1857), 23.

4. "the bitter-sweet of a white-oak acorn...": Henry David Thoreau, *The Writings of Henry David Thoreau: Journal XIV* (Boston: Houghton Mifflin, 1906), 265.

5. "such a foul feeder": Vincent M. Holt, *Why Not Eat Insects?* (1885).

6. "privilege of the cabin": Christopher M. Parsons and Kathleen S. Murphy, "Ecosystems under Sail: Specimen Transport in the Eighteenth-Century French and British Atlantics," *Early American Studies* 10, no. 3 (Fall 2012): 523.

7. "old wife of Crete": Agnes Arber, *From Medieval Herbalism to the Birth of Modern Botany* (Oxford: Oxford University Press, 1953), 317.

8. "highly expert old women": Otto Brunfels, *Herbarum vivae eicones*, vol. iii, (Strasbourg: Johann Schott, 1530–32), 13.

9. "was not ashamed to be…": Arber, *From Medieval Herbalism to the Birth of Modern Botany*, 318.

10. "As the world decays…": William Westmacott, *A Scripture Herbal* (1694).

304

Chapter 2: Heavy Beasts with Mushrooms and Wild Honey

1. "the hog had no heart": Felipe Fernández-Armesto, *Near a Thousand Tables: A History of Food* (New York: Simon and Schuster, 2002), 123.

2. "privileged for wild beasts": John Manwood, *A Treatise and Discourse of the Lawes of the Forrest* (1598).

3. "his two chaps": Aneurin Owen, ed., *Ancient Laws and Institutes of Wales: Comprising Laws Supposed to be Enacted by Howel the Good*, vol. 1 (London: G.E. Eyre and A. Spottiswoode, 1841), 287.

4. Joan Thirsk, *Food in Early Modern England: Phases, Fads, Fashions 1500–1760* (London: Continuum Books, 2007).292.

Chapter 3: Fish, Fin, Shell, and Claw

1. *The State of World Fisheries and Aquaculture 2018* (Rome: Food and Agriculture Organization of the United Nations, 2018).

2. "the best food the Sea affords": Richard Ligon, *A True and Exact History of the Island of Barbados* (1657).

3. "never eaten anything more appetizing": Peter Lund Simmons, *The Animal Food Resources of Different Nations* (New York: E. & F.N. Spon, 1885), 226.

4. "much like veal": C.R. Markham, ed., *The Hawkins' Voyages during the Reigns of Henry VIII, Queen Elizabeth, and James I.* (London: Printed for the Hakluyt Society,1878).

5. "an Act Agaynst the Killinge": Alison Rieser, *The Case of the Green Turtle* (Baltimore: Johns Hopkins University Press, 2012), 113.

6. "creolean degeneracy": Susan Scott Parrish, *American Curiosity: Cultures of Natural History in the Colonial British Atlantic World* (Chapel Hill: Omohundro Institute and University of North Carolina Press, 2006), 103.

7. "a greater abundance of purer and freer spirits": Thomas Parker, *Tasting French Terroir: The History of an Idea* (Oakland: University of California Press, 2015), 130.

8. "between that of veal…": Richard Bradley, *The Country Housewife and Lady's Director in the Management of a House, and the Delights and Profits of a Farm* (London: Printed for D. Browne, 1732).

9. John Timbs, *Club Life of London*, vol. II (London: Richard Bentley, 1866), 276.

10. "generous spirit...": *The London Magazine, Or, Gentleman's Monthly Intelligencer* 24 (1755): 229.

Chapter 4: Salmis of Roasted Fowl

1. "merchantable commodities": Michael Lewis, ed., *American Wilderness: A New History* (Oxford: Oxford University Press, 2007), 22.

2. "nothing but roast meat": Rev. Francis Higginson, *New England's Plantation or a Short and True Description of the Commodities and Discommodities of that Country* (London: Michael Sparke, 1629).

3. "If I should tell you": William Wood, *New Englands Prospects* (1634).

4. "within a few miles" Richard Hooker, *Food and Drink in America* (Indianapolis: Bobbs-Merrill, 1981), 12.

5. "too tedious": Hooker, *Food and Drink in America*, 13.

6. "turning of the earth": Joan Thirsk, *Alternative Agriculture: A History from the Black Death to the Present Day* (Oxford: Oxford University Press, 1997), 23–4, citing speech in House of Commons on Enclosures (Hist. MSS. Com. MSS. of Marquis of Salisbury, Part VII, 541–3), 1597.

7. "You look around...": Roderick Nash, *Wilderness and the American Mind* (New Haven, CT: Yale University Press, 2014), 42, citing Sidney Smith, *The Settler's New Home; or the Emigrant's Location* (1849).

8. "One of my primary...": Eli Whitney, letter to Oliver Wolcott, cited by Ruth Schwartz Cowan, *A Social History of American Technology* (New York: Oxford University Press, 1997), 7–8.

9. "clothed to his toes": H. Clay Merritt, *The Shadow of a Gun* (Chicago: F.T. Peterson, 1904), 261.

10. "thing in season": Thomas F. De Voe, *The Market Assistant* (New York: Hurd and Houghton, 1867), 20.

11. "genuine Southern negro": Scott Giltner, *Hunting and Fishing in the New South: Black Labor and White Leisure after the Civil War* (Baltimore: Johns Hopkins University Press, 2008), 171, quoting C. W. Boyd in *Outing*, vol. XIII (1889), 401.

Chapter 5: Forest Flesh with Roots and Tubers

1. "Whoever shall kill a stag": James B. Whisker, *Hunting in the Western Tradition* (Lewiston, NY: Edwin Mellen Press, 1999), 50, citing William the Conqueror.

2. "suffocating wilderness": H.M. Stanley, *In Darkest Africa*, vol. 1 (1890).

3. "travellers' happy hunting": Dugald Campbell, *Wanderings in Central Africa: The Experiences & Adventures of a Lifetime of Pioneering & Exploration* (1929), 143–44.

Chapter 9: Nests and Blooms

1. Annie Brassey, *The Last Voyage* (London: Longmans, Green, 1887), 177.

SELECTED BIBLIOGRAPHY AND FURTHER READING

Carr, Archie. *So Excellent a Fishe: A Natural History of Sea Turtles*. New York: Natural History Press, 1967.

Cronon, William. *Changes in the Land: Indians, Colonists, and the Ecology of New England*. New York: Hill and Wang / Farrar, Straus, and Giroux, 1983.

Cronon, William, ed. *Uncommon Ground: Rethinking the Human Place in Nature*. New York: W.W. Norton, 1996.

Fletcher, Nichola. *Charlemagne's Tablecloth: A Piquant History of Feasting*. London: Weidenfeld & Nicolson, 2004.

Greenberg, Paul. *American Catch*. New York: Penguin, 2014.

Harris, Marvin, and Eric B. Ross. *Food and Evolution: Toward a Theory of Human Food Habits*. Philadelphia: Temple University Press, 1987.

Hochschild, Adam. *King Leopold's Ghost: A Story of Greed, Terror, and Heroism in Colonial Africa*. Boston: Houghton Mifflin, 1999.

Luchetti, Cathy. *Home on the Range: A Culinary History of the American West*. New York: Gillard Books, 1993.

Mabey, Richard. *Weeds: In Defense of Nature's Most Unloved Plants*. New York: Ecco, 2011.

Merchant, Carol. "Gender and Environmental History." *Journal of American History* 76, no. 4 (March 1990): 1117–21.

Mianda, Gertrude. "Colonialism, Education, and Gender Relations in the Belgian Congo: The Évolué Case." In *Women in African Colonial Histories*, edited by Susan Geiger, Nakanyike Musisi, and Jean M. Allman, 144–63. Bloomington: Indiana University Press, 2002.

Montanari, Massimo. *The Culture of Food*. Translated by Carl Ipsen. Oxford: Blackwell, 1996.

Ortega y Gasset, José. *Meditations on Hunting*. Translated by Howard B. Wescott. New York: Charles Scribner's Sons, 1972.

Paulme, Denise. *Women of Tropical Africa*. Abingdon, UK: Routledge, 1963.

Plante, Ellen M. *The American Kitchen 1700 to the Present: From Hearth to Highrise*. New York: Facts on File, 1995.

Ponting, Clive. *A Green History of the World*. London: Sinclair-Stevenson Limited, 1991.

Pratt, Mary Louise. *Imperial Eyes: Travel Writing and Transculturation*. New York: Routledge, 2008.

Schiebinger, Londa. *Plants and Empire: Colonial Bioprospecting in the Atlantic World*. Cambridge, MA: Harvard University Press, 2004.

Shepherd, Gordon M. *Neurogastronomy: How the Brain Creates Flavor and Why It Matters*. New York: Columbia University Press, 2012.

Stoler, Ann L. *Carnal Knowledge and Imperial Power: Race and the Intimate in Colonial Rule*. Berkeley: University of California Press, 2002.

Thirsk, Joan. *The Rural Economy of England: Collected Essays*. London: Hambledon Press, 1984.

Tsing, Anna Lowenhaupt. *The Mushroom at the End of the World: On the Possibility of Life in Capitalist Ruins*. Princeton, NJ: Princeton University Press, 2015.

Whisker, James B. *Hunting in the Western Tradition*. Lewiston, NY: Edwin Mellen Press, 1999.

Woolgar, Christopher, Dale Serjeantson, and Tony Waldron, eds. *Food in Medieval England: Diet and Nutrition*. Oxford: Oxford University Press, 2006.

Yates, Barbara. "Church, State and Education in Belgian Africa: Implications for Contemporary Third World Women." In *Women's Education in the Third World: Comparative Perspectives*, edited by Gail Kelly and Carolyn Elliott, 127–51. Albany, NY: SUNY Press, 1982.

INDEX